The Only True America

The Only True America

Following the Trail of Lewis and Clark

David Hauser

Writer's Showcase
presented by *Writer's Digest*
San Jose New York Lincoln Shanghai

The Only True America
Following the Trail of Lewis and Clark

Writer's Showcase
presented by *Writer's Digest*
an imprint of iUniverse.com, Inc.

For information address:
iUniverse.com, Inc.
620 North 48th Street, Suite 201
Lincoln, NE 68504-3467
www.iuniverse.com

ISBN: 0-595-10056-2

Printed in the United States of America

For my original companions on the Trail:
Alison
Karen
Luch
Yayoi
After almost twenty years, here it is!

Introduction

Many years ago I was teaching at an eastern college which encouraged unusual academic projects during a six-week term from late April through May. This was primarily so that students could get to summer internships and available jobs before people from other colleges. But it also made study trips—to Greece, Italy, England, Asia, wherever—possible in advance of the tourist season. I was determined to take advantage of the opportunity to get away, but I was unqualified to lead foreign-study tours, so I began to speculate on the possibility of a trip to the American West, which I had "discovered" some years earlier. I needed, however, a more specific subject matter.

Rummaging through the Library one day, I hit upon the Lewis and Clark Journals in Bernard DeVoto's abridgment and immediately knew I had found the locus for my study tour. The day-to-day record of their exploration up the Missouri, past both friendly and hostile Native Americans into lands no white men had ever seen, the gut-wrenching story of their agony portaging the Great Falls and crossing the Rockies, their entrance into the strange world of the Columbia Gorge and finally their sight of the Pacific Ocean—all this mesmerized me. Like so many others, I had become instantly caught up in what was unfolded in the Journals—the drama of their day-to-day adventures, the magnificent competence of the leaders, and their eventual triumph over most forms of adversity. While I had of course been vaguely familiar with their names, I had known nothing much of the details of their journey, either because the schools I attended didn't include it in the curriculum, or, more likely, I hadn't paid enough attention. In any case, their story intrigued me and began to fill in the blank spaces of my own inner map. Four venturesome students signed up to spend two weeks reading the Journals and preparing for the trip, then four weeks on the road traveling in my van, tent-camping along the way to the Pacific and back, more or less following the route of Lewis and Clark. At last I am getting to fulfill my promise to those students to write a book which will, in some measure, reflect our shared experience and its aftermath for me. To them I have dedicated these pages, for without them they would never have been written.

Since then I have been "on the Trail," in whole or in part several times, nowhere near as often as some who make a virtual summer ritual of trail-visiting, and not as systematically and purposefully as others who have canoed, hiked, driven to, even lived in places I am unfamiliar with. Because of the physical limitations of age I am primarily a car camper, who therefore often misses as much as he sees by not going more slowly by canoe or on foot. By no means am I trying to pass myself off as an expert on the history of the west; my background has been as an interpreter of texts. Nor am I to be viewed as a travel guide who has visited all the places of interest along the Trail. In fact, my account sometimes reads as a series of missed opportunities. But what I have experienced has had its effect on me and has led to the reflections here, which may be relevant to the lives of others as well as myself.

I must, however, first report on a curious phenomenon. Yes, my travels have been initiated by the journals of Lewis and Clark, but of course they are on modern highways and are composed of my experiences along those highways (and sometimes byways). But the more time I spend on the road, and the more I observe contemporary life along the route of the explorers, the more I am driven back into the past. It isn't the case that I can look at the country through their eyes; one of the recurring themes along the Lewis and Clark Trail is that little remains the same as it was then, since even the very courses of rivers have changed and the "ravages" of civilization have altered the landscapes. A fundamental achievement of the Ken Burns television program on Lewis and Clark was the ability to discover images along the Trail without roads and power lines and dams in the way. And, moving as it can be, the attitude of nostalgia for an irrecoverable past is not my primary response, even though I respect this perspective and admit that some of today's best writing on the West takes this point of view, as, for example, in Ian Frazier's *Great Plains* and Dayton Duncan's *Out West*.[1]

Instead, I find that, in a way that is curious, the past and the present are more tightly intertwined. The history of the West is a history of roaming, of displacement. At the same time, virtually every town which has survived (and many that haven't; the ghost town is mainly a western phenomenon) has its "cultural center" (a nicely ambiguous term), its historical museum. Older residences are carefully marked and listed even when they are not preserved. Even individual trees are nurtured in the towns, as if they are historically significant, which, of course, they are. And often momentous events are not so far back in time nor so lost in complexities as is sometimes the case on the Eastern seaboard. We know, for example, the exact site of the village in which Sakagawea lived among the Hidatsas in North Dakota, because of oral testimony and the still-visible earth depressions of their lodges. The process of change over the last two centuries creates its own narrative. The very newness of the country to our eyes seems to make its past more intelligible, and this makes sense out of the flow of time.

Finally, that is what I am trying to do here—to tell the Lewis and Clark story in the light of my story and some of what has happened in between. The first few times I traveled the West I was overwhelmed, like everyone else (including Lewis and Clark), by the natural scene in all its vastness, magnificence, and, above all, its *difference*. But on further visits I found myself drawn to the towns and small cities as well, which exist in the landscape in ways that have tended to be obscured in the east. What I hope will emerge is a glimpse of changes in the society and the landscape of the West which are sometimes tragic but also sometimes hopeful, offering the promise of a valuable future to those who participate in it. Poised next to the damaged civilizations of Native Americans and the disappearance of once-viable small towns are vibrant communities along the Missouri and the Columbia, which may be leading the way to what successful urban life will look like in some future time. Wallace Stegner, one of the wisest of students of the West, was fond of talking, in a guarded way, of what he called the "geography of hope," the West as the freshest of America's regions with a chance to become something unprecedented and unmatched in the world.[2] On the other hand, some of the best writing from the region today records a measure of personal despair and self-destructiveness, which may be the result of the death of hope. The jury is still out. But I believe I catch glimpses of this hope in places along the Trail like Sioux City and Yankton and Bismarck and Great Falls and Astoria and maybe even Portland. This account, then, is meant to serve as a word to those who live under very different conditions on both east and west coasts that there is, in fact, the possibility of a meaningful existence in the vast middle of the nation.

My title, in all its presumption, comes, fittingly enough, from Thoreau. There is a marvelous story in the chapter of *Walden* entitled "Baker Farm" about John Field, a recent Irish immigrant, and his family, who literally dig out a living from the Concord countryside by turning over meadows for nearby farmers with a spade or bog hoe at the rate of ten dollars an acre. This is body-wracking and mind-numbing labor. Thoreau patiently explains to the family how they can get ahead: they could build their own tighter, more comfortable house in a month, as he has, for what they now pay for one year's rent; if they didn't use tea, coffee, butter, meat, or milk, as he doesn't, then they wouldn't need so much cash and would not have to work so hard, as he doesn't; if they didn't work so hard, they wouldn't have to eat hard to "repair the waste of the system," and so get caught up in the circle of consumption. It is the one place I recall in all of *Walden* where Thoreau lectures another person directly, and it has as little effect as most lectures. For in spite of the difficulty of their lives and the lack of the prospect of improvement, the Fields rated it a gain in coming to America, where you could at least get tea and coffee and meat every day. Now in one of his stunning explosions of narrative into symbolism, Thoreau says, "But the only true America is that country where you are at liberty to pursue such a mode of life as may enable you to do without these..." A land of individual freedom of action, like these United States? Not quite. He continues: "and where the state does not endeavor to compel you to sustain the slavery and war and other superfluous expenses which directly or indirectly result from the use of such things."[3]

Setting aside for the moment the entire radical economic theory implied in that last phrase, it is clear that the "only true America" for Thoreau does not exist within the constitution and political arrangements of any existing nation-state. But that does not mean that it does not exist at all. In order to measure the success or failure of anything real, there must be an ideal, and it is in the *imagining* of it that the "only true America" can be said to exist. Ultimately, then, we are all poets of our own destiny. And the more inclusive and comprehensive our imaginations become, the more vivid such an image of potential reality will be. Perhaps the final meaning of the "Corps of Discovery" is not what it gleaned of the geography, the peoples, and the natural history of the West, nor how the exciting story of epic proportions inspires and informs us about the human spirit. Its meaning consists of what it contributes to our own sense of the possibilities of the land each of us inhabits, how it feeds our imaginations. There is plenty here for all.

I also want to attempt something else, which may seem more ambitious. I want to see if I can to some extent recover the image of America that the trip impressed on the imaginations of Lewis and Clark themselves. The Journals reverberate with the openness of these men to the totally new worlds through which they were passing and the unexpected climate and weather and the new experiences with Native Americans and animals that their previous life east of the Mississippi had never prepared them for. We can, to some extent, trace their journey from men reared with the values and attitudes of their time, which had been tested in the Old Northwest, to encounters with events and people far beyond anything their backgrounds had ever led them to anticipate.[4] Being men of the Enlightenment, as this was understood in America, they were forced to confront the magical and holistic acceptance of the natural world embodied in the lives of Native Americans, as well as a natural world of power, violence, beauty and indifference to men's' concerns that the Enlightenment had never conceived of. In the process they were, of course, changed, and I believe that each of them returned with different images of the "only true America." In order to develop this theme, my intention is to pursue particular passages in the Journals as more than historical statements. I read them as elements in the transformations (or lack of them) that Lewis and Clark undergo. Such reading is, of course, based upon presuppositions about personality and the ways experience is absorbed, and I will try to be as open about these presuppositions as I can. Even more central to me than viewing the Journals as historical documents is to see them as ways the imagination tries to make sense of a larger world.

It has become a cliché to say that Lewis and Clark failed in the primary purposes of the journey, that they found no practical Northwest Passage and they created enmity with key tribes that was to fester for generations, even up to today, but they succeeded in leading to later development (sometimes read as exploitation) of the West. There is another way in which they can be said to have succeeded. Thoreau and most Easterners found their ideal in a particular place, and the search for roots has always been an American dream ("We'll build a sweet little nest/Somewhere in the West/ And let the rest of the world go by," says a popular song from the 1920's). But as the journey of Lewis and Clark emphasized (although did not invent), "moving on" has also become a means of expressing one's ideal; like no other people in human history Americans have celebrated being "on the road." Some readers, like James Ronda, have found the

Journals to be the Odyssey of our American experience; Dayton Duncan is fond of comparing the Journals to *Pilgrim's Progress*.[5] But the journey homeward to nation, family, and a just world, which occupies Odysseus, does not happen for Lewis. And only in the most tenuous way can the adventures of Christian as he journeys toward the Heavenly Gates be compared to Clark. Because of their friendship and their total agreement on matters of leadership and decision-making, we have tended to see Lewis-Clark, one character. Graphic artists have struggled to find images to differentiate them, Lewis with his dog Seaman, Clark with his mapmaking instruments, just as writers have developed stereotypical labels, Clark the bad speller, Lewis the skilled rhetorician. But their differences were far greater than this. In fact, they may well have come away from the Expedition with diametrically opposed responses to their experiences, which I label the "landscape of promise" and the "landscape of despair." It is no accident that both views still exist and inform our understanding of today's west, and, ultimately, our own futures.

So my narrative will be double-tracked, perhaps even schizophrenic at times, trying to ride the two horses of 'then' and 'now', dealing with the differences between past and the present, only occasionally the similarities, trusting that both will join at some point before I end, but not apologizing if they don't. For both can offer insights, even if at a level beneath speech. Lewis and Clark, I believe, learned more than they expected or even intended. They learned that the life of reason, which had been bred into them, was insufficient for the lives they were to lead. They received an initiation into a larger world from the Native Americans they encountered and from the vast natural world they traversed. And, paradoxically, I have had reaffirmed for me that there is still room for reason in the tumultuous and chaotic world of our times. Perhaps what brings our stories together, then, is the ways in which they can complement each other. But you must be the judge of that.

1   Duncan's book (New York, 1987) is a highly engaging account of his personal adventures along the Trail, as well as something of the background of the Expedition. Frazier's work (New York, 1989) is a profound meditation on the past and present of the region, told from his highly personal, even idiosyncratic point of view. Both are remarkable pieces of writing.

2   I encountered the phrase in his Introduction to *Where the Bluebird Sings to the Lemonade Springs* (New York, Penguin,1992), p. xv, but a lecture, "A Geography of Hope," delivered at the University of Colorado appeared in A Society to Match Our Scenery (Boulder, 1991).

3   I have used the Riverside Edition of *Walden*, edited by Sherman Paul (Cambridge, MA, 1960), p. 141.

4   In spite of the contemporary interest in Lewis and Clark, we have no up-to-date authoritative biography of either man. John Bakeless, *Lewis and Clark: Partners in Discovery* (New York, 1947) was useful for its time but left too many holes in its fabric, and Richard Dillon, *Meriwether Lewis* (New York, 1965), wrote a sensible account based on then-available material on Lewis. Jerome O. Steffin's *William Clark: Jeffersonian Man on the Frontier* (Norman, OK, 1977) makes no pretense at focussing on Clark's life. This leaves Stephen Ambrose's *Undaunted Courage: Meriwether Lewis, Thomas Jefferson, and the Opening of the American West* (New York, 1996), whose success is more due to the narrative retelling of the Expedition's adventures than to any new information about its leaders.

5   Ronda, one of the most thoughtful students of the Expedition, has edited a collection of essays entitled *Voyages of Discovery* (Helena, Montana Historical Society Press, 1998), in which one of his contributions, "'A Darling Project of Mine': The Appeal of the Lewis and Clark Story," pp. 327–335, develops this idea. Duncan has made the Bunyan analogy in lectures several times.

CHAPTER I

Albemarle Origins

The object of your mission is to explore the Missouri river,
& such principal stream of it, as, by it's course and communication with the waters of the Pacific ocean, whether the
Columbia, Oregan, Colorado or any other river may offer
the most direct & practicable water communication across
this continent for the purposes of commerce.

Thomas Jefferson to Meriwether Lewis, 20 June 1803[1]

Accounts of the Lewis and Clark expedition usually begin with the
party setting off up the Missouri on May 14, 1804, from their winter
encampment at Wood River, Illinois. About a hundred years after the
expedition returned, however, another journal surfaced which began
with Lewis's departure from Pittsburgh with the keelboat and two
canoes on August 31, 1803, picking up Clark and other members of the
expedition recruited by Clark, and, in more or less detail, describing
their journey down the Ohio River to the Mississippi and thence to
their winter quarters across the Mississippi from the mouth of the
Missouri. It is legitimate and instructive, then, to begin the journey

from its source at Pittsburgh. But the expedition has a rich background, for which it is necessary to go back further in time and elsewhere in place, to Albemarle County, Virginia, where the three major actors— Jefferson, Lewis and Clark—all had their origins and where the idea of the expedition was formed, as we often hear, in the mind of Jefferson.

What most of us non-Virginians think of first when we look toward the past, I would guess, is the world of the planters, whom we imagine as they thought of themselves—aristocratic ladies and gentlemen living a refined life (on the basis of the labor of their slaves) in the great plantation houses of the Tidewater country. Genealogy is big in Virginia, and many contemporary citizens of the State work hard to trace their roots back to these families. The world of the Tidewater was a rural one, with self-contained estates, the houses not nearly so grand in the eighteenth century as our imaginations would have them, built on water as deep as possible along Chesapeake Bay, and the Potomac, York, Rappahannock, and James Rivers, so that hogsheads of tobacco could be directly loaded on ships.[2] The economy was based almost solely on tobacco, or rather credit for future tobacco, since everything purchased abroad was charged to the next season's crop. Virtually no one had much cash. This was of course a precarious way of life, but even more so when the destructive effect of tobacco on the soil was taken into account, for it could exhaust the sandy Tidewater soil in two or three years, where fields then had to lie fallow for thirty years before again being marginally usable. The solution to this problem, however, seemed simple—acquire more land, which appeared inexhaustible.

Very early in the colony's history there were those who looked to the west for more and more land which could, it was hoped, enable the planters to break the dependence on credit from the merchants of England and Scotland. And for those without the ability to buy Tidewater land or who could not inherit it, the west seemed to be the answer The famous expedition of Lieutenant Governor Spotswood in 1716 to the Piedmont country and beyond—the Governor plus twelve of his political allies from the House of Burgesses, 30 servants, fourteen soldiers, and four Indian guides, accompanied by every form of alcoholic beverage known in the New World—was to enrich the participants and did so magnificently, one land grant as large as 100,000 acres. (By the way, the Governor founded the Order of the Golden Horseshoe, based on the present given to each of the gentlemen who drank—and drank—the King's health on George Mountain, and this exclusive club carried considerable social and political clout in Virginia's early days. Thomas Jefferson's grandfather possessed one of these Horseshoes.)[3] Especially after marriage into the ubiquitous Randolph family, the Jeffersons were one of the larger landholders in this new West, at the eastern foot of the Blue Ridge Mountains, in the area which was separated off from Goochland County to become Albemarle County, just about the time Thomas Jefferson was born. Peter Jefferson, Thomas's father, had surveyed and made maps of much of this country and was named its first colonel of militia. One of his best friends, Dr. Thomas Walker, laid out the town of Charlottesville a few years later. Peter Jefferson attained a measure of local fame for his role in the legendary expedition of 1746, which mapped much of the Shenandoah Valley while encountering hardships of epic proportions. Peter owned a good deal of land, but his life style and character did not much resemble the planter class of Tidewater. Life in the Piedmont was far simpler, less luxurious and profligate, and more attention was of necessity paid to work and to the natural world around them than that of high society, although this is not to imply that crude pioneer mores prevailed. But much of the uneasiness with slavery was to come from these Piedmont residents, who tended to value individual merit and initiative more highly than birth or class.

While Thomas Jefferson went to college in Williamsburg, enjoyed the intellectual stimulation found there, and as a lawyer had to attend to much of his court business in the provincial capital there, his home was in the west, and he spent as much time as possible in Albemarle County, where a unique society had grown up amid the forests. Moreover, his livelihood for several years depended on the west. Augusta County, beginning at the western slopes of the Blue Ridge and extending to the Mississippi, was where almost all of the young lawyer's business in land claims adjudication came from. In later life, his republican ideal of small landowners creating a society based on enlightened self-interest grew in part from his focus on the agricultural settlement of the west, not on the trade-and-credit world of the eastern seaboard, which he too often found himself caught up in. His neighbors included numerous Meriwethers, Lewises, and Clarks, although the latter family moved a county or so away from bordering Jefferson's property, so that William was born in Caroline County, still however, west of the Fall Line and thus separated from Tidewater by the lack of easily navigable streams. When William was a teenager the family moved to the west, what today is Kentucky. Meriwether Lewis, too, spent much of his youth away from his birthplace in Albemarle County, for after the death of his father and the remarriage of his mother the family moved to the Georgia frontier for a time. But he returned to manage the land holdings in Albemarle County, and his mother remained there the rest of her life. Wherever Jefferson, Clark, and Lewis lived in later years, then, each identified himself to himself as a product of the Piedmont.

These men, then, were all Westerners in background, outlook, and future prospects. If they were to live as gentlemen, even western gentlemen, they had to look further west for their prosperity. And this meant land. George Washington, a Tidewater gentleman of the first rank, also did all he could to salvage his fortunes in the west, especially since the soil at Mt. Vernon was so poor and exhausted he could not continue to grow tobacco. He spent considerable time traveling in today's western Pennsylvania, Ohio, West Virginia, and Kentucky, primarily so that he could collect parcels of land. But he saw no other value there. As the journals of his trips to the west testify, he despised the people even while he manipulated and connived to gain more land.[4] There is almost a feverish quality evident in these real estate ventures. A story from early in his career illustrates his energy in pursuing profit from the west. He tenaciously tried to persuade General Forbes to take his army west on the road cut by General Braddock years earlier in the campaign against Ft.Pitt, even though it was miles and miles out of the way. He became a laughing stock among Forbes' staff for his insistence. But he owned land along that road and would have been able to gain income from tolls if it became the established route west.[5] On another occasion warrants were issued for his arrest in some obviously shady land dealings in Pennsylvania.[6] But Jefferson based his vision of the future on the west, not for reasons of personal enrichment but on his belief in the kind of republic he foresaw, and Lewis and Clark were intimately acquainted with it, both in their upbringing and their early careers as Army officers. They liked the west and were comfortable there.

———————

On my first visit to Charlottesville one midsummer day the temperature hovered around the 100-degree mark. The atmosphere was so palpable with humidity (the mountains are called the "Blue Ridge" with reason) that the view from the expensive inn perched on the side of the mountain at the entrance to the Skyline Drive would be like peering into a pan of dirty dishwater. Mile upon mile of rolling green forest was only hinted at below. The attendant at the last gas station said of my air-conditionless van, "All you can do is roll down the windows, turn the wings around, and drive faster." He was right. Throughout my time in the town the local people kept telling me that you get used to the humidity, but when it was necessary to think about each breath, I wondered.

But growing things prosper in Charlottesville, and one's first impression in late July is of trees and gardens everywhere. The town rests in the valley of the Rivanna River (one of nineteen celebrations of

Queen Anne's name found among Virginia's rivers), hardly a river, more of a creek. Yet since it flowed into the James, it was a main avenue of transportation in the early days at those seasons when there was enough water to float poled flatboats. The green-shaded, winding streets and individual lots seem to become part of some large-scale landscape plan. This is a prosperous town and an expensive one. A fundamental source of wealth must be the University and the many start-up ventures that all universities these days seem to spawn, some of which are visible on Highway 29 on the edge of town. Upscale shops abound in the downtown area and in the outlying shopping centers. And, of course, there is "old money" which has been inherited. Some well-to-do residents commute to the Washington area by personal jet, and some nearby estates are known to contain heliopads. Horse farms dot the valley, with steeplechase races in spring and fall (nothing so common as harness or track racing) and club polo-playing as well. There are also tax-write-off wineries in the area and the tourist attractions like Michie Tavern, Monroe's home, Ash Lawn-Highland, and, the greatest of them all, Jefferson's Monticello, where nearly a half million visitors come each year, as if to a religious shrine.

Like most southern towns, Charlottesville, named after George III's queen, is not old by New England standards, since society was not organized around urban areas in Virginia. There is only one remaining eighteenth-century building in the downtown historic district. During the years of the Revolution, Charlottesville had direct experience of warfare only once, and that briefly by British raiders, but it became the site of a large-scale prisoner-of-war camp. Four thousand prisoners taken at Saratoga were marched over six hundred miles south to an installation a few miles west of the present town. The only remaining trace of the camp is in the name of a street, Barracks Road, and a nearby shopping center. Instead of a central commons, as in more northerly towns, a two-acre courthouse bloc was established at the perimeter of Thomas Walker's original town plan. One observer in the 1790's described Charlottesville as a courthouse, six taverns, and a handful of houses, and the population then was about 600 people. No church existed until the 1820's. The foremost authority on the area points out that during its early days Charlottesville was a small, rural county seat "almost untouched by improvements...."[7] The area around the Courthouse soon was developed with commercial buildings, which in turn have been demolished for a park. In order to maintain as many as possible of the early nineteenth-century shops and houses, other public buildings were dispersed around the edges of the original central area, so that there seems to be no genuine town center. Yet today the Historic District along Main St. has become an attractive brick-paved pedestrian mall with full-sized trees and interesting shops, and the surrounding area holds an upscale hotel and low-lying office buildings. There are fine memorial statues to Jefferson, Lewis and Clark, George Rogers Clark, and others liberally scattered around the town.

Many of the Charlottesville residents I have met have been friendly and outgoing, in an impersonal sort of way. I especially remember a man named Richard, who staffed the gift shop of the hotel I was staying at and who looked like Captain Kangaroo. When he learned I was from upstate New York, he had a story for the occasion. It seems that several members of his old Virginia family (he got this into the story early) were temporarily living in the Schnectady area, and Richard remembers visiting them when he was a boy. He was deeply puzzled by the habit New Yorkers had of greeting each other by naming another state. When he could no longer bear the mystery he asked his mother about such strange behavior, but she didn't understand what he meant. "But, Mama," he recalled, "When they meet they always say 'Hawaii.'" Apparently suppressing her laughter, she tried to explain that not all people were the same, not like us. The point of the story was to illustrate Richard's main criticism of New Yorkers: they talk too fast. He also claimed that a people whose idea of breakfast was Danish and coffee committed sacrilege daily. The conversation, while amusing, made me wonder what other ways were used to divide the "us" from "them" when I wasn't around. For the subtext of the anecdote clearly spoke to the social differences of Virginian and New Yorker, southerner and northerner, to the detriment of the latter. Yet it is important to note this ordinary man's narrative skill and the fact that while disarming me he was able to criticize my kind and me, no mean rhetorical feat.

West of the Historic District lies the University and all the shops, restaurants, and watering holes which always surround a university today. But before reaching the Rotunda it is necessary to pass by the massive UVA Health Sciences Center and Hospital, modern white buildings, which extend for what seem to be blocks and blocks. Auto and pedestrian traffic are both heavy around here. It doesn't seem possible that there are enough sick people in the area to keep all these staffers busy (and there is another hospital on the other side of town), but there are more signs of hurrying here than anywhere else in Charlottesville. The size of the University is masked by the hills, ravines and trees, which obscure many of the buildings. Most are redbrick versions of college buildings found everywhere. But the Rotunda is something else. Designed and built by Jefferson as the Library and academic center, Palladian in form and conception, with its residential arcades forming wings off each side and the well-kept gardens surrounding them, all placed on the extensive lawn—this center of the University is very special. At one point in his retirement Jefferson devoted all his energies to the building of the University, one of the only three accomplishments of his life he wanted to be memorialized on his gravestone (the others being the authorship of the Declaration of Independence and the Statute of Virginia for Religious Freedom). The Rotunda contains oval-shaped rooms with hourglass center halls between them. The dome itself with its skylight served for a hundred years as the University Library (with books chosen and supplied by Jefferson). The Rotunda was completely gutted by fire at one point in its history and was redesigned by Stanford White, who looked to improve on the original, but it has been since reconstructed according to the original plans and stands today as one of the nation's architectural jewels.

Jefferson had planned for a community of learning, an "academical village," by having faculty and students share living space in the arcades and the pavilions, which stretch down the sides of the "Lawn," the open area behind the Rotunda. He asked one of the most learned and thoughtful scholars in America, James Madison, to be its rector. He even hoped to sneak in an education in architecture by displaying every variety of classical forms in the various pavilion designs and types of columns. But he was bewildered by the occasional vandalism of broken windows and scribbled graffiti, seemingly common wherever young people of spirit have gathered. When he had all gambling banned from campus, the rector's window was smashed and a deck of cards and a pair of dice thrown through the opening. Today the arcades, the inner row called East and West Lawn, with the ten Pavilions, faculty apartments and classrooms, the outer row called the Ledges, are still used for their original purposes. Students apply for the honor of living here, even though they must wander down the covered loggias in their robes to take a shower, no matter what the weather. Across a campus road is the Alderman Library, the modern center of the University.

When I first visited the University for a conference, I remember drinking coffee outdoors next to the Library when faint sounds of martial music drifted across the road from the Rotunda area. As the piping and drumming grew louder and louder, eight young men dressed in heavy antique dress uniforms of blue and red came into view, marching toward me in somewhat ragged formation. The fife and drum players had red uniforms trimmed in blue, the flag bearers and the remainder the reverse. This was the standard practice of revolutionary times, so that commander and enemy alike could identify the musicians, the former to use them as a rallying point for the troops, the latter to save their powder and shot. This was part of the Monticello Guard, one of the oldest continuous military organizations in the nation, tracing its roots to the 1740's; it had distinguished itself in wars ever since. The young men marched to the steps of the University building, where they presented the colors and then played the "Star-Spangled Banner." Then they marched off to where they came from, presumably to head for their day jobs.

Today, as two hundred years ago, the heart of the area is Monticello, just a couple of miles out of town and located on a "mountain," really a hill. All the promotional material about the area begins here. Monticello has become a genuine national monument, and it seems a sacrilege to have allowed modern houses to be built on a nearby higher hill, so that they look down on it. Monticello was Jefferson's life-long hobby. When his birthplace, Shadwell, burnt in 1770, he moved to the hill that he had been leveling for construction of a house since 1768. He lived in a one-room brick structure today called the South Pavilion, where he brought his bride, Martha Wayles Skelton, two years later while the work continued. Many books have been written about Monticello, its domestication of Palladian and Roman architecture to the Virginia countryside, its ingenious features, such as the kitchens, stables, and workshops connected to the main house by an underground passageway out of sight under the terraces (which served as their roofs), the 1000-feet long vegetable garden and large orchards where Jefferson experimented with new plant varieties and also fed the population of about 150 people, the well-planned flower beds around the house and along the Roundabout, the oval walkway surrounding the house, and above all the beauty and serenity of the union of the natural and the man-made. The house also furnishes insights to Jefferson's personality. I am especially fond of learning about his obsession with time; clocks are to be found everywhere, and at the foot of his bed is a handsome one, which, when it became light enough to see its hands, told him it was time to rise. The fact that the main foyer became a museum of western Indian objects and animal bones, so that visitors could pick up this preoccupation, also tells us a good deal about his interests. We are fortunate to have remaining today so many of Jefferson's notes, drawings, and records, since we can see that his achievements do not consist of a series of accidents but are the result of meticulous attention to detail and constant planning.

Monticello faces west, toward the Blue Ridge Mountains, but its builder never ventured very far across those mountains, as his father and grandfather had, to physically travel in the West, which was virtually another of his creations. (Among other accomplishments, by the way, Jefferson authored the first Northwest Ordinance of 1784, never adopted but the precursor of the Northwest Ordinance of 1787, which developed the grid pattern for surveying land used thereafter in every new survey; he also provided a plan for how these territories were some day to become states; and he limited the spread of slavery). And throughout his life the content of the word "West" kept changing. At first it was the Shenandoah Valley, then Kentucky and the Ohio Valley, then the Mississippi and New Orleans, and only later the Louisiana Territory, on the far side of the Mississippi. But he knew the West—as a series of ideas. He probably knew more of the theory of the continent's geography than any contemporary did. The symmetry of the old Four Rivers theory lived on in Enlightenment thinking, that the land was drained from a central highland to the East by the St. Lawrence through the Great Lakes, to the South by the Mississippi, to the North by the Red and/or the Nelson, and so it stood to reason that there must be a River of the West. The idea was seemingly confirmed in 1792 by the mapping of the mouth of the Columbia by the American seaman Robert Gray. The new nation could profit immensely if it could be the first to find the source of the Columbia and use this water route to deliver goods across the country and thence to the Orient. At the very least the heralded fortunes in furs could come to Americans instead of the British, who were approaching the area from the Canadian north. Perhaps even more important, the West in American possession could serve as a buffer to prevent English settlement south of Canada; Jefferson throughout his life saw the British as natural enemies of the new

Republic, and here was a way of minimizing their influence. In a more concrete way than other Virginians who had proclaimed that the State extended to the Pacific Ocean, Jefferson looked forward to the day when the nation would embrace this territory and Americans would settle there, even though he always hoped for orderly settlement east of the Mississippi first. There are places in his writings that sound very much like the doctrine of Manifest Destiny to be articulated decades later. The phrase "empire of Liberty" is his creation.

The story of Jefferson's attempts to obtain more first-hand knowledge of the West is well known. Shortly after the end of the war, he approached George Rogers Clark about leading a party to head off the British, who were rumored to be putting together a team for exploring the country "from the Mississippi to California." Clark agreed it was necessary but his own debt-ridden situation prevented his going. While in France Jefferson learned of a plan for Louis XVI to send an expedition to the Pacific Northwest, and he met a great American talker and daredevil named John Ledyard, who persuaded Jefferson that, accompanied only by his two dogs, he could traverse Russia, thence to the Northwest, and across the country, ending up at Washington, where he would give his report. He actually started out, but got arrested in Russia and shipped back to his starting point. He later committed suicide in Africa while on an equally unlikely venture to explore the sources of the Niger. No one has remarked on the fate of the dogs. In 1790 Henry Knox, then Secretary of War, thought it important to send a secret intelligence mission up the Missouri to ascertain the disposition of the tribes there. Lieutenant John Armstrong was nominated, got as far as the Mississippi, determined realistically that more resources than the Secretary was willing to commit were needed, sent in a budget requisition, and that was that. And in 1793 primarily through Jefferson's efforts, the American Philosophical Society sponsored a subscription drive that raised one thousand pounds (with the help of donors such as George Washington and Alexander Hamilton) to be paid to the explorer who could make it to the Pacific and back. Once again Jefferson thought he had found the right man, this time the French botanist Andre Michaux. But by the time Michaux had reached Kentucky, Jefferson discovered that he was in the pay of France to help to take over Spanish territory, and so Jefferson shamefacedly recalled him.

So far this reads like comic opera material. But the events of the following year raised the stakes considerably and created a sense of urgency in the mind of Jefferson. After a first expedition involving great pain and difficulty had ended up by mistake in the Arctic, Alexander Mackenzie made it on his second try to the Fraser River and then into the Straits of Georgia at Vancouver Island. There, on a rock he painted the inscription "Alexander Mackenzie, from Canada, by land, the twenty-second of July, one thousand seven hundred and ninety-three." His Journal was not published until 1801, but Jefferson had undoubtedly heard this news earlier, and it must have seemed to confirm his worst fears, that the British were once again moving toward conquest on the continent. When he read the Journal the following year his attention would have been drawn to Mackenzie's urging the British government to build a series of forts from Lake Winnipeg to the Pacific coast to forestall American expansion and Russian incursions. At the same time, Mackenzie reported that westward flowing water was found after only a one-day portage and while that river was not navigable, the strong possibility existed that further south the same proportion would obtain. In effect, the way to the Pacific might be open and easy, the western mountains bearing the same relation to the Pacific as the eastern ones did to the Atlantic. "It was this simple fact of imaginary geography that gave birth to the Lewis and Clark expedition," says the geographer John Logan Allen.[8]

Long before the Louisiana Purchase made the vast territory between the Mississippi and the Rockies an American province, then, Jefferson was hard at work learning everything he could about the area, which he knew would inevitably become the future of the new nation. Since virtually nothing was known for certain west of the Mandan villages on the Missouri, where traders had visited, first-hand exploration was essential. Jefferson's negotiators were hard at work trying to buy New Orleans, which was vital for the development of the Old West, since any foreign government could impede the shipping of goods from the Ohio-Mississippi trade and thereby stifle growth in the region. Jefferson himself began to plan the future of the new West. And this even before the surprise offer of the French to sell the entire Louisiana Territory. Undoubtedly some of those irrecoverable conversations between Jefferson and his private secretary Meriwether Lewis during the early years of his presidency focused on such exploration. Lewis's imagination had been inflamed for many years prior to this by the possibility of such exploration. And by 1802 Jefferson had procured British and French passports for Lewis under the guise of a mission to add to the store of scientific knowledge. He was rebuffed by the Spanish, who were less inclined to pay their respects to Enlightenment rhetoric and more concerned with political realities. As Lewis began to recruit men for the trip he was instructed to keep its true purposes a secret, so he always spoke of it as a mission to the upper Mississippi region, except when he wrote the truth to Clark. Jefferson was determined to learn more, even if that knowledge had to be obtained illegally. Yet when it finally came through in 1803 it was characteristic of Jefferson to agonize over the constitutionality of the Purchase without congressional approval even as he rejoiced in the opportunities it opened up.

For our purposes some major questions need to be addressed. For example, why Lewis? It had been almost twenty years since Jefferson considered an army man for the task of exploring the Missouri Basin. Lewis had once, in 1792, volunteered his services to Mr. Jefferson to explore the West but was not seriously considered, presumably because of his youth and inexperience, in spite of the reputation he had earned from childhood on as an outdoorsman and a cool head. There is a story of how as a ten-year-old in Georgia he was the only one who had thought to put out a campfire which would have given away the position of his group of adults to Indians attacking in the area.[9] Because of the scholarly detective work of Donald Jackson we are certain why Lewis was selected by Jefferson to be his private secretary. One of Jefferson's first concerns as President was the reduction of the standing army to save money (he didn't believe in a national debt) and to reverse the trend toward ominously authoritarian trappings found among the Federalists. Twice already an army had been turned on the new country's own citizens, in Shay's Rebellion in Massachusetts and the Whiskey Rebellion in Pennsylvania. Moreover, John Adams had named a group of new officers in the lame-duck period after his defeat but before Jefferson's inauguration, and in Jefferson's mind the effects of an enlargement in force implied by this increase posed a threat to ordinary citizens (it wasn't as threatening as it sounded—there were proportionately far more officers than fighting men). Meriwether Lewis had spent nearly five years in the army serving in the Northwest where almost all the army was to be found, and was, as we shall see, uniquely qualified to evaluate both the competence and the political sympathies of the officer corps. His first job for Jefferson was such an evaluation, which today we still have in his handwriting.[10]

This was the immediate task, but there were others for which Jefferson needed someone he could trust, one of his own kind, almost family. Lewis served as a liaison with Congress and even read the first of what was to become the State of the Union Address to Congress (Jefferson avoided public occasions whenever he could, in part from shyness, but more, I suspect, to avoid any taint of authoritarian leadership by speechifying—he had the example in mind of how Patrick Henry could sway a legislature without making much sense). Moreover, everyone, even a genius like Jefferson, needs to talk out certain ideas informally to make sure they are utterable, and no one ever had a better audience than Lewis was for his mentor. In his memoir for Lewis after his death, Jefferson spoke with intimate knowledge of the Lewis family, almost his neighbors, whom he knew so well that he was aware of some "hypochondriac affections," which today we would probably call depression, hanging over "all the nearer branches of the family." He adds, "While he lived with me in Washington I observed at times sensible depressions of mind; but, knowing their constitutional source, I estimated their course by what I had seen in the family."[11] Nevertheless he strongly implies this was the cause of Lewis's death. Interestingly, no one else, anywhere, ever mentioned such an infirmity in the Lewis family, which calls Jefferson's judgement into question. But that is another story. He also stated that so long as Meriwether was active no trace of this illness surfaced. In spite of this, Lewis was, so far as we know, Jefferson's only choice to be his assistant.

But so far nothing has been said about Lewis's choice to command the expedition. It is usually pointed out that in all of Jefferson's previous descriptions of qualifications for such a role a high degree of interest in and knowledge of scientific procedures was prerequisite. Jefferson wanted not only a Northwest Passage but also a glossary of all Native American languages, anthropology of tribal mores, botanical and zoological knowledge, and, of course, flawless maps made of the territory along the way. And Lewis possessed very few of these skills, no matter how much his army experience fitted him for exploring. In fact, little about those army years proved to be distinguished. He joined the Virginia militia as a private in an apparent burst of patriotism to follow George Washington and the army of 13,000 to crush the Whiskey Rebellion in western Pennsylvania. At this point in his life there is no indication that he harbored any sympathies for the victims of a new "taxation without representation." From a letter to his mother we learn that he considered the rebels to be traitors, as Washington did, and he was delighted that "our leading men are determined entirely to consume every attum of that turbulent and refractory spirit that exists among the Incergents." But the real reason was probably boredom with his life running a farm. Nothing else in the letters of this time indicates much more than a desire for adventure and a thrill at the gusto of military life, although he shrewdly remarks on the poor logistics of the "Watermelon

Army," which was perpetually ahead of its supplies and forced to forage off the Pennsylvania countryside and farms, to the disgust of most Pennsylvanians. He wrote his mother from Pennsylvania that "I am quite delighted with a soldier's life."

When the Rebellion fizzled out, Lewis volunteered to stay on in western Pennsylvania with a small force to keep the peace, and he received a commission in the Virginia militia, which was to last for six months, after which he was expected to return to Locust Hill. But at the end of that period the opportunity arose for a commission in the regular army and he immediately accepted it, in spite of his mother's strong desire that he return home to carry his weight there. How he received a commission at the very time the army was being reduced in number is not at all clear. Washington had once proposed giving priority to veterans (and children of veterans) and to "young Gentlemen of good families, liberal education, and high sense of honour;"[12] Lewis matched these criteria, even if his formal education was sketchy. But Washington went on to say that in no case should any be appointed "who are known enemies to their own government," and Lewis had addressed his mother as "Citizen Lucy Marks," in the fashion of the French Revolution, which could have been dangerous to his prospects if it were known. His association with Jefferson was firm, but it is doubtful that knowing Jefferson was so black a mark to the Federalists at this time as it would be in another year or two. While his only remarks about the army in his letters have to do with the uniforms and the pomp and the dinner parties, he must have distinguished himself in some way to gain his commission, even in this time of vague perquisites for the job, of which there seemed to be three. First, a commanding appearance, physical energy, stamina, and courage, respectability, and a keen sense of personal honor were expected. Then, too, an officer had to demonstrate practical skills such as keeping records, handling administrative routine, enforcing discipline, and leading troops through tactical maneuvers. Finally, that something Washington had called "liberal education" was needed, the ornament of a gentleman, or at the very least some formal schooling for the sake of polish.

Lewis served briefly under General Anthony Wayne and was present at the signing of the Treaty of Greenville in August 1795. Here he would have had the occasion to observe the native chiefs and listen to their speeches, as well as watch them as they consumed Ft. Greenville's supply of whiskey. Apart from one trip from Detroit to Pittsburgh with a Native American guide, this was the extent of his special knowledge of the Northwest Indians, although when he was stationed at Fort Pickering on the Mississippi, he did spend some time studying the Cherokee ways and language. He shared in the unruliness—and drunkenness—of his fellow officers, and got into serious trouble as a "loose cannon" when a court-martial was held on charges that he had entered another officer's house when intoxicated, insulted him, and disturbed the group of fellow officers gathered there. Lewis was forcibly ejected and challenged the officer to a duel. Dueling was strictly forbidden by the Articles of War, even if it was often practiced; Wayne repeatedly urged officers to find other means of settling their disputes than by troubling the army with courts-martial, and on at least one occasion permitted an officer killed in a duel to receive partial military honors.[13] If Lewis had been found guilty this would have ended his military career, but in its wisdom the court saw otherwise and acquitted him. He was transferred to new duty, first serving for a few months in a rifle company commanded by Captain William Clark and then spending most of the next four years roaming the Ohio Valley as special messenger and paymaster to the scattered army posts from Forts Detroit and Fayette (Pittsburgh) to Fort Washington (Cincinnati) and elsewhere. (Some scholars believe that he was secretly charged with an important intelligence mission at this time, namely evaluating the location of Indian tribes and the extent of their sympathies to the British, but I can find no evidence of this.) Like many other officers, he was also sizing up the lands he passed through for future investment and potential profit.

And he later accepted assignment as a recruiting officer in Charlottesville, which enabled him to be near home while earning hard-to-come-by cash, since officers were paid two dollars for every recruit they signed up.

The point is this: on the basis of his resume Lewis was not especially qualified for the responsibilities Jefferson was about to confer upon him. His behavior sometimes seemed immature for his years, his thoughts a bit superficial, his judgment suspect. There will be later questions about his judgment as well. When it becomes clear that the expedition will be unable to start up the Missouri during 1803 and will spend the winter in camp, Lewis writes to Jefferson that he intends to make use of the extra time by exploring in the direction of Santa Fe. This could have been a disaster, for the Spanish were paranoid enough without what they would perceive as an American invasion, and given the slowness of the mails, Jefferson is held in suspense for weeks until he can release his breath when he learns that Lewis has changed his mind.

Again, why Lewis? Apart from the family connection and his upbringing as a true son of Albemarle, in a particular letter written to his mother there is more than a hint of a special quality that would appeal to Jefferson. In May 1795, just after reenlisting, Meriwether received an urgent letter from his brother Reuben telling him how much their mother wished his return to Locust Hill. His reply directly to her needs examination:

> So violently opposed is my governing passion for rambling to the wishes of all my friends that I am led intentionally to err and then have vanity enough to hope for forgiveness. I do not know how to account for this Quixottic disposition of mine in any other manner or its being affliected by any other cause than that of having inherited it [from] the Meriwether Family and it therfore more immediately calls on your charity to forgive those errors into which it may at

any time lead me. Tho all I shall ask at present is that you will
not finally condemn me untill next fall at which time it will
be my task personally to plead an excuse for my conduct.[14]

What is going on here? Lewis has chosen a highly elaborate way of
apologizing for not returning home immediately and announcing that
he will be home in the fall. In a manner partly playful, partly analytical
(a tone that he used at other times with his mother), he blames her for
his "rambling," since he has inherited his "Quixottic disposition" from
her side of the family, in contrast to the wishes of "all my friends." But
can his army service on the frontier serving his country by helping to
make the West safer for settlement aptly be described as "rambling"?
Hardly. And then, too, everyone knows that he will be scouting out land
warrants and investments, as most officers did, in order to assist the well
being of his family. This is not rambling. In fact, he is claiming, his
failure to return home at this time is because of his need to satisfy the
dictates of *duty* and *honor*, in spite of other claims made upon him. But,
taking this a step further, he implies he behaves the way he does because
of her, and hence he has learned how to satisfy duty and honor because
of her. The final sentence, with its metaphor of courtroom procedure
(condemnation and pleading), expresses his total confidence that he
will be exonerated of all blame for his behavior. All this, by the way,
from someone who is twenty-one years old.

Jefferson the attorney would have been delighted with the quality of
the argument here, as well as the expression of dedication to honor and
family. He would understand that here was a mind of first-rate ability,
probably capable of absorbing the crash courses in botany, zoology,
medicine, celestial navigation, ethnography, and, most of all, geography
that would be needed for the upcoming expedition. Evidence of Lewis's
capabilities as an outdoorsman had been evident throughout his life.
His rapid advancement in the army presumably testified to his skills in
leadership, and his time as paymaster, as well as his years running the

family farm at Locust Hill, proved that he possessed the meticulousness and forethought needed for the tasks of supplying the expedition and recording its progress. Lewis was one of very few officers who had strong Republican sympathies, as his evaluation of the officer corps indicated. And he had the advantage of living with Jefferson and learning the more subtle political issues involved in the mounting of the expedition. Apart from questions about Lewis's lack of a scientific education, the only doubts Jefferson must have harbored concerned Lewis's judgment.

A corollary question occurs: why not Clark? The Jefferson and Clark families were even closer neighbors; at one time the Clark property bordered Jefferson's. Thomas and George Rogers were rumored to be childhood friends, and we know that he was the first person Jefferson invited to explore the west. Although the Clarks had moved closer to Tidewater in Caroline County before William was born and then moved again some fourteen years later to the frontier of Virginia known as Kentucky, they were widely known as gentlefolk and highly respected. The story of William's army years must wait for a full biography, but we know it was thoroughly successful. He was with Wayne's army at the Battle of Fallen Timbers, he had conducted supply and intelligence missions to the Mississippi, and he had distinguished himself in an Indian attack when eighty or so men under his command escorting a pack train of 700 horses made it through to resupply Fort Greenville because of his coolness under fire.[15] He left the army to assist his family, thereby revealing an admirable sense of duty and responsibility. George Rogers had underwritten his army personally during his western campaigns in the Revolutionary War, confident that he would be reimbursed by the Virginia Legislature and the federal government. But it was not to be, and so his final years were spent in legal entanglements fending off creditors. William showed his dedication to his brother by spending virtually his full time managing those affairs. We learn from a letter written to Nicholas Biddle after Lewis's death that during the years he was living on his "farm in Kentucky" he visited the "Eastern States and

Washington" frequently, where he became "acquainted with President Mr. Jefferson."[16] Tantalizingly, he does not mention visiting with Lewis, which he probably would have done if these visits occurred after Jefferson became President, as the letter seems to imply, since Lewis arrived to live with Jefferson less than two months after the Inauguration. But we have no record of these occasions.

As we shall have many chances to see, Clark possessed the professional and personal qualities needed to command a successful expedition in as great or greater measure than did Lewis. Moreover, his work on his brother's behalf had led him to become a skilled surveyor and map-maker. He was more familiar than Lewis with Native Americans, at least eastern tribes, and less judgmental in assessing them. What he lacked was a "liberal education," indeed much formal education at all, and he tended to be quiet and reserved in social situations. If Jefferson had ever considered him to lead the expedition, it is likely he would have rejected him on the grounds of his supposed inability to handle scientific inquiry and, perhaps, diplomatic niceties. At any rate, Jefferson named no one until Congress approved a $2500 appropriation for western exploration on February 28, 1803. In his memoir after Lewis's death Jefferson recalls how Lewis "renewed his solicitations to have the direction of the party."[17] But it is clear from what follows in that memoir that Jefferson had already made up his mind Lewis was the one.

From March (Congress took almost six weeks to approve Jefferson's request—affairs moved at a quicker pace in those days) through July Lewis was incredibly busy. We are not privy to the extended conversations that must have taken place with Jefferson, which would be instructive. But by mid-March Lewis left for Harpers Ferry to pick up fifteen of the Army's newest rifles and to oversee the construction of a metal boat frame which could fold up and be covered with hides when needed (this sounds suspiciously like an idea of Jefferson's, but, given Lewis's degree of distress when the boat failed, may have been his own). There he was detained for a month. Then it was on to Lancaster to spend time learning celestial navigation with an eminent scholar for another month. By May 10 he had arrived in Philadelphia, where he began his crash courses in medicine, Indian ethnography, natural history, and more navigation, all with scientists who were Jefferson's friends and colleagues in the American Philosophical Society. Even more impressive is the record of his purchases to supply the expedition.[18] Again, he and Jefferson must have begun the itemizing of what was needed, but Lewis had to place the actual orders, oversee their receipt, and see to their shipping to Pittsburgh by wagon. The expedition was to include ten to twelve members, but Lewis was already thinking ahead; his basic order for everything from rifles to blankets was for fifteen participants for a two-year campaign. (Only later, when the velocity of the Mississippi current was encountered, was it clear that more men would be needed, and they were recruited along the River and supplied from St. Louis.) In addition, he had to plan for the trade goods and presents to be used with the tribes all along the way. We have the careful accounting of his purchases, as befitted a former paymaster, and we remain amazed at how detailed his thinking about provisions was.

By mid-June Lewis was back in Washington. On June 19 he wrote to Clark inviting him to share command (more of this later). On June 20 he received Jefferson's detailed instructions, which had been written in consultation with his cabinet officers Madison, Dearborn, Gallatin, and Lincoln. Whatever agreements had been hammered out in private conversations, it was nevertheless necessary to specify in writing what was expected. The instructions run to almost six crowded pages and reveal more than might be expected in a committee document.

First of all, they are addressed to "Captain Meriwether Lewis" of the First Regiment of Infantry of the U. S. of A. We should always remember that this is a military expedition, then, and will proceed under military discipline and law on orders from the Commander-in-Chief. This will not be a footloose group of bushwhacking adventurers off on a spree. The instructions contain the imperatives of orders, which obviate misunderstandings. They provide the authority for recruiting the members and gathering the supplies before stating the fundamental overriding purpose:

> The object of your mission is to explore the Missouri river, & such principal stream of it, as, by it's course and communication with the waters of the Pacific ocean…may offer the most direct & practicable water communication across this continent for the purposes of commerce.[19]

For a long time scholars have agonized over Jefferson's motives for creating the expedition, whether he hoped primarily to expand the nation or promote scientific knowledge. Some ingeniously hold that for an Enlightenment man they were one and the same. But there should be no question: in his highly organized prose he opts "for the purposes of commerce." Virtually everything in these instructions relates to this. Certainly the urgent pursuit of knowledge about Indian tribes is focussed on their role as trading partners or as obstacles to trade. Even interest in their religion and morality is expressed so that they may be more easily "civilized" and thereby assimilated to purposes of trade. They are to be treated in "the most friendly & conciliatory manner which their own conduct will admit," in order convince them "of our dispositions to a commercial intercourse with them." The party's safety is not to be jeopardized because this would deprive Jefferson of the information that has been gathered, and he gives seemingly specific instructions (not really specific at all) about how they may return home with what they have learned. Instead of sending a ship to the mouth of the Columbia, Jefferson gave Lewis a letter of credit to be drawn on anywhere in the world, so that, if necessary, the party could sail around the world on its way back to the East Coast on any ship they happened to find.

The tone of the entire document is peculiar. Some matters are treated in far greater detail than necessary for orders, as if Jefferson wanted to summarize everything he knew or thought he knew, as in his discussions of rivers south of the Missouri, or the lengthy paragraphs on caution in confronting hostile forces or the procedures for providing succession of command to head off "anarchy, dispersion, & the consequent danger to your party, and total failure of the enterprise." He even proposes that a copy of the journal Lewis is ordered to write be made on birch bark, as if this material were universally available. Granted, these are serious issues, but single sentences could have clearly and concisely handled them. It is almost as if Jefferson hopes to cope with every problem the party will encounter and thereby join it in his imagination when he cannot in fact.

But there are two items in the instructions that are not explicable in the terms above. One sentence in a list of "other objects worthy of notice" such as soil, climate, volcanic appearances, and minerals speaks of "the animals of the country generally, & especially those not known in the U.S."; another deals with "the remains or accounts of any which may be deemed rare or extinct." Strictly speaking, Jefferson did not believe in the extinction of entire species, but only individuals, and there is no commercial benefit to be gained from these observations. Lewis and Clark took both injunctions seriously and especially in the matter of new birds and animals and plant species have been celebrated for what they reported. And if there are exceptions to commercial benefit, perhaps I am overstating Jefferson's passion for trade. Another detail may speak to such a possibility.

Jefferson emphasizes the need to explore the *southern* tributaries of the Missouri, presumably to clarify the extent of Spanish interests and claims and where the Rio Grande and the Colorado Rivers have their sources. Lewis is warned away from the northern tributaries as already explored by the British. But in the Journals we see that special care all along the route is given to the *northern* ones; it is, after all, Lewis's extensive exploration of the Marias that leads to bloodshed with the Blackfoot tribe. And comments on Jefferson's draft by Gallatin stressed the importance of the north in relation to future settlement and to block English incursions.[20] It is likely that private instructions were given to Lewis to explore to the north. Madison may have provided a key to understanding when he pointed out to Jefferson (who had asked his cabinet for suggestions to his draft) that emphasis be placed on the commercial goals of the expedition to repel "criticism of illicit principal objects of the measure." The only illicit object would be to define a *de facto* American boundary with the British beyond current understandings. A recurrent theme in the early years of the Republic is the desirability of annexing Canada or major parts of it. The instructions, then, not only put into writing the principal commercial objects of the mission and give an inexperienced commander specific guidance beyond what would normally be deemed necessary, but also in all probability intentionally try to mislead observers from perceiving the full imperialistic intentions of the expedition.

After all the subtleties and intrigue of international diplomacy, it must have been a great relief to get underway and lose oneself in action. The Journals are unique in the annals of exploration in their thoroughness and detail. And in the minds of many readers, they provide the closest thing we have to an American epic. But before we, too, get underway, it may be helpful to spend a moment explaining something of the journals' proceedings, for they have a rich and perplexing history of their own, so much so that an entire book has been published on the subject.[21] Moulton spends a good deal of time in his recent edition on their construction and eventual publication.[22] At no less than four places in his formal charge of June 20 Jefferson instructs both captains to keep daily records of their experience, and he thinks it a good idea for the sergeants to do so as well. And write they did, becoming, as Donald Jackson has stated, the "writingest explorers in history."

The final words in Clark's hand on Sept. 25, 1806, five days after the party landed at St. Charles, Missouri, and the unpacking had begun were these: "a fine morning we commenced wrighting &c." This suggests that what had been done along the trail were notes and that the journals were a polishing of rough drafts done after their return. But there would have been very little time for this, since they were celebrities, to be feted all along the East Coast before returning to their new official duties in St. Louis. And at other times it is clear that the finished entries were done very close to the events they describe. Moulton prints Clark's field notes next to his final entry for the day, so that extensive revisions in tone and emphasis can be seen. The captains had much time at their disposal during the winter at Ft. Mandan and again at Ft. Clatsop, where they undoubtedly brought their writing up to date, as they sometimes did during other pauses from the daily grind of travel. When Lewis died in 1809 he was on his way east with his manuscript of the journals, possibly untouched since their return three years earlier, even though it was to be his responsibility to get them into shape for publication, since he was the more literary of the two. Fortunately, the journals were recovered and together with Clark's, made their way to Philadelphia. Lewis had arranged for publication and had presented a prospectus to get subscribers for what was to be an expensive publishing venture: one volume of the narrative, another of the scientific observations, and a gigantic version of the map Clark had made of the territory covered, the first of its kind with any degree of accuracy. But Clark felt inadequate to the task of putting the material in publishable shape, the original publisher went bankrupt, and Jefferson seemed to have lost interest, so that his influence was not exerted. Finally, the independently wealthy Nicholas Biddle took an interest in the manuscript and worked long and hard to produce what he called the history of the expedition, editing the Journals' narrative but leaving the scientific work to others. His version was published in 1814, but the second publisher immediately went bankrupt as well, and only 2000 copies were ever printed. It took Clark two years to see a copy. The manuscripts on which this version was based were deposited in the library of the American Philosophical Society in Philadelphia, where they remain today.

With little promotion and waning interest in a country that had moved on to war with England and a new market civilization, the Journals dropped out of sight for most of the century (although in his novel *The Prairie* James Fenimore Cooper does mention the expedition three times). They were revived by a new annotated edition of Biddle's History in 1893 by Elliot Coues, for many years an army surgeon and an eminent ornithologist. A much more inclusive edition of the Journals in eight volumes followed in 1904–05, edited by Reuben Thwaites, head of the Wisconsin State Historical Society, who published all the scientific material, as well as journals of the sergeants and other journals entries by Clark not part of the original version. But by the 1980's the time was ripe for the beautifully annotated and edited version of the Journals recently completed by Gary Moulton and the University of Nebraska Press, which will remain the standard for years to come. In addition to the popular and excellent abridgment by Bernard DeVoto (my introduction to the Journals) in 1953, there have been several inexpensive recent versions, notably that by Frank Bergon for Penguin in their Nature Classics series. There is even an on-line version of the Journals prepared by college students so that web-surfers can vicariously follow the explorers day by day.

Like everything else about the expedition, the Journals are a genuine collaboration. Some days we have both Lewis and Clark writing independent accounts, some days Clark is clearly copying from Lewis, some days we have two entries from Clark, both his original field notes and his revised version. But for large stretches of the journey Clark is our main source; there are about 400 days with no entry from Lewis. In some cases it is clear that Lewis wrote nothing. In the trip down the Ohio he left blank pages in his notebook equal to the missing days, and near the end of the expedition after he is wounded he tells us he is laying down his pen. But we have nothing of the trip up the Missouri the first spring and summer, and nothing but a few spotty entries at first of the desperate journey down the Bitterroots, the interlude with the Nez

Perce, the tumultuous ride down the Columbia, and the building of Ft. Clatsop. Whether his entries for these days are missing or never written is difficult to say. The scholar Donald Jackson believes that we can point to places which indicate journal entries were lost, but others like Gary Moulton speculate that, for whatever reasons, for long periods of time Lewis simply did not keep up the writing.[22] This is all the more evident, since in purely literary terms Lewis is the more accomplished writer. The big moments—the appearance of the Great Falls, the portage, the tension-filled trip up the mountains to the Missouri's sources, the encounter with the Shoshonis, the stock-taking passages as the expedition enters new phases—all are Lewis at his best, and we will have occasion to explore most of them in detail. But Clark, it seems to me, has never received his due for his thoroughness and his accuracy, his buoyant, sometimes naïve expressions of delight and wonder, and his tight-lipped presentation of moments of crisis, as in the encounter with the Teton Sioux. Clark, too, is the master of the one-liner as he continually sizes up the territory they pass through, and his "Oh, the Joy" as he believes they have finally made it to the Pacific reverberates through the reader's consciousness. His bizarre and totally unsystematic spelling has probably encouraged the notion that he was really not very verbal (his punctuation isn't much worse that Lewis's or, for that matter, Jefferson's). In fact, as I have lived with the Journals, I have come to trust Clark when I have occasional suspicions about Lewis's genuineness.

The reader's patience is required to let the cumulative effect of the Journals sink into consciousness, but when this occurs they become remarkably hypnotic and yet dramatic at the same time. They are clear in main outline even when obscure on some details. They are totally absorbing in conveying the experience of a daily advance into the unknown with adventures and sights beyond what have ever been experienced by white American men. In this regard they resemble the entire genre of science fiction which explores planetary travel and its wonders. But in the final analysis they remain unique in annals of the past, a point where historical writing and literary revelation merge in a special way. In addition to encounters with the unknown, dealt with through skill, courage, and dedication to the values which have sent them forth, Lewis and Clark must deal with the world beyond nature as they have understood it, and they must confront themselves in the light of these encounters. We know how the story turns out, but what become most compelling are the details of their and our discoveries along the way.

1 Donald Jackson, ed., *Letters of the Lewis and Clark Expedition, with Related Documents, 1783–1854* (Urbana, University of Illinois Press, 1978), I, 61.

2 Rhys Isaac's *The Transformation of Virginia, 1740–1790* (New York, W.W. Norton, 1982) beautifully supplements the usual economic and political histories of the region.

3 I have taken the account of the Spotswood expedition from a lecture given by Kevin Hartwick, Univ. of Maryland, at the 27th Annual Meeting of the Lewis and Clark Trail Heritage Foundation on July 30, 1995.

4 Hugh Cleland, *George Washington in the Ohio Valley* (Pittsburgh, Univ. of Pittsburgh Press, 1955), pp. 255–288.

5 Thomas A. Lewis, *For King and Country: The Maturing of George Washington, 1748–1760* (New York, HarperCollins, 1993), pp. 241–258.
Lewis reports that General Forbes advised one of his staff "to consult Colonel Washington, although perhaps not follow his advice, as his behavior about the roads was no ways like a soldier" (258).

6 Cleland, p. 288.

7 John Hammond Moore, *Albemarle:Jefferson's County, 1727–1976* (Charlottesville, for the Albemarle County Historical Association by the University of Virginia Press, 1983), p. 30.

8 John Logan Allen, *Lewis and Clark and the Image of the American Northwest* (New York, Dover Publications, 1991), p. 178. The University of Illinois Press originally published this work in 1975 as *Passage through the Garden: Lewis and Clark and the Image of the American Northwest*. It is a fascinating and profound

exploration of the meaning of the expedition from the perspective of a philosophically minded geographer.

9   Much of the material on Lewis's life is from Richard Dillon's biography, *Meriwether Lewis: A Biography* (New York, Coward-McCann, 1965). This episode is reported on p. 12. Stephen Ambrose, *Undaunted Courage: Meriwether Lewis, Thomas Jefferson, and the Opening of the American West* (New York, Simon & Schuster, 1996), has been widely read but adds little to our knowledge of Lewis apart from his time on the westward expedition.

10 Donald Jackson, "Jefferson, Meriwether Lewis, and the Reduction of the United States Army," *Proceedings of the American Philosophical Society,* 124 (April 1980), 91–96 reprinted in James Ronda, ed., *Voyages of Discovery: Essays on the Lewis and Clark Expedition* (Helena, Montana Historical Society Press, 1998), pp. 59–71.

11 The "Memoir of Meriwether Lewis," a letter from the ex-President, was prefaced to the first edition of the Journals material in 1814, edited by Nicholas Biddle into *The History of the Lewis and Clark Expedition,* and has appeared ever since, causing much mischief concerning our view of Lewis. We will have occasion at a later time to examine it in greater detail.

12 Cited in William B. Skelton, *An American Profession of Arms: The Army Officer Corps, 1784-1861* (Lawrence, University Press of Kansas, 1992), p.24.

13 Skelton, pp.55–56.

14 Cited in Ambrose, p.43.

15 Jerome O. Steffin, *William Clark: Jeffersonian Man on the Frontier* (Norman, Univ. of Oklahoma Press, 1977), p. 22, summarizes the report on this adventure found in Clark's own journals of the period.

16 *The History of the Lewis and Clark Expedition,* ed. Elliott Coues (New York, Francis P. Harper, 1893), I, lxxii.

17 *History,* p.xxi.

18 We have the full records in Jackson, *Letters,* I, 69–99.

19 These instructions have often been reprinted. I use the version in Jackson, *Letters,* I, 61–66.

20 Jefferson requested comments on the Instructions from his cabinet members, and their responses can be found in Jackson, *Letters*, I, 32–36.

21 Paul Russell Cutright, *A History of the Lewis and Clark Journals*, (Norman, Univ. of Oklahoma Press, 1976.

22 Moulton contains as part of the Introduction to his edition a section entitled "The Journal—keeping Methods of Lewis and Clark," II, 8–35. The treatment of this question comes to a conclusion on pp. 20–21. His discussion is so exhaustive that it would be presumptuous to disagree with him! A full reference is as follows: Gary E. Moulton, *The Journals of the Lewis and Clark Expedition* (Lincoln, Univ. of Nebraska Press, 1986–1997), 12 volumes. The first volume consists of maps relating to the Expedition. All further references, unless otherwise noted, will be to this edition.

CHAPTER 2

"The Most Beautiful River in the Universe"

Arrived at Bruno's Island 3 miles below [Pittsburgh] halted a few minutes…being invited on by some of the gentlemen present to try my *airgun*…. Mr. Blaze Cenas being unacquainted with the management of the gun suffered her to discharge herself accedentaly the ball passed through the hat of a woman about 40 yards distanc cuting her temple about the fourth of the diameter of the ball; shee fell instantly and the blood gusing from her temple we were all in the greatest consternation supposed she was dead by [but] in a minute she revived to our enespressable satisfaction, and by examination we found the wound by no means mortal or even dangerous; called the hands aboard and proceeded to a ripple of *McKee's Rock*.

Lewis, August 30, 1803 (*Journals*, II, 65).

Today the gleaming skyscrapers of the Golden Triangle, that point of land where the Ohio River is created (as we all learned in school) by the juncture of the Allegheny and Monongahela, cast their shadows over what in 1803 was the entire settlement. Nothing remained of the old French Fort Dusquesne, and when the last threat of French domination had ended with the fall of Fort Niagara on Lake Ontario, English hopes for settlement and profit looked to the Ohio Valley. William Pitt insisted on a stronghold that would "maintain his Majesty's subjects in undisputed possession of the Ohio," meaning the entire territory of the Old Northwest. To serve as a base for the taming of the often rambunctious Native Americans of the area, a huge pentangle-shaped ditch was dug, ramparts formed of dirt twenty feet high were thrown up (local timber had been exhausted earlier), and the resulting structure was named after the Prime Minister. Even before Fort Pitt was completed, it began to fill up with refugees from the rampaging Chief Pontiac and his braves.[1]

Fort Pitt's one moment of "glory" came in 1764 when the Indians attacked continuously for five days and nights before withdrawing, sensibly concluding that the cost to take it would be too great. Immediately thereafter, an expedition led by a Swiss professional soldier named Col. Bouquet, containing 1500 Pennsylvania and Virginia militiamen, relieved the Fort. The army was fresh from a victory the previous year over the Shawnees and Delawares at Bushy Run, where the Indians had been outsmarted. Boquet's mission was to "chastise the savages," and after almost self-destructing, the army marched to the Muskingum River and so intimidated the gathered tribes that they sued for peace and returned over 200 frightened prisoners. This was one of the few triumphs in this region that white men were to enjoy during the eighteenth century.[2]

The Fort remained, staffed by American troops throughout the Revolutionary War, serving as a base for operations such as George Rogers Clark's expeditions down the Ohio to the Mississippi; the flatboats that transported his army were built at the area of the Fort and he was supplied there. General McIntosh left from Fort Pitt with orders to clear out the Wyandots in the Sandusky region (where he was attacked by the infamous Simon Girty), and it was also from here in 1781 that Daniel Brodhead left to burn Coshocton and other villages, slaughtering along the way with particular ferocity (such as the personal tomahawking of a chief while he was sitting in negotiations). Soon after this the Fort was decommissioned, in part because no use could be found for it, in part because is was a huge moldering and eroding pile of mud and weeds, incapable of being maintained. Today only a single blockhouse remains in Point State Park to commemorate the "undisputed possession of the Ohio."[3]

When Lewis was serving in the Army in the Northwest during the latter half of the 90's, he carried dispatches from Ft. Detroit to a new fort on the Allegheny River side of the point called Fort Fayette. From here, too, he set out on paymaster runs down the Ohio to Wheeling and Cincinnati (Fort Washington). By all accounts Fort Fayette was a flimsy affair and played little part in future history, except for a moment when citizens attempted to take it over during the Whiskey Rebellion. It also served quietly as a supply depot and military lockup during the War of 1812. But it was the focus of a growing settlement. In 1792 the town beside Fort Fayette had 36 "mechanics (clock-makers, saddlers, and the like), two brickyards, three or four boatyards, and, nearby at least two sawmills."[4] Its first genuine tycoon (of many to come), James O'Hara, bore the title of Quartermaster General, and made a good thing of provisioning and equipping the armies fighting Indians in Indiana and Illinois, sending goods downriver in flatboats built for the purpose.The fact of settlement, however, did not mean that the town was an oasis of civilization. One observer described it as "a parcel of abandoned wretches" who lived like "so many pigs in a sty." Sunday mornings were rarely celebrated by churchgoing but instead furnished a prime occasion for drinking, which meant fighting, commonly consisting of eye gouging, so that a higher than normal proportion of the population

were one-eyed. The law was sporadically enforced at best; while mayhem was regularly occurring on all sides, a man was horsewhipped by
the court and then fatally shot for kicking another man's dog.[5]
Pittsburgh in this era was called a "Sodom." Views of the entire western
Pennsylvania area were colored by the way the participants in the
Whiskey Rebellion were portrayed along the Eastern seaboard as rab-
ble-rousing, law-avoiding ungovernable troublemakers, although it is
possible to make the case that they were merely taking seriously the
promises of the Revolution, that there was to be no taxation without
representation. But no one could accuse most of them of gentility.
Absentee landlords owned much of the area's property, understandably,
and wealth became concentrated in the hands of a few. So there were
genuine grievances. But these were not, in general, polite petitioners of
the government. The federal census in 1800 (handwritten) tells us that
there were 304 residences in the village itself, but other estimates of the
population in the greater area put it at nearly 95,000 (from 33,000 at the
end of the War).

   Today, of course, Pittsburgh is a different matter, although shrunken
in size from its population of over 700,000 in 1950 to about half as
many today (the five-county area, however, supports about 2.2 million
people). The story of its economic transformation from steel and grime
capital of the nation to high-tech and white-collar center of the eastern
Midwest has been told often and with considerable self-congratulation.
From the mid-seventies on, one mill after another closed, so that
unemployment in Pittsburgh by 1983 was officially at 14.7%,
unofficially much higher. But by 1985, only two years later, Pittsburgh
was named the most livable city in America by a national publication
(although for whom was not addressed), and in 1989 shared such a
designation with San Francisco and Seattle. Obviously, the change from
a smoky industrial base to a more sanitary economy was underway
before this time, so that to the concentration of old wealth already there
was added the prosperity of burgeoning new enterprises, such as

medicine and biotechnology, which today employ more people than any other sector of the area economy.⁶ Such progress has not come without its price; like every other large eastern city, maybe all large cities, the traveler cannot help but notice that just beyond the opulence of the downtown area, block after block of burnt out, partly abandoned but partly occupied tenements still stands as testimony to our failure to create a livable society for all.

After all the discussions with Jefferson, all the intensive studying in Philadelphia and Lancaster, all the careful purchases of supplies and arms in Philadelphia and Harpers Ferry, it was here to Pittsburgh that Lewis came to learn who would accompany him. On July 18 he received Clark's affirmative reply to his letter of invitation of June 20. One major preparatory task remained—the building of the keelboat. Lewis would take it down the Ohio, pick up Clark and the "nine good men from Kentucky," as well as Clark and York, his slave, near Louisville, move on to Ft. Massac and then the garrison at Kaskaskia to gather other volunteers, and finally that season journey up the Mississippi to their eventual winter quarters beside the Wood River in Illinois. The original idea, Lewis tells Jefferson in an April letter from Lancaster, was to contact Congressman William Dickson at Nashville and ask that he find a builder for a keelboat there, so that Lewis could sail from the Tennessee River to the Ohio, and pick up more volunteers for the expedition from South West Point, an Army base in Tennessee. Over a month later Lewis mentions from Philadelphia that he had written again to Dickson because he had heard nothing from him, even though he had sent $50 on account (we have no record that he ever did hear from Dickson). Because the season was slipping away (Lewis still hoped that the Corps of Discovery could start up the Missouri before winter set in), he did not wait for a refund but left Washington for

Pittsburgh so quickly he forgot his wallet, his dirk, and his favorite bridle, arriving on July 15. (Jefferson forwarded the wallet, but we don't know what happened to the rest).

One of the several mysteries that perplex Lewis and Clark enthusiasts is this keelboat—who designed it, who built it, and what precisely it looked like. From many references in the Journals, together with Clark's drawings, we know enough about its appearance, so that it has been reconstructed at least twice recently. While the design bears some traces of the mechanically-aptituded mind of Jefferson, its rudiments were common enough on the Ohio by this time. Throughout the latter half of the eighteenth century flotillas of flat-bottomed skiffs known by the French (who were the boatmen of choice) as "bateaux" navigated the Ohio, sometimes so flimsily built that they traveled downstream and were torn apart when they reached New Orleans or Pensacola, salvaged for the planks. In the 1760's Philadelphia firms began to systematically enter the "Illinois trade" to Kaskaskia by building boats in the Fort Pitt area, but these ventures were not very profitable, since British goods coming upriver from New Orleans were still cheaper. But the Revolution dramatically altered that equation, and the River became a veritable highway with throngs of Tories (and the apolitical as well) heading west by barge, and soldiers and materiel shipped back and forth. George Rogers Clark, for example, left for Illinois in 1778 from the Monongahela boatyards with 150 men in six bateaux. The first recorded engagement on the Ohio involved three American boats armed with swivel guns meeting ten British ones coming down the Wabash River and capturing seven of them.[7]

But these were flatboats, either of the "Allegheny" or "Mackinaw" types, often with a cabin or shelter, able to float on a "heavy dew" and highly unstable in adverse weather or when meeting obstructions such as bars or floating logs. About 1800 a keel consisting of a 4-inch-square beam on the bottom was added to the design, and this provided a measure of stability, especially when the boat was towed, as well as absorbing the shock of collisions with rocks or logs. These keelboats, characteristically 40 to 80 feet long with a beam of seven to ten feet, pointed at the bow and sometimes at the stern as well, often carried a mast for mounting a sail, and added seats for rowers. They must have looked vaguely like miniature Spanish galleons. They drew about two feet when loaded. They were spoken of in terms of their load, as carrying, for example, 60 or 100 barrels of salt.[8] Apparently the rudiments of the keelboat were so standardized by 1803 that Lewis did not have to specify to Dr. Dickson many details of design. And apart from the modifications added by Clark at the Wood River encampment, primarily the cargo hatches that could be fixed in an upright position to provide defense against attackers, the Corps of Discovery's keelboat (why didn't it ever get recognized with a name?) resembled its Ohio River counterparts.

This leaves the question of who built it. On two occasions, in letters to Jefferson and to Clark, Lewis gives us spirited accounts of his frustrations with the unnamed builder, who was, according to Lewis, a drunkard and poor manager of his workers. He had calculated before arriving there on July 15 that he would leave Pittsburgh on August 5, but, "most shamefully detained by the unpardonable negligence of my boat-builder," he found at that time the planking barely underway and the builder at odds with his workmen, who eventually walked off the job. Lewis threatened him "with the penalty of the contract, and exacted a promise of greater sobriety in future," but threats had little effect. Lewis considered the possibility of purchasing two or three pirogues (large canoes), hoping to find a keelboat down river, but the local merchants persuaded him (whether rightly or not—keelboats were built at Wheeling and Marietta, but we don't know if any were available at the time) that chances of success were very slim. He did buy the pirogues, anyway, as his stock of goods grew, and one of them may have been the "white pirogue" that accompanied the party all the way to the Great Falls in Montana. The latter part of August saw Lewis spending most of his time as a stand-in foreman, "alternately persuading and threaten-ing" the workmen, not very effectively, it seems. He tells Clark as an illustration of their dilatoriness that it took twelve days for them to pre-pare the poles and the oars.⁹

Why all the hurry? Apart from understandable excitement to be underway, Lewis still believed that the Expedition could set off up the Missouri before winter, although his faith in this possibility must have been waning by now. More immediately, the level of the Ohio was dropping to record lows. Locals, "those who pretended to be acquainted with the navigation of the river," (his exasperation with the entire place is evident) told him it was impracticable to think of descending the River at this season.¹⁰ He was to take this advice to the extent that he transported many of the supplies by wagon to Wheeling, where the River deepened, and he was to off-load others into the pirogues. The keelboat was finally finished at 7 a.m. on July 31st, Lewis tells Jefferson, it was immediately loaded, and he was underway by 10 a.m.

For someone capable of making and executing such detailed plans for provisioning his command and purchasing the needed supplies within a budget (mostly), Lewis seems guilty of casualness in the highly important matter of selecting his boat builder. Maybe he had been familiar with builders who were at work there during his tour of Army duty and perhaps selected one whose career had since gone downhill. A problem with this idea is that it seems likely he would have mentioned his recollection somewhere, and, so far as we know, he never did. It is more likely that he had asked for a recommendation from someone whose contemporary knowledge of Pittsburgh was better than his own. That someone would almost certainly have ties to the army, since the army was the best customer for boats. And the bill was to be sent directly to the government (I've found no one, however, who has been able to locate the bill in Washington; it could have been destroyed by fire during the War of 1812, as so many government records were). At this point, I thought I could step in and with my well-honed research skills get some immediate results, so I headed for Pittsburgh and the formidable resources of the Pennsylvania Collection at the Carnegie Library. I had phoned ahead for help with printed materials from the year 1803 and learned of the files of the *Pittsburgh Gazette* available there. What I was looking for was a list of local boatbuilders, maybe some gossip about who among them was losing business to the bottle, or had labor troubles, or maybe even lawsuits or a bankruptcy reported in the public press. In addition, the librarian suggested that I might be interested in something-called *Cramer's Almanac* for 1803, and that it would be waiting for me when I arrived. It was, and proved to be just what the named implied, a day-to-day weather forecast, along with some planting lore and moralizing one-liners in the manner of Poor Richard—in short, no help at all. Also waiting for me were two envelopes of newspaper articles dealing with the shipbuilding industry at Pittsburgh. When the articles dealing with World War II were set aside (Pittsburgh produced thousands of landing craft, as well as Liberty ships and even smaller warships at this time), and the accounts of the colorful early steamship days were sorted out, a few remained on the keelboat era, and they paralleled the material in the Baldwin's book. No help here, beyond the few names mentioned in Baldwin, which I proceeded to follow up in the massive catalog of genealogy in the Pennsylvania Collection. But one fact soon emerged: boatbuilders were apparently beneath the notice of genealogists, and merchants fared not much better, unless they became merchant princes.

Not to worry, I thought, since the microfilm of the entire run of the Pittsburgh *Gazette*, the West's earliest newspaper, awaited me Surely in the give-and-take of daily commerce I would find ads from boatbuilders, boats for sale, maybe even bankruptcy notices from drunken boatbuilders. To be on the safe side, I started reading from June 11, 1802, and amid the bits of national news, proclamations from the President and congressmen, landings of famous Europeans in

Boston and New York, merchant ads announcing goods just arrived, want ads about lost horses, and bankruptcy notices, in the very first issue I found an ad which read: "Kentucky Boats at Wheeling Dennis Cassat to furnish boats for descending Ohio." This was surely getting somewhere, for although Kentucky boats had a reputation for inferior workmanship, and Lewis would have avoided them (Mississippi boats had somewhat higher rails, were normally better caulked and altogether more stable), and although the ad was from Wheeling rather than Pittsburgh, nevertheless it was on track to more promising material. And sure enough, on March 11, 1803, this ad appeared: "Mississippi Boats for Sale 40–45ft. Built in the best manner with Chimnies and Pumps compleat. For sale by Tarascon Brothers, James Berthoud & Co. (Front and Market Sts.)" This merchant house apparently retailed products of the adjoining boatyard on the Monongahela side of the point, with blacksmiths and rigging and sail lofts, as well as a stores warehouse nearby. The boat for Lewis was to be much bigger, but I was getting closer. Then—nothing! There was a gap in the microfilm until 1806! When I later checked the film of the *Gazette* at other libraries I found the same gap. The *Gazette* for two years had simply vanished, and I have never been able to locate those issues elsewhere.

If I couldn't find the builder, I thought, I might be able to locate the person who recommended the builder. And one name kept appearing in the annals of early Pittsburgh with some frequency, Major Isaac Craig. He had served with distinction in the Revolution and had been a survivor of the Valley Forge winter. At one point he had been seriously wounded but returned to active duty. In the 90's he showed up in Pittsburgh as Quartermaster, and it was he who outfitted General Anthony Wayne's river expedition against the Indians of the Old Northwest, including, in all probability, letting the contract for the building of the boats. He knew George Rogers Clark, and from a comment in one of Lewis's letters to Jefferson, he appears to have been acquainted with Meriwether Lewis as well. He left the Army in 1801 at

Jefferson's inauguration and became a Pittsburgh merchant and later owner of a sawmill, a glass factory, and other enterprises. Could Lewis have asked him to recommend a boatbuilder? Possibly, but probably not, for one major reason. Craig must have left the Army because of his Federalist Party roots. Before leaving office John Adams had packed the officer corps with loyal Tories, probably because of his mistrust of the "radical republican" about to take his place. We know that one of Lewis' first tasks as Jefferson's private secretary was to annotate the politics and competence of all 250 of the Army's officers, as a prelude to dismissing many. Jefferson wanted to shrink the Army as well as get ride of political appointees, so there was not much of a future for a confirmed Tory major, and Craig was astute enough, apparently, to see this. But this makes it highly unlikely that Lewis would then go to Craig, who, if he shared the general Tory antipathy towards Jefferson's western interests, would not have much invested in the success of any expedition requiring a keelboat.

My Pittsburgh research thus came to an inconclusive and humbling end. But I returned to the Letters and found a far more plausible candidate for the source of the boatbuilder recommendation and a possible reason for its being a bad recommendation. On the day Lewis arrived in Pittsburgh at 2 p.m. he writes to Jefferson at 3 p.m.: "I have not yet seen Lieut. Hook nor made the enquiry relative to my boat...."[11] Moses Hooke was a young officer who had joined the First Infantry in 1799, had served under Capt. Daniel Bissell (whose name will reappear), sustained a broken leg when a tornado struck the encampment in Indiana where he had been stationed, and since January, 1803, had been serving as the commander of Fort Fayette. This sentence could refer to two different but equally urgent activities. Lewis may be saying he needed to check in with the person who had already been instructed by Secretary of War Dearborn to give every possible assistance to Lewis in provisioning, including furnishing him with "eighteen light axes": In addition, he needed to learn of the progress made on the boat construction with its builder. Or the sentence could suggest that he had not yet checked with Hooke *about* the boat. A year later Dearborn charges Hooke with the procuring of a boat capable of transporting fifteen men with baggage and to draw little water, probably to return some Osage Indians back to their tribe.[12] This indicates that the Commander of the Fort was expected to be able to expedite such an order. And tucked away in Lewis's accounting for the expenditures of the trip is this entry: "March 28, 1804: for amount disbursed by Lt. Moses Hooke between July & Novem. 1803 for ferriage &for a boat, outfits, &c."[13] By itself the entry is inconclusive but it is probable that the total cost of the boat was covered here. The fact that the recommended builder turns out to be a bad one in Lewis's case could be chalked up to Hooke's inexperience, since he had only been in Pittsburgh since January. Perhaps the recommended builder had done work for the Army in the past that had been satisfactory.

At any event, Lewis and Hooke hit it off. Lewis writes to Jefferson on July 26, within two weeks of arriving at Pittsburgh: "…in the event of Mr. Clark's declining to accompany me Lieut. Hooke of this place has engaged to do so, if permitted; and I think from his disposition and qualifications that I might safely calculate on being as ably assisted by him in the execution of the objects of my mission, as I could wish, or would be, by any other officer in the Army."[14] What holds up the possible appointment is Hooke's responsibility for public accounts and stores and the difficulty in finding someone to take over this job. Lewis suggests as a likely candidate for interim manager until another officer can be assigned to Ft. Fayette the name of Isaac Craig! Secretary Dearborn gives Hooke permission to go with Lewis once his duties have been turned over, and we are on the verge of creating the Lewis and Hooke expedition, or, more likely, the Lewis expedition, since Hooke is his junior in rank and experience. Then on August 3, in one of the more affecting letters in American history, Lewis received Clark's response: "This is an undertaking fraited with many diffeculties, but My friend I do assure you that no man lives whith whome I would perfur to undertake Such a Trip &c. As your self...."[15] The personalities of Jefferson and Dearborn hover over this entire movement, like Greek gods watching the actions of mortals; Dearborn's laconic response to Jefferson is that Clark's acquiesence "...is highly interesting, it adds very much to the ballance of chances in favour of ultimate success."[16] Although Lewis has been given considerable latitude in making choices about personnel (and will show bad judgement in at least two cases where he invited unsuitable candidates to come along), we almost hear a sigh of relief from the elders.

As previously noted, Lewis left as soon as the boat was ready. Accompanying him was a detachment of seven soldiers, a pilot who was paid seventy dollars to conduct Lewis to the Falls of the Ohio at Louisville, and three "young men on trial," whose names we will probably never know. But the journey almost aborts before getting very far along the River, as the passage at the beginning of the chapter testifies. How do we explain this bizarre episode? Why did a man in such a hurry to leave stop so soon to socialize with a group of strangers, even if one of them may have been an acquaintance? What could he have gained? During the winter ahead Lewis will spend a great deal of time in St. Louis while Clark is left to train the party on the Illinois bank, but he has a purpose in this socializing. He is making business contacts with men who can provide supplies and information on conditions along the Missouri. But here there is apparently no such justification. Do we chalk it up to adolescent showing off and youthful exuberance? It is not a good omen for the enterprise ahead, except that it bodies forth a *resurrection,* the possibility of a new life, in the apparent death and revival of the unnamed woman who was shot in the temple. But Lewis seems unaware of any symbolic overtones in this episode and hurries on to talk about the difficulties of navigation, almost as if, while he was duty bound to report on the incident, he did not care to dwell on it. Or as if he was whistling his way past a bad dream to make it go away. This was not, after all, an episode that a would-be Enlightenment gentleman would care to dwell on.

The River was very low that season, and much of the Journal of this leg of the trip involves descriptions of how they pushed, lifted, dug, even hired horses and oxen to pull them over the bars. When a boat was grounded, there was a universal rule that all hands must jump overboard and help to get it underway. Baldwin tells us that once when Louis Phillipe of France and his brothers were traveling the Ohio in the comparative luxury of the cabin, even they responded to the call, "You kings down there! Show yourselves and help us three-spots pull off this bar!" [16] It took from Sept. 1 to Sept. 5 to make it to Stubenville, at the time a small settlement with, as Lewis says, "several respectable families residing in it." By Sept. 7 they reach Wheeling, the site of Fort Henry, "now gone to decay", where Lewis finds the supplies he had sent overland in good order, and where he establishes two habits that will stay with him for the entire trip: acute and sometimes remarkable observations of the natural world around him, and prolonged visits with locals It is as he leaves Wheeling that he provides us with the account of thousands of squirrels swimming across the River to no apparent purpose, except to delight and entertain his Newfoundland dog, Seaman, who had been purchased in Pittsburgh for twenty dollars, a good price for a dog. And it is in Wheeling that he spent time with some government officials headed for the "Mississippi Territory" who happen to be good Jeffersonian Republicans. He behaves as if he will some day run for political office.

It is here, too, that we find another of those occasions that reveal Lewis's sometimes-questionable judgement. In a letter to Jefferson written from Cincinnati a week or so later, Lewis outlined his plan for journeying down towards Santa Fe during the winter, since it has now become impossible to start the expedition before the following spring. This was the first that Jefferson had heard of this. But the Santa Fe side excursion, through Spanish territory, would not be welcomed by the

Spanish, to say the least, and could jeopardize the entire Missouri plan. Just a few years later Pike's expedition to the Southwest was intercepted by the Spanish, and Pike and his men were imprisoned. We know that at one time a Spanish army was out looking for the Corps of Discovery as well, but in the wrong places. Jefferson and those of his inner circle among the Cabinet are obviously dismayed, and must have begun to have second thoughts about their choice for a leader. Jefferson sent instructions to head off this imprudent bit of high spirits, but a letter took a long time to reach its destination.

Even in Wheeling there is a problem. Lewis met there the son of one of his Philadelphia tutors, a Doctor Patterson, who was a physician apparently interested in trying his fortunes in the Illinois Territory. On a very brief acquaintance Lewis invited him along, saying that a physician has not been authorized for the expedition but implying that there would be time that winter in St. Louis to gain Jefferson's permission. Lewis was especially taken with the doctor's collection of medicines, reportedly valued at one hundred pounds. Dr. Patterson was to wind up his local affairs and meet the boat the following day. Whereas Moses Hooke may or may not have been a suitable second-in-command, Dr. Patterson clearly was not up to the rigors of the journey, since it was generally understood that he was a chronic alcoholic. Fortunately, for the history of the expedition (and probably of our country), he never showed up and the party sailed without him.

There is no trace today of low water from Pittsburgh to Wheeling along the river called "Oyo" by the Iroquois, which the French took to mean "beautiful river," but which in fact may mean "great white water" (a nice stage-Indian sound to it), "river of the white foam," or "bloody river" (also appropriate, given the fierce struggles along its banks, to say nothing of the hog-butchering). Zadoc Cramer's *The Navigator*, the

bible of Ohio navigation, called it "the most beautiful river in the universe," and even de Tocqueville, lapsing into that hyperbole which
seems to have always accompanied perceptions of the West, wrote: "The
Ohio waters one of the most magnificent valleys in which man has ever
lived."[19] The nineteen dams and locks responsible for its domestication
(which replaced an older set of 51) insure a consistency of water level
unknown in Lewis' day, and the channelization completed by the Army
Corps of Engineers in the 1930's make it relatively easy to navigate.
From a snag-laden, channel-shifting, shoals-creating series of hazards,
much like the Missouri, the Ohio has become a "chain of lakes," in one
observer's phrase.[20] Even the Falls of the Ohio at Louisville, once a series
of rapids dropping about twenty feet in three miles, have been tamed to
a strong riffle, although at high water the northern passage toward the
Indiana side, called Indian Chute, was never dangerous, and there were
records of voyagers having gone over the Falls without even realizing it.
Over its 981 miles from Pittsburgh to Cairo, where it flows into the
Mississippi, it drops 430 feet, an average of less than six inches per mile,
enough to keep the volume of water moving in a noticeable current but
not enough to present many serious hazards.

   To the untrained eye the remains of the earliest inhabitants of the
Valley, the Mound Builder Indians, are indistinguishable from natural
hills. The Mound Builders vanished centuries ago, and no one knows
why or where they went. The fecund land has served as favorite hunting grounds for many Native American tribes. In the 1660's LaSalle is
reported to have voyaged down the River from his Quebec base by taking what was to become the preferred French route, from Lake Erie
down the Allegheny to the Ohio. He apparently made it as far as the
Falls, where his companions abandoned him, leaving him to find his
way back alone. This proved to be good preparation for his later travels
down the Mississippi. Another enterprising Frenchman named Celeron
deposited metal plates in several tributaries in 1749 (some of which
have been recovered) with inscriptions announcing that the Ohio and

all the streams flowing into it were henceforth the property of King Louis XV.[21] We will encounter this strange French habit of burying metal plates all the way to the Dakotas.

But after the French and Indian War the British took over in 1758, and five years later the Crown proclaimed any settlement west of the Appalachians was forbidden, an edict surely as ignored as any in history. The exploits of George Rogers Clark "pacified" much of the region north of the River, so that settlement became safer, if still far from peaceful. After the Revolution the River soon became our first interstate highway, and with the Northwest Ordinance of 1787 the border between slavery and freedom as well. Squatters were constantly settling on land the Indians deemed their ancestral hunting grounds, conflicts would develop, the army would move in to remove the squatters and tear down their buildings, and they would almost immediately ooze back and rebuild. At this time the two sides of the river developed differently. On the southern bank the Virginia pattern of metes and bounds land survey, where ownership was determined by topographic landmarks and "tomahawk blazes," produced large farm holdings sustained by the institution of slavery (this pattern held also for the southeast corner of today's state of Ohio, which was the property of the Virginia Military District of Ohio). But the north side of the river was surveyed by the federal government using the township and range system, whereby a north-south, east-west grid of six-square-mile townships was surveyed into mile-square sections, which in turn were easily divisible into farms of 220, 180, 90 or even 40 acres.[22] I once lived in Oxford, Ohio, where one of these townships had been set aside at the beginning of the nineteenth century to form Miami University, and the land on which residents built their homes could not be purchased but had to be leased from the state.

In the early days of the river's settlement the natural world remained relatively pristine. Passengers on the steamboats (which began running in the teens) watched otters, beavers, and muskrats in the shallows, and deer swimming in the current. One writer says that migrating squirrels crossed the water in such numbers that "they formed thick gray rafts, blocking traffic." 100 to 200-pound fish were not uncommon, and one catfish was caught with "the greater part of a suckling pig" inside it.[23] Buffalo still roamed the area; some of the first trails through the woods followed routes widened and defined by their passage. This was the region of numerous fossil beds and near the site of the mammoth remains that Clark later sent to Jefferson, which helped him refute the continental theory that in the New World species were smaller and weaker than in the Old. The most famous natural resident of the area, the passenger pigeon, traveled in vast clouds which darkened the sky until the degradation of their habitat and the wholesale slaughter by hunters made them extinct.

In addition to abundant farmland the area had rich resources of iron ore, coal, and salt, which laid the foundation for industrial development. In the early 1800's 65 charcoal furnaces in the Valley turned out pig iron for foundries in Cincinnati, Pittsburgh, and Columbus. An industrial empire began to flourish, centered on Ironton, site of the Hanging Rock iron region, and Portsmouth in Ohio, and Ashland in Kentucky (on today's West Virginia border). Much of the ordnance used by the North in the Civil War came from this region. Further west, Cincinnati became the nation's first meat packing center, as corn-fed hogs from a wide area were sent there for slaughter; Mill Creek there became known as "Bloody Run." Proctor & Gamble evolved from the availability of salt and pork fat for soap. But the product most in demand was Ohio Valley coal, which was mined to the point where coal slurry and oil slicks eventually killed off untold species of marine life and poisoned many of the feeder streams, as well as eroding the land. Paradoxically, then, the very bounty of the Valley contributed to its decline, which lasted until the completion of the rebuilding of the river. As late as the 1950's little was being done to control the pollution of the Ohio from the industrial, municipal, and farming wastes dumped into it.[24]

To get a better "feel" for the region, I once drove the full length of the Valley from the Golden Triangle to Cairo, Illinois, where the Ohio empties into the Mississippi. Along the highway on the bluffs to the north of the River after crossing the McKee's Rocks Bridge, there are some fine old Victorian homes visible, before the newer but still substantial residential areas of Avalon and then Sewickley are approached. Always on the flood plain beneath and to the south are the train tracks, yards, and acres and acres of mills, mostly abandoned or even demolished, leaving rusting nightmare shapes or vast grass-free plateaus to scar the surface of the land. The heart of the steel industry had been to the east, along the Monongahela—the storied names of Hazelwood, Homestead, Braddock, McKeesport—forming a 23-mile continuous stretch of furnaces, mills, and fabrication plants where once 100,000 workers were employed and where one firm, the Mesta Machine Company, owned a mile-long plant, the largest under one roof in the world. But there was enough steelmaking left over for plants the size of the Aliquippa Works to develop in this region, a facility covering 725 acres and extending for seven miles along the south shore of the Ohio, and Neville Island, where 50 different heavy industrial concerns once flourished and the Dravo Corp. built and launched hundreds of ocean-going ships and landing craft during World War II. Aliquippa today, on the south side of the River, is a town struggling to survive. Its population is half of what it had been, the 14,000 jobs in the J&L Steel mill long gone, its closest supermarket four miles away, its Russian Orthodox Church burned to the ground by firefighters to spare it the fate of gradual decay. A developer has tried to interest buyers in 600 acres of the old mill site but so far without results.[25] Today the few remaining active sites where stacks emit scrubbed plumes of white smoke bear signs proclaiming "Wheeling-Pittsburgh" and "JTV", not the history-laden names of U.S. Steel, Carnegie, Jones & Laughlin or Republic, all merged, gone, or in other lines of work. But the many railroad tracks indicate that plenty of goods still move in and out of this city. The yards at Conway are among the largest I have ever seen.

And there are always barges moving up and down the Ohio, massive strings of them pushed in both directions, some the length of several football fields. Many hold coal, and there are places along the River where coal is mined and conveyed directly to the barges, so that there are no separate loading operations. Petroleum products and chemicals, too, are prominent among the barge loads. It is not uncommon to see storage tanks, chemical refineries, and power plants all at the same location. There are rusting donkey rigs along parts of the Valley, but most of them are no longer pumping. And then there are the reactors— Shippingsport, the first nuke in the nation, is there, and Beaver Falls, and near the Ohio line is a sign proudly boasting of Ohio's fourteen nukes. More spectacular are the huge stacks of the coal-fired plants that dot the Valley, some so tall that their tops vanish into the clouds on an overcast day. The idea is to prevent the particulate matter from dropping close to their source; even the least of animals know enough not to foul their own nests. But of course this means that the sulfur dioxide produced creates acid rain, which falls hundreds of miles away, driven by the prevailing winds to New York's Adirondack forests and the New England mountains, changing the balance of nature so that lakes die and trees languish. And from the general shabbiness of the areas around these plants, it doesn't appear that the local residents prosper very much. Portsmouth, Ohio, for example, the site of one of the East's three uranium enrichment plants for weapons and civilian use, has seen its population cut in half in the last 60 years. Where does all this energy go? We like to think that it is used for the benefit of the people along the river, and some of it is. But much more has gone to satisfy the enormous appetite for energy needed to create plutonium.

Most of the time along the stretch of the river bordered by West Virginia and Ohio the river's gorge is well defined and not very broad, unlike that of the Missouri. There is no hint that the river isn't deep, no sign that it sometimes could be necessary, as for Lewis, to get out and walk. But it's no Columbia, either. Instead, it appears to be a peacefully flowing gray-green stream usually about 100 yards wide. To the amateur's eye it appears that when one bank goes up steeply into hills and bluffs, the other shore broadens out some distance, so that hills on that side are set back quite a distance. There is probably a law known to all geologists that explains this. But one effect is that there appear to be few places with equal-sized settlements directly across the River from each other. There is a stinging in the eyes produced by the succession of industrial monuments (why are most of the chemical plants on the West Virginia side of the river?) Past Weirton, Steubenville, and Wheeling the terrain begins to change as the road winds around the border of the Wayne National Forest to a sharp bend in the river near Marietta, where the Valley broadens out. The Muskingum River enters the Ohio here and was in flood stage when I first saw it. When the level of the Ohio rises, the feeder streams back up, since the changes in elevation are typically very slight. This pattern prevails in most parts of the Midwest and seems to begin about here.

Nevertheless, most of the town of Marietta is built high enough so that the floodwaters were having little obvious effect. A town of some 15,000, Marietta (named after Marie Antoinette) was the first settlement in the Northwest Territory (although it has to contest with Clarksville, Indiana, for the honor; apparently the controversy turns on the meaning of "town"). It has a rich history. Founded by a group of New England Revolutionary War officers banded together as the Ohio Company of Associates, who had purchased 1,5000,000 acres from Congress, the town was meant to embody an ideal environment, an Eastern society shorn of its flaws and raised to a higher cultural plane. A majority of these men were members of the Society of the Cincinnati, a cross between a lobbying group for soldiers' back pay and pensions and an exaltation of republican patriotism. The town was to be a place "where the veteran soldier and Honest Man should find a Retreat from ingratitude," a society unlike that of the squatters, where interdependence, urban development, manufactures, and social stratification were to be overseen by a firm authority and secured by churches and schools. Their town plan embodied such a vision of order: the city was to be built in 60 rectangular blocks, all streets were to be 100 feet wide, four blocks were to be provided for public use and all others divided into house lots of 90 by 180 feet. The Indian mounds were to be made the center of the city, where the stockade was to be built and named Campius Martius, the streets parallel to the Muskingum were numbered, the perpendicular ones named after distinguished members of the Society of the Cincinnati, with Washington as the main street. In spite of these careful plans, life in Marietta never worked out quite as planned, since the squatters surrounding the growing town simply ignored the founders' wishes, as they had ignored all other governmental directives, and settled where they pleased and lived however they wished, usually not in accord with the plans of others.[26]

Marietta today displays many handsome and well-restored buildings, which bear witness to its aspirations. It is fond of citing a phrase from *National Geograpic* calling it a "picture perfect postcard of a town." Marietta College has beautifully landscaped grounds, one of the most elegant Victorian buildings houses the Chamber of Commerce, a recently renovated mansion called the "Castle" is used for community events, and the downtown area appears prosperous with several upscale shops and bustling traffic. While it hopes to become a tourist destination, the town remains mainly a service center with some light manufacturing. The largest employers are city, county, and state governments with colleges (two of them), metal fabrication (the Steel Workers Union has a presence in Marietta), and Ohio Power and Shell Chemical (both big non-union operations).

I was interested in what was shown on the map as the Historical Society building, which turned out to be an 1854 structure across the Muskingum in a district called Ft. Harmar, but it was not really a historical society in the usual sense, merely a historical house. Two other institutions serve that purpose. A few blocks north of the central shopping area in a parklike setting on the Muskingum is the Ohio River Museum, an evocation of steamboat days.Down at the wharf is a handsome sternwheeler, one of several in working order in Marietta, which bills itself as "the Riverboat Town" and each summer hosts a riverboat festival. While this has its interest, the people there directed me up a hill to another museum within easy walking distance to satisfy my interest in the history of boatbuilding and river navigation. And this place, the Campus Martius Museum of the Old Northwest, turned out to be a remarkably useful institution, with historical displays and a small research library of quality. Still thinking I might learn something about Lewis's keelboat (the people at the Carnegie Library in Pittsburgh told me that the best collection of material on Ohio riverboats was to be found here), I met with a researcher who had information about boats built at Marietta and about the army personnel stationed in Washington County at the turn of the century, but he could only point me toward some titles in the Museum's library for further information. Even though I was at a dead end in solving the riddle of Lewis's keelboat, someday I would like to return here to study the Old Northwest.

After passing the mouth of the Kanawha River at present-day Parkersburg, West Virginia, where Lewis saw clouds of passenger pigeons for the first time and on Sept. 18 negotiated Letart's Falls, a half-mile of rapids and the largest obstacle to river navigation apart from the Falls at Louisville, Lewis's journal breaks off until Nov. 11. Why? Nobody knows, but this introduces the pattern to be found throughout the expedition of long lapses in Lewis's contribution to the Journals. Whether he stopped writing or whether pages have been lost is the subject of intensive scholarly examination, and while the best reasoning seems to point to lapses in writing, we must remember that some writings may have been lost. No one, for example, knew of the existence of the Ohio River Journal for a hundred years or Clark's field notes until the 1950's, and it is possible that other fragments may appear some day. But in this case Lewis left blank pages in his notebook which would just about equal the number of days he skipped, and so it looks like he intended to go back at some future time and provide entries for the missing days on the Ohio. The party remained a week in Cincinnati, as we learn from Lewis's letters, not the Journals.[28] Lewis visited the fossil beds at Big Bone Lick, Kentucky, which had so stimulated Jefferson's imagination. By mid-October Lewis reached Clarksville, on the Indiana shore, across from Louisville. We can only speculate about the meeting with Clark and the "nine good men from Kentucky" he had recruited and about the conversations during the two weeks at Clarksville. Lewis and Clark had a lot to catch up on.

Beyond Portsmouth the country broadens out and begins to look more Midwestern than Appalachian, with subsistence farming and some animal raising. Since the hills have receded, the Ohio itself floods regularly, and fifty or sixty miles out from Cincinnati there are many cabins, cottages, even campgrounds on the banks which are often underwater. Mark Twain would have recognized this country as being like "life on the Mississippi," with a permanent population of "river rats," who have to adjust to frequent flooding. At this point the best way around Cincinnati is to get on the Interstate, which leaves the Ohio River and cuts through the Kentucky hills, so that the traveler is spared dealing with the city. By the time the road returns to the River, we are in Indiana, dumped onto a potholed two-lane highway, which, nevertheless, has a magnificent view of the River, with more strings of barges, and the occasional massive power plant (Ohio has no monopoly).

My destination for the morning was Madison, an early river town that prospered in the decades following Lewis's passage as a transfer

center; one of the earliest railroads in the Territory connected the farm-
lands of central Indiana with Madison . But by 1850 the railroads had
bypassed the town, and it stagnated as a minor service provider for an
area known today as "Little Switzerland" (for no apparent reason; the
hills look more like Pennsylvania). In another of what will become a
long string of personal failures along the Trail, I could not reach the
town by way of the river road because it was flooded, or, where the
waters had receded, the pavement had been badly damaged. Instead, I
was detoured for what seemed like hours on former wagon roads or
maybe some of those buffalo trails winding over much of southernmost
Indiana. When I finally arrived at Madison, it was to be disappointed.
There were some antebellum structures but mostly in bad repair.
Clearly, time has not been as kind to Madison as to Marietta, and I soon
moved on.

Surely, I thought, there would be more of interest at Clarksville,
founded in 1784 by George Rogers Clark and the center of a huge grant
to him and his men, their reward for service during the Revolution.
Although for much of his retirement George Rogers lived at Mulberry
Hill, on the Kentucky side, originally his father's home, in his later years
he built a cabin called Clark's Point on the Indiana side. In his final
years he lived at Locust Grove, the home of his sister, also on the
Indiana side. William had retired from the army primarily to handle the
chaotic finances of his brother, who had supported his troops by notes
on his own property, for which he was sure he would be reimbursed by
the Virginia legislature. But it was not to be, and so creditors hounded
the old hero until his brother dealt with them as competently as he had
commanded his brigade. But today, there are few signs in Clarksville of
a rich family legacy, although Locust Grove is being restored.

Beyond the town's name, and the name of a state park of small
distinction, there is little here to remind us of the past. The Falls have been
reduced to a minor rapids and the town seems to be given over to
miscellaneous industry and looks like a lower-middle-class bedroom

community for Louisville across the bridge. Beyond the G.R.C. Wayside on the River, on the other side of the bridge approach was a Colgate factory with a massive clock, probably about 15 to 20 feet in diameter, not quite a match for those other Colgate clocks in Newark and Reading, reportedly the first and second largest in the world, but pretty good for Indiana, and a reminder of how time has passed.

From this point on, there are not many roads along the river, testament to recurrent flooding. The land flattens out further, until the coal country of Illinois is reached. I was able to get to the river at Metropolis, however, another of those town names in this part of the world that never came to denote reality. Thebes and Cairo on the Mississippi are the counterpart of upstate New York's, Rome, Syracuse and Ithaca but are further from the glamour and splendor of the originals than these. There is even a place, barely existing, called Future City. Metropolis, however, boasts a statue of Superman larger than movie-size (you can't talk about the "life-size" of a comic strip character). I thought that some enterprising merchants seeking a distinction that fate had not provided renamed their town to pretend it was the scene of this superhero's exploits. But I learned this was not the case; the original town name had been Metropolis City, shortened only to square more completely with reality (and, one would like to think, to avoid redundancy). The statue is about fifteen feet high, and Superman faces us directly in full color with legs firmly planted and arms upraised, a grim expression beneath his forelock. The base of the Statue reads "For justice and truth—and the American Way." Just down Main Street a mile or so is a Big John supermarket with a statue fully the equal of Superman in size but with a bag of groceries in each arm and an ingratiating smile. Clearly, his occupation is less stressful.

More interesting is the site of Ft. Messac, on the edge of town. It was built by the French as Ft. Messiac in 1757, ceded to the British in 1763, who were only there a year, but long enough to Anglicize the name. The Fort was razed by the Chickasaw but rebuilt by the Americans in 1794 for the benefit of Anthony Wayne's Indian campaigns. Lewis and Clark recruited two good soldiers here. Today the Fort, the first Illinois state park, is in the process of being rebuilt, and it offers an excellent view of the lives of soldiers on such duty. Situated on the bluffs overlooking the river, with the stockade and blockhouses in place and its ancillary cooking and sanitary facilities being reconstructed, it does not take much imagination to place oneself among the 100 or so soldiers who at one time were stationed here, keeping an eye open for troop or Indian movements up and down the River.

While in the "neighborhood," I had to check out another statue, this one of Popeye at Chester, Illinois, where a bridge crosses the Mississippi. Popeye was harder to find, since instead of being downtown or on the highway, he was in a postage-stamp-sized park by the bridge across the Mississippi, called Segar Park, named after Popeye's creator, who must have come from here. Popeye was considerably smaller than Superman, maybe six feet high, not painted but dark gray in coloration, and something of a disappointment in his bare little spot of ground. Perhaps this was fitting; it always seemed to be the supporting cast of Olivoyl, Sweepea, Wimpy, and Bluto that lent their appeal to Popeye. From this point on, we will deal only with real-life superheroes.

Lewis again picked up his Journal entries at Fort Messac, if only for three more weeks. From that time until April of 1805 all entries will be those of Clark. We learn that as they left Massac Lewis suffered from a severe fever, the "ague" we call malaria, typical in this fever-ridden country. Clark had had it earlier. A few decades later Harriet Beecher Stowe describes the pestilential bottomlands of Cincinnati, which were to claim the life of her husband recently out from the East to head up a new seminary. A dose of Rush's famous pills seemed to cure Lewis temporarily, but these fevers recurred across the continent for both Lewis and Clark.

Lewis makes no mention of the broad confluence of the Ohio and the Mississippi at today's Cairo, apart from some measurements of latitude and longitude. This majestic sight is best viewed from the point at Ft. Defiance Park, which often can be completely under water. Lewis has only this to say on Nov. 16: "Passed the Missippi this day and went down on the other side after landing at the upper habitation on the opposite side," an opaque sentence if ever there was one.[29] The point, I imagine, is to convey the excitement of crossing the swift Mississippi, for the next few days describe Cape Girardeau and the Missouri side of the river. The other item of note to Lewis on this day was the offer by some Delawares of three beaver skins for his dog, which he scornfully refused. But at this point Lewis and Clark have come to the end of the somewhat languorous cruise down the Ohio and are about to face what will be their destiny for much of the next two years, battling upstream on two of the continent's mightiest rivers. Their genuine adventures are about to begin, and their world will be enlarged beyond recognition.

1   Much of the comes from Walter O"Meara, *Guns at the Forks* (Pittsburgh, Pittsburgh University Press, 1965), 22. 218–24.

2   We have Bouquet's account of this expedition in Mary Darlington, ed., *History of Col. Henry Bouquet and the Western Frontiers of Pennsylvania, 1747–1764* (NewYork, Arno Press, 1971), a reprint of a privately printed edition of 1920.

3   The broader picture is presented in R. Douglas Hurt, *The Ohio Frontier: Crucible of the Old Northwest, 1720–1830* (Bloomington, Indiana University Press, 1996), pp.49–58.

4   Esp. Hurt pp. 83–86.

5   Leland D. Baldwin, *Pittsburgh: The Story of a City* (Pittsburgh, Pittsburgh University Press, 1938), p. 115.

6   Thomas P. Slaughter, *The Whiskey Rebellion: Frontier Epilogue to the American Revolution* (New York, Oxford University Press, 1986), p. 64.

7   Frank Toker, *Pittsburgh: An Urban Portrait* (University Park, Pennsylvania State Press, 1986), p. 16.

8   The most complete source for this period on the Ohio River is Leland D. Baldwin, *The Keelboat Age in Western Waters* (Pittsburgh, Pittsburgh University Press, 1941), pp. 6–17.

9   Baldwin, *The Keelboat Age,* pp. 42–47.

10 *Letters,* I, 121–122; 124.

11 *Letters,* I, 112.

12 *Letters,* I, 110.

13 *Letters,* I, 203.

14 *Letters,* II, 423.

15 *Letters,* I, 113–114.

16 *Letters,* I, 110–111.

17 *Letters,* I, 117.

18 Baldwin, *The Keelboat Age,* p. 72.

19 Found in Robert L. Reid, ed., *Always a River: The Ohio River and the American Experience* (Bloomington, Indiana University Press, 1991), "Introduction," by Reid, p. xi.

20 Scott Russell Sanders, "The Force of Moving Waters," in Reid, p. 20.

21 Sanders, p. 12.

22 Sanders, p. 10.

23 John A. Jakle, "The Ohio Valley Revisited: Images from Nicholas Creswell and Reuben Gold Thwaites," in Reid, p. 55.

24 Sanders, p. 14.

25 Hubert G. H. Wilhelm, "Settlement and Selected Landscape Imprints in the Ohio Valley," in Reid, pp.66–79.

26 "Aliquippa, Pa. Still Coping After Loss of Steel Mill," *New York Times*, 6 July 1997, A22.

27 Hurt, pp. 180–183.

28 *Letters*, I, 126–127. This letter to Jefferson contains everything we know about this period of time along the Ohio.

29 *Journals*, II, 87.

CHAPTER 3

Between Two Worlds: Mississippi Interlude

On my arrival at the Comds. dwelling [at Cape Girardeau] I was informed that he had gone out with his family to attend a Horse rase...I pursued him to the rase grown found him and delivered him my credentials...the rase was just over before I reached the grown...this seane reminded me very much of their small raises in Kentucky among the uncivilized backwoodsmen...they are almost entirely emegrant from the fronteers of Kentuckey & Tennessee, and are...men of desperate fortunes, but little to loose either character or property—they bet very high on these raises in proportion to their wealth; it is not uncommon for them to risk the half or even the whole of their personal property on a single wager....

Lewis, November 23, 1803 (*Journals,* II, 106)

The Great River Road passes through Cairo, which has never lived up to its geographic potential as the point where the Ohio and the Mississippi merge. Apart from its few years of glory as a major supply depot for Grant's western armies and its role as symbol of freedom for the South's escaping slaves, time has passed by Cairo. Stretched out on a narrow peninsula between the two rivers, it has depended on the rich agricultural floodplains for what cash it can muster, and frequent flooding of this low country makes this problematic. In spite of one fine public building, the town library, it is a predominantly poor place; the liveliest spot in town seems to be the bean storage elevator. Driving up the Mississippi, one encounters even more depressing sights: the remains of a place called Cache (no pun intended, I'm sure), which appears to have been both flooded and burned; a crossroads named Olive Branch, which advertises itself as the "goose hunting capital of the world" because of its commercial farms where people pay to shoot birds.

It must have been at this point as they left the Ohio behind and entered the full current of the Mississippi that Lewis and Clark understood the need for more men to power their way up the Missouri. Jefferson's earlier planned explorations had envisioned one or two explorers, maybe accompanied by a dog, sauntering through the West so as not to alarm whatever tribes they might encounter. The original plans for this expedition had been predicated on about a dozen recruits. But the powerful current of the Mississippi made it excruciatingly difficult to propel the keelboat upstream. It became necessary to cross and recross the river, remaining in the lee of bends to make any headway at all, and even then the best they could do was about a mile an hour of totally exhausting poling, rowing, paddling, or towing. And the Missouri, they had heard, was even swifter than the Mississippi. No wonder they rested at Cape Girardeau.

Near the end of November, 1803, the party had worked its way upstream to the settlement there, composed, Lewis tells us (Clark is sick during these days), of 1,111 persons and governed by a French Canadian named Louis Lorimer, a successful trader. Lewis found his family attractive, especially his wife, a half-blood Shawnee who dressed in the style of her people, and a daughter "remarkably handsome & dresses in a plain yet fashonable stile or such as is now Common in the Atlantic States among the respectable people of the middle class." Note that "style" and "respectibility" go hand in hand, as we might expect from Lewis. He goes on and on about her: "she is an agreeable affible girl, & much the most descent looking feemale I have seen since I left the settlement in Kentuckey..." (*Journals*, II, 107–108).

He attends the scene of a day of horseracing and finds that the participants there make an impression of a different sort altogether. Decisions of the judges were ignored, fights broke out, and thievery was openly displayed. But with a condescending tolerance Lewis reports that such behavior is only to be expected, since these settlers are the dregs of Kentucky and Tennessee. The tone is peculiar for Lewis, from whom we have come to expect a reportorial point of view. The behaviors he chronicles—in addition to the above, he goes to great length to tell how steep the wagers are in relation to the poverty of the participants—sound remarkably familiar to those who have read about colonial Virginia. There is a passage on horse racing in Rhys Isaac's book, *The Transformation of Virginia:1740–1790*, that almost exactly parallels what Lewis writes.[1] Isaac is describing, to be sure, the generation prior to Lewis's own, and points out that the practice of English course racing began to be adopted in the Tidewater by the 1750's. But it is highly probable that the flat-track, quarter horse contest was still the only type of racing in the Piedmont during Lewis's youth there. I can find no references to oval racetracks in Albemarle and Orange Counties in the eighteenth century.[2] And, after all, many of those the despised settlers from Kentucky and Tennessee came originally from Virginia. But Lewis is an officer and is working hard at being a gentleman, and so he must delineate his status by separating himself from these common Westerners. He illustrates anew how important such status was to him, and, indirectly, how precarious it was. We should expect a more relaxed attitude from the man who had been the President's private secretary and a captain in the United States Army, but on the edge of an ordered society, status becomes more difficult to preserve.

At Kaskaskia they exercised the option given by Secretary of War Dearborn and recruited perhaps as many as a dozen more volunteers (clear statements of which men were recruited at what points are rare).[3] Here we encounter another of the many sources of confusion caused by the errant course of rivers. Kaskaskia and Fort Kaskaskia are two different places, today separated by the Mississippi. Jesuits, who followed the Kaskaskia Indians when they migrated from the Peoria area about 1703, founded the town of Kaskaskia. The town grew around the site of Pere Marquette's Mission of the Immaculate Conception and became a commercial center of some importance to the French, so that they built a small fort on the hills overlooking the town and the River. This fort did not compare in grandeur with Ft. Chartres a few miles upriver, which was reported to have walls eighteen feet thick, but it had the advantage of being above the floodline and thus was not eroded. When the Jesuit order was suppressed in France, the French abandoned their forts in this part of the world, and, removed their soldiers from the town of Kaskaskia as well. The British moved in. They never bothered with the fort on the heights but instead fortified the old mission in the town and called it Fort Gage. During the Revolution, the British had word that George Rogers Clark was on the way upriver to take Fort Gage, and so the garrison mounted an eagle-eyed watch on the river. But Clark outmaneuvered them by a daring march overland to sneak up behind them and gain their surrender without a shot being fired. And so the American history of the area began, although many of its citizens were still French. By the way, George Rogers Clark found the overland strategy so beguiling that it was from here he marched his weary rag-tag band of Kentucky militia back across today's Illinois, a land in flood during the winter, so that he reported his men knee-deep in water much of the way, to Fort Vincennes, which he captured in one of the most celebrated victories of the war.

After this, chaos began to reestablish itself. Since the territory was still technically part of Virginia, Governor Patrick Henry appointed a county leader named John Todd, who found it not personally fulfilling to try to teach self-government to these (mainly) Frenchmen with little support in manpower or cash from the impoverished state of Virginia. So he quit, leaving in his stead an even less effective fellow named Richard Winston. About this time John Dodge, an adventurer from Connecticut with some vague backing from the Americans at Bellfontaine (the entire area was known as American Bottom) arrived on the scene and apparently knew a good thing when he saw it. He took over the Fort, gave himself the title of captain commandant, and began a reign of terror by arresting Winston, chasing away the local court, and imposing tribute on the hapless local citizens. He was only one of the many bandits in the area, perhaps the best organized. Dodge finally left after eight years of tyranny, and the local residents burned down the Fort in the hopes that his kind would never return. [4]

Meanwhile, the town of Kaskaskia grew, became an important trade center for Mississippi and Ohio cargoes, and eventually had an American army garrison stationed there. It later became the first capital of the new state of Illinois. But between them the floods of 1844 and 1881 wiped out the town, and, even more interestingly, radically changed the course of the Mississippi. It now began to follow the bed of the Kaskaskia River to the east and created a twenty thousand-acre island portion of Illinois territory on the *west* side of the River. Notable in this village is a state memorial housing a 650-pound bell, called "Liberty Bell of the West." Louis XV gave it to the colonists, and it cracked when it was rung to celebrate George Rogers Clark's victory over the British in 1778.[5] And this is why Ft. Kaskaskia is not the same as the town or garrison of Kaskaskia! The site of the old fort remains today on the Mississippi bluffs looking across the water to the place where once there was a town. Just north of it along the Great River Road the fine French-style house of the trader Pierre Menard, which still stands today as a public attraction, was completed early in 1803, in time to be seen by Lewis and Clark. Years later Menard was to be a partner of Clark's in the Missouri Fur Company, but there was no indication at this time that the explorers were aware of him and his Missouri trade experience or even of his house.

———————

The only way to approach Kaskaskia today is by way of a rickety bridge across the Kaskaskia River from St. Mary's, Missouri (or as a billboard proclaimed, "St. Marie"—the French element still very much alive). The road leading to the Church of the Immaculate Conception and the Kaskaskia Bell is called the King's Highway, and it does not refer to Hanovers or Windsors. About five miles along the road, a sign appears, stating, "Kaskaskia—Pop. 18." But there is no trace of a village even of that size. When the Mississippi moved to the east in 1881, it also cut out the ground underneath the village, so that house after house slipped into the water. The flood of 1993 completely submerged the island and took away most remaining signs of habitation. The Church, founded by Father Marquette in 1749, still stands, together with the Bell, and a house or two, which don't look very permanently occupied. The Bell is housed in a temple-like enclosure behind a metal grill. Pressing a button during those hours when no human guide is present (which I gathered was most of the time) can open its doors. There is a good view of the Bell, for there are no distractions, apart from the old checkerboard linoleum tile on the floor. Like the better known

Philadelphia Liberty Bell, it is definitely cracked. The remainder of the Island is extensively farmed, with corn and soybeans, the signature of Missouri, everywhere. In fact, this is the first glimpse I have had of farmland with no farmsteads in sight; there will be much more of these views farther west.

Upriver is the very old and historic village of St. Genevieve, the earliest settlement in Missouri, today a thriving tourist town with several antique inns, a good-looking restaurant or two, and many quaint boutiques with the ornamental ironwork we associate with French influence. Clearly, this is a favored weekend getaway spot for St. Louisians. The land here slopes up sharply from the River, so that today there is no sign of flooding (the townspeople learned the hard way by being flooded out several times before rebuilding back from the River), and the slope continues into the town, where at the crest of the hill is a massive Catholic Church dominating the entire area. The evident prosperity goes back some time. Maybe the huge working quarry on the outskirts of town has something to do with it. Fort Chartres, a powerful French outpost, is supposed to be somewhere around here, but I never did find it.

Clark took the boat party up the river from here while Lewis traveled by horseback to Cahokia, on the east bank, and then went across the River to St. Louis to meet the Spanish authorities still governing the area, even though it was in French territory just recently purchased by the United States. This is one of the lesser sources of confusion in a confusing time. The Spanish denied Lewis permission for his party to cross into Missouri until sovereignty had been officially transferred, but this was not scheduled for three more months, July 4, to be exact. But Lewis had given up thoughts of ascending the Missouri until spring, anyway, and was looking for a place for a winter camp. It so happened that a fur trader he met at Cahokia offered a 400-acre tract on the Illinois side of the Mississippi, directly across from the mouth of the Missouri, where a small river named Riviere du Bois entered the Mississippi.[6] Clark took the party there and set up camp, where he spent the winter in monotonous training routines. He also recruited some locals for the expedition, while Lewis spent most of his time in St. Louis arranging for supplies for the augmented party, as well as gathering every scrap of further information he could find about what lay upstream. It is likely that Lewis learned everything about the Missouri that was then available.

The name 'Wood River" is a misnomer. The original name 'Riviere du Bois' referred to a person not trees. "Wood's River" would be more like it.[7] Nevertheless, the mistake stuck. At the turn of the nineteenth century the Missouri entered the Mississippi directly opposite the mouth of this small steam, so that Clark wrote about the muddy water from the former flowing with such force that it crossed all the way to the east bank of the latter (the Mississippi is at least a mile wide at this point). But the courses of all the streams have changed so much that the site of the original encampment is reckoned to be on today's west bank a couple of miles further north. Or maybe even under the waters of the Mississippi—no one is quite sure. When the builders of the Illinois Lewis and Clark Monument had to determine where to put it, they hit upon an ingenious solution: they kept the same relative positions by siting the monument directly across from the current mouth of the Missouri, next to something called the Cahokia Diversion Canal, which takes the place of the Wood River, now two miles to the north.[8] It isn't even in the town of Wood River but south of there, within the town limits of a place called Hartford.

The first time I saw the Monument, a concrete pedestal supporting eleven pylons representing the states through which the Expedition passed and flying the flags of the United States, the United States in 1804, and the flag of Illinois, it was a humid, mosquito-infested early May day. The place was not only free of other visitors but seemed desolate, and vandals had defaced some of the plaques. Yet through the straight, full trees growing from the river flats there seemed to be a spectral light, which suggested the presence of rangy, tough soldiers at drill, marching back and forth through the heavy air, getting through another boring day of training until it was time to leave. The nearby town of Wood River, built around a Standard Oil refinery in the first decade of this century, retains the odors of a refinery town, which can quickly put an end to fantasies about the past. When I once stopped at the modern town library to ask for directions to the monument, no one there could recall where it was, although some vaguely remembered hearing about such a thing, even if none of them, lifelong residents, had ever visited it. After a couple of phone calls they placed it for me, but we learned that the most recent flood had destroyed the access road. A year later I tried again and saw through a gap in the levee the sight of a suspicious shining, even though the barricades of the previous year had been removed. While the road had been partly repaired, it was under about six feet of water, so that I couldn't yet get a glimpse of the monument. Several men dangled fishing lines into the Canal, testing their luck. It was comforting to see that this had become a choice spot for fishermen, who probably didn't know or care about Lewis and Clark but who at least made use of their territory. Plans are underway to construct an ambitious Lewis and Clark Interpretative Center in the area in time for the Bicentennial in 2003.

The monument area is part of the East Bank's urban blight best typified by East St. Louis, a few miles to the south. In 1797 the site of a ferryboat crossing, later incorporated as Illinoistown, and near the once thriving settlement of Cahokia, East Saint Louis is on the American Bottoms, the name once given to the Mississippi's flood plain, and is ringed by hills, called the Illinois Bluffs. The area once flourished as a stockyards and meatpacking center, a rail hub (at one time the second largest freight yard in the nation), later as a steel and chemicals producing town. Thousands of African Americans were drawn from the Deep South by the promise of jobs during World War I, but they were used mainly as strikebreakers, and in 1917 this precipitated bloody riots which involved hangings and scalping and the burning of hundreds of residences. Nevertheless, blacks continued to be brought in, 10,000 at one time by an aluminum company, again to break the unions, but after encouraging this migration, the company soon shut down and moved further South. A renaissance of sorts occurred during the Second World War, when abandoned factory buildings were used for the manufacture and warehousing of war materiel and army personnel lived and worked here. But it was a bitter flowering, for the kind of prosperity created led to prostitution, gambling, and links to organized crime.[9] I once visited East St. Louis in the early fifties, when around the St. Louis area the very name was synonymous with sin, and an evening spent there was considered a rite of passage for young middle-class white men. The bachelor party I attended crossed the river to see topless "dancing," at that times a daring adventure for Midwestern youth.

But today there are no jobs and little hope. The population peaked in 1945 at 80,000; today it is less than half of that and virtually all African American. The federal Department of Housing and Urban Development calls it "the most distressed small city in America,"[10] These two realities are all but openly linked by state officials, who blame the city's problems on mismanagement, cronyism, and fraud. The state of Illinois has taken over the city's finances.[11] The State Board of Education has taken over the wretchedly unfit schools, described by Jonathan Kozol as repeatedly closed by backups of raw sewage, and surrounded by mounds of uncollected garbage. There are few textbooks and little office or science equipment, a shortage of teachers (because of cuts in the budget), the lowest tax base per student and the highest property tax rate in the state. The only new industry in years (the old industries remaining have had created for them shadow towns, like National City, so that they aren't liable for East St. Louis taxes) has been a riverboat casino. An energetic mayor, Gordon Bush, used the proceeds to pay back salaries, buy new police cars and fire trucks, and put more officers on the streets and in the fire stations while reducing property taxes.[12] But the needs are still greater than resources, and the city is a long way from becoming livable.

This was brought home to me forcibly when one weekday not too long ago I drove through the downtown area of the city at noontime. Block after block of stores were boarded up or, more often, burnt out, with litter and garbage piled everywhere. I could find only a beverage store and a newsstand and two bars open for business. But the streets were crowded with men, some of them engaged in conversation but most standing and staring either at me or straight ahead, like the living dead. Even though nobody moved very much I felt menaced, so I locked the doors of my rusty nine-year-old van, which was the best looking vehicle in sight (although there was very little traffic—apparently most residents can't afford to drive). This was the most desperate urban landscape I had ever seen. As I left the downtown area, things didn't get much better, although there were at least people moving in and out of one fairly new governmental building, apparently the welfare office. There is a branch of the University of Southern Illinois nearby, but it no longer offers classes and instead is a social services center. The signs of fire among the houses were unmistakable, so that only a small proportion of buildings was fit for habitation. One house that had not been touched by fire had a couple of pots of bright geraniums on the porch, and they stood out as a beacon of attenuated hope. But there were few such signs. According to Kozol, what is not visible might even be worse—the industrial pollution, the arsenic, mercury, and lead in the soil, the residue of toxic substances that caused a creek bed to smoke by day and glow by night, the clouds of poisoned air—as the bodies and brains of children receive their share of permanent damage.[13] When I finally found my way to the Interstate, I breathed easier again. Once on the highway, of course, I was able to ignore the city and move around it to the middle-class outposts on the Bluffs, which are also able to ignore it. In fact, although East St. Louis is the largest city south of Springfield, it was left off the map of Illinois not long ago, and the telephone directory that serves the region does not list residences or businesses there.[14] The inference is that there are those who wish it would disappear.

One of the recurrent motifs of this book will be how the smaller cities along the Lewis and Clark Trail may well offer a glimpse of social organization that works to provide more satisfying ways of life for their residents. But at the very beginning of the trip stands a caution and a reminder that we have barely begun to understand how we can make our cities livable. As long as East St. Louis exists, optimism must be tempered.

1   (New York, Norton, 1982), pp.98–101.

2   In fact, the staff at the Orange County Historical Society (Madison's home county) commented that the river bottoms in the Piedmont were almost always too narrow to accommodate an English racing oval.

3   In an Appendix to the *Journals*, II, 509–529, Moulton summarizes everything We know about all the members of the Corps of Discovery.

4   Much of this material is found in Robert P. Howard, *Illinois: A History of the Prairie State* (Grand Rapids, Eerdmans, 1972), pp.37–46.

5   Howard, p. 37.

6   Ambrose, p. 123, reports these details. Lewis twice mentions he has not seen the Wood River site when he writes to Jefferson, but he tells us nothing about now he settled on it. Neither Moulton nor Jackson contains these details, nor do other basic sources (Dillon, Bakeless, or Coues) mention them.

7   *Journals*, II, 132n.

8   Ann Rogers, *Lewis and Clark in Missouri*), St. Louis, Meredco, 1993), p. 130.

9   Jonathan Kozol, *Savage Inequalities* (New York, HarperCollins, 1991), pp. 7–39, contains as its opening chapter a discussion of East St. Louis.

10 Kozol, pp. 7–8.

11 I have followed these issues in the *St. Louis Post Dispatch* throughout November and December of 1997.

12 Janet Ward, "East St. Louis Mayor Gambles and Wins," *American City & County* (Argus Press, 1995), vol.110, 70–71.

13 Kozol, pp.10–11; p.17.

14 Kozol, p.18.

Chapter 4

"We're Bound away, Across the Wide Missouri"

Note the Commanding officer is full assured that every man of his detachment will have a true respect for their own Dignity and not make it necessary for him to leave St. Charles—for a more retired Situation—W.C.

> Ordway, May 16, 1804 (*Journals*, II, 234)

a Sergeant and four men of the Party destined for the Missourri Expidition will convene at 11 oClock to day on the quarter Deck of the Boat, and form themselves into a Court martial to hear and determine (in behalf of the Capt.) the evidences adduced against William Warner & Hugh Hall for being absent last night without leave; contrary to orders;—& John Collins 1st for being absent without leave—2nd for behaveing in an unbecomeing manner at the Ball last night—3rdly for Speaking in a language last night after his return tending to bring into disrespect the orders of the Commanding officer.

> Ordway May 17, 1804 (Journals, II, 235–236)

What must have passed through the mind of Clark on May 14, 1804, looking out across the Mississippi to the mouth of the Missouri as he set out from the Woods River camp to begin the trip of a lifetime, or for that matter, of many lifetimes? We will never know, because the Journals present him as full of the business before him. Are the boats loaded properly? How far can we realistically plan on getting today? Will the rain and current affect our progress? Are the men as ready for what lies ahead as I can possibly expect? Perhaps he lacked the leisure to think very seriously about the distant future, as Lewis will do dramatically from time to time along the Trail. Or maybe he had nothing to say. But later on Clark will reveal himself as a man of considerable imagination and appreciation for the scenes around him, and so it is fair for us to speculate about the excitement and even awe he must have felt at that unparalleled moment.

The Missouri is the continent's longest river, besting the length of the Mississippi by three miles.[1] It had long been a river of mystery. No one, including the Native Americans, knew its sources or knew that the river that began at the Three Forks in Montana was the same one that emptied into the Mississippi. Centuries earlier Coronado had been told of the existence of the Missouri by Indians in Kansas, and he had believed it to be the River of the Holy Spirit, which DeSoto had discovered in Florida.[2] Jefferson, of course, was sure that it originated within a few miles of the Columbia, so that a minor portage was all that was required to open up trade with the Orient. Although Clark gave no indication of knowing it, he was heading upstream midway between the most difficult times of the year. The Missouri has two flood periods annually. The first, from around the beginning of March to the end of April, results from rapid snowmelt on the plains and the breaking of ice jams on the tributary streams, as well as the main river itself. This causes greatest damage in the upper basin, but of course all that water does eventually come downstream. The second, called the "June rise," is caused by the mountains' snowmelt and often heavy widespread spring rains in the lower basin. These floods increase the dangers of navigation. There was a saying among rivermen that the trouble with navigating the Missouri was that you had to take a boat with you.

Marquette and Joliet "discovered" the Missouri during the June rise. Hearing a great roaring and thinking they were approaching a dangerous rapids on the Mississippi, Marquette reports the following: "I have seen nothing more dreadful. An accumulation of large, entire trees, branches, and floating islands was issuing from the mouth…with such impetuosity that we could not without great danger, risk passing through it."[3] Clark must have encountered some of this, because he found out that, contrary to what appears reasonable, boats on the Missouri must be loaded more heavily in the bow than in the stern. The normal procedure makes it too easy to ride up on floating logs and snags and thereby endanger the boat's hull. The very first day out they encountered three logs that almost sank the keelboat. He ordered the boats to be unloaded and repacked at the first opportunity, when they rested at St. Charles. It also became clear that one of the pirogues lacked the manpower to keep up with the others, so that the distribution of the crew had to be altered. The plan was to sail to the village of St. Charles, where they would meet Lewis, pick up the supplies he had arranged for, perhaps more crewmen as well, together with any further information about upriver conditions, and be on their way. While Clark and the men were battling the newly discovered conditions on the river, Lewis journeyed from St. Louis to St. Charles with a group of "rispectable inhabitants", got caught in a thunderstorm and stopped under shelter for a picnic, his last such polite entertainment for a long, long time, even if dining al *fresco* was to become habitual. The Corps of Discovery would pause in St. Charles for several days, so that the officers could be suitably feted and sent on their way.

The three crew members court-martialed for leaving their posts to observe a ball (actually, they apparently made themselves more of an embarrassment than that; we can only imagine their notion of witty commentary on the genteel proceedings and the repartee concerning the ladies present). They must have been only too aware that this was their last opportunity for such merriment, and so it is understandable why they left their posts to steal a peek at the finery. And it is difficult not to appreciate their energy and enterprise in finding a way to celebrate their last evening in civilization. But we are sharply recalled to the fact that this is a military expedition travelling under the Articles of War, and that their act was not primarily one of discourtesy or rudeness, but a disobeying of duly constituted orders. All winter long military discipline had been drilled into the men. It would become essential for survival many times along the way. If at the very beginning of the journey such flagrant disobedience was tolerated, there was no way of telling how discipline would disintegrate later on. So two of the men were found guilty of being absent without leave and sentenced to 25 lashes "on their naked back," but mercy was recommended because of their former good conduct. The third was found guilty of all three charges and sentenced to fifty lashes without any mercy to be shown. The Captains carried out precisely what the court recommended with swiftness and a lack of comment. Military law was upheld with no room for questions or quibbles. Undoubtedly the severity of the latter sentence resulted from Collins's language "tending to bring into disrespect the orders of the Commanding officer," which could not be tolerated. At this point the issue seemed simple, the resolution equally so. Reason called for the stark imposition of law; not to do so resulted in potential chaos.

When I set about to recapitulate their travels, it seemed only appropriate that I, too, begin at the confluence, from a point closer than the view across the Mississippi, which tended, anyway, to be obscured almost constantly by strings of barges pushed up and down the River by sturdy tugs. I had revisited the magnificent Gateway Arch on the downtown riverfront and its useful prelude to the Lewis and Clark exploration, the twelve-foot-high David Muench photographs on the walls, together with appropriate excerpts from the Journals. At my last visit there was a sign next to the full-sized westward-facing figure of Thomas Jefferson saying that when funds became available he would be transformed into a "life-like" speaking, moving model who (which?) would answer spectators' questions. Apparently the road to the Disneyfication of the American heritage is not without potholes. After driving through a business district which seemed perpetually under construction and through areas containing all the ancillary enterprises a city needs, from produce warehouses to foundries to tiny repair shops, through working-class neighborhoods with a high number of bars and large ornate old churches on the high ground, I came to some residential districts with peculiar names like Bellfontaine Neighbors and Spanish Lake on my way to what the map showed was a possible road to the confluence at a place called Columbia Bottoms. St. Louis, for whatever reason, has some colorfully named areas—Black Jack, Champ, Shoveltown, and Fee Fee among them. The unmarked road had a gate across it, but the gate was open, so I entered what was little more than a track so washboarded and rocky that a screw from my van's headliner worked its way out, even though I was travelling no faster than five miles an hour. I drove past mile after mile of corn and soybeans and some farm machinery (which indicated the purpose of the road) toward the treeline, which is inevitable along the Missouri, until I came to a low levee. I could have driven over it, but the road on the other side dwindled to less than a track, and I didn't want to risk getting stuck in an area where, for all I now knew, I would not be welcome. So I parked, grabbed my camera, and started hiking past some good-sized pools of standing water and more soy beans in the intense heat of a Missouri summer afternoon. After a few minutes I did not seem to be getting any closer to the treeline, the rivers were nowhere in sight, and frankly, I was afraid of sunburn. So, defeated, I headed for St. Charles instead, where I knew I would get my first close-up look at the Missouri.

St. Charles, across the River, is an interesting place, built on essentially three levels. On the level of the Interstate bridge are the town heights, with residences on tree-lined streets and Lindenwood College, a small liberal arts institution, which billed itself at the turn of the 20th century as the "Wellesley of the West."[4] On a lower level closer to the river are the commercial and governmental centers and the "Old Town" area, containing the first state capitol, many original buildings remade into upscale shops and restaurants, as well as a further historical area which remains to be refurbished, and "Frenchtown," once a workingman's neighborhood and today the site of many antique shops. Down on the River is a waterfront park and further historic buildings—an old woolen mill, the Katy depot, and a floating riverboat-casino named the "Goldenrod." This entire area was under water during the flood of 1993, but Old Town was spared, even though there were no tourists for over two months because the media frightened people away.

Time will inevitably be measured in this part of the world from the flood of 1993, which far surpassed those "100-year" or "500-year" projections that engineers are fond of making in order not to overbuild. Recorded history had seen nothing like it, nor had residents even been prepared for its possibility. Levees along the entire Mississippi-Missouri system had been constructed over the years in careful ways, and together with the massive dams upstream on the Missouri, they had for the most part sufficed to keep the water from the majority of people, even though some flood plain, low-rent areas where the "river rats" lived were inundated again, as often in our time as we read of in Mark Twain's. But levees can be topped, broken, or breached, and when a "sand boil", a subterranean discovery by the water of permeable soil in the levee, occurs, the levee can blow with the sound of a freight train. Over one hundred levees along the Mississippi and the Missouri did one or more of these things in the spring of 1993. The town on Kaskaskia Island disappeared, and only six houses were considered salvageable. Two million acres, about twenty percent of Missouri's cropland was under water. Every bridge along the Missouri between St. Louis and Kansas City except two was closed or washed away.[5] There were all kinds of stories, including the bravura adventure of how the breakaway Burger King floating restaurant, normally moored by the Gateway Arch, was saved by pursuing tugs, which kept it from crashing into floodwalls by skillfully nudging it to safety, to the slow-motion horror of the overwhelming of the Des Moines, Iowa, waterworks, where a city of 250,000 had to endure twelve days before a toilet would flush, a shower would function or a fire hydrant would gush anything but air, nineteen days before there would be water fit for drinking or cooking.[6] It needs to be emphasized that Midwestern floods are not like eastern or western ones, where the high water, destructive as it may be, roars through, does its damage, and allows the cleanup to begin. These floodwaters stayed around for six weeks or more, excruciatingly prolonging the misery and the danger.

I was to make one more doomed attempt to view the confluence by driving from St. Charles to a long finger of land between the two rivers. I passed a huge complex of factory buildings where McDonell-Douglas builds missiles. Once out of the city I went through tiny communities with names like Orchard Farm and Black Walnut, marked by fruit trees and unmistakable white frame German Lutheran churches, to the small town of Portage Des Sioux, where the Mississippi rolls on, by, and often over the peninsula. The five hundred or so residents of the region are accustomed to floods, but the '93 flood cut off the area for sixty-two days, and the confluence moved sixteen miles north of its usual location. It is easy to see why this flat area regularly is overrun: across the Mississippi River are bluffs hundreds of feet high that act to channel the waters in that direction. Every square foot of the peninsula is planted in corn and soy beans, apparently nourished by the frequent applications of upriver silt and profitable enough to make the occasional need to replant worth the cost and effort. I wondered, though, since the level of prosperity in the area seemed low, as if people weren't doing all that

well, even though there were some tidy little brick houses in the town
which revealed few signs of flood damage. The one place in town where
comfortable life-styles were to be seen was at the marina, where many
St. Louis sailors apparently prefer to dock. But I still faced defeat; the
road petered out in marshes and silt near the bridge over the rivers, as
if it was not intended that anyone should approach from this direction.
So once more I failed to make it to the confluence and returned to St.
Charles, humbled by mighty waters.

The town of St. Charles was founded in 1769 by a Frenchman named
Louis Blanchette, "le Chasseur," who had married a Pawnee woman and
met a tribe of Dakotahs whose chief turned out to be another
Frenchman. They hit it off right away. Blanchette called the settlement
"Les Petites Cotes," and he was named commandant by the Spanish,
who claimed that the St. Charles district extended all the way to the
Pacific. After the Louisiana Purchase it became an outfitting station for
those heading west, and Zebulon Pike's expedition to Colorado also
started from here about the time Lewis and Clark returned. In one year,
1821, over 6000 wagons headed west from St. Charles.[7] One of its first
local industries was the manufacture of castor oil, for which Lewis and
Clark were customers. The first Missouri State Capitol was housed in
modest buildings still to be seen in Old Town, called Peck Row,
primarily, it seems, because the Peck brothers were willing to lease the
buildings for as little as $100 per year. The legislators were so rowdy that
the townspeople began to have reservations about housing them. At one
point over the chair of the Speaker of the House was this scribbled this
motto: "Missouri forgive them. They know not what they do."[8]
Nevertheless, this unruly crew hammered out a constitution, and five
years later the capital was moved upriver to a new town which Senator
Thomas Hart Benton wanted to name "Missouripolis," but which
instead was named the "City of Jefferson" and later transposed into a
more pronounceable "Jefferson City." Within a few years the St. Charles
area became the home of many German immigrants, so that in the

1830's two-thirds of the town's residents were German speakers, part of the "German belt" that grew up on both shores of the Missouri extending westward to include Hermann and the Rhineland-like wineries which are within about 50 miles of St. Charles.

———————————

On Monday, May 21, with the boat reloaded, the crew returned to its usual state of sobriety, and the memory of the floggings still fresh, the Corps of Discovery left St. Charles to the huzzahs of the spectators on shore. On May 23 they stopped at the mouth of the Femme Osage River to pick up the Fields brothers, who had been sent on ahead to purchase some corn and butter. Clark reports that "Many people Came to See us," but the most illustrious resident of the region, Daniel Boone, was not among them. Lewis and Clark knew that he lived nearby, but they made no effort to pay their respects. Apparently they did not think that he could furnish information about what lay upstream that would interest them. He would have been seventy years old but still vigorous with thirteen more years of life and very much an active participant in the region. A few years earlier the Spanish in St. Louis were surprised by the arrival of a man from Santa Fe, who claimed he had been commissioned by the Spanish throne to open a trade road. The French also claimed the territory as part of the confused history of the area, and the Spanish hoped to head off these claims, so they hired Daniel Boone to become commandant of the district and administer it. In spite of his fame Boone had lost most of his land in Kentucky and was in debt, so the offer of 850 acres of prime Missouri bottomland was appealing. He functioned as sheriff, judge, and jury in the Femme Osage region by 1800 and conducted court on his property near today's hamlet of Matson, under what became known as the "Judgement Tree." But he apparently still missed the frontier, so in 1805 he moved to his son's property at Boonslick, another 100 miles further west, to the extensive salt deposits there, near what was to be the town of Franklin, across the River from Boonsville. This was to become a well-known highway, for by 1821 the Santa Fe Trail originated here, by 1840 the Oregon Trail branched off from the Santa Fe, and by the 1850's the California Trail forked from the Oregon.[9] Even today the two-lane highway west from St. Charles is known as the Boonslick Trail.

Daniel Boone's homestead is hardly the humble residence the name suggests. He had had a good deal of practice in moving from place to place and had obviously learned how to make his family comfortable. Touted as "Missouri's Gem" by the billboards scattered all over the region, the main house is a large structure of native blue limestone with walls two-and-a-half feet thick and with ten fireplaces (five have mantels carved by Daniel from black walnut trees once on the property). In addition, there are several sturdy outbuildings. The most striking feature, however, is the setting; this is beautiful rolling country much like that of his beloved Kentucky and even today the land remains very fertile. The homestead itself has become a commercial tourist attraction with fake rustic signs posted on virtually every tree, reminiscent of some of the California redwoods ("Drive through the tree with a shop in it!"). A tall fence has been erected to keep the nonpaying gawkers from a free ride. Even so, there is a kind of dignity about the area when you turn away from the hucksters' tawdriness.

But down the road (or several of them) is a far different and virtually forgotten monument to Boone. Along a deserted backcountry road, atop an isolated knoll reached by a steep set of weathered concrete steps with an old pipe railing for support, lies a shaded family graveyard where Daniel and his wife were originally buried on what was once his daughter's property. No crowds, no signs here, only a bronze plaque on a five-foot boulder, surrounded by a group of gravestones with names I didn't recognize. Daniel's wife Rebecca was buried here (she died seven years before him) and Daniel, too, for a while. Then both sets of remains were relocated to Kentucky. Next to the boulder were a register and a plea for donations to keep up the area. Boone had nothing but trouble with governments all his life, and today not one of them is apparently interested in maintaining his memory at this site.

———————————————

Two days later along the River another of those breathtaking events occurred which could have ended the entire enterprise. As he often did, Lewis had been exploring the bluffs on foot, while the flotilla proceeded on, when he slipped and fell, or, as Clark enigmatically tells it: "Capt. Lewis near falling from the Pencelia of rocks 300 feet, he caught at 20 foot" (*Journals*, II, 249). That's all we learn about that! I assume Clark means that Lewis fell twenty feet, not 280, since that might take the fight out of a man. But even twenty feet can forcefully bring home one's mortality. On May 25 they arrived at the tiny settlement of La Charette, near present-day Marthasville, where five families lived, the last outpost of whites they were to see in over two years. They now were truly the Corps of Discovery.

You cannot drive along the Missouri at very many places and keep the river in view, the way you can drive along the Hudson or the St. Lawrence, the Niagara or the Susquehanna. Or even the Mississippi on the Great River Road. Hard experience has taught the treachery of the Missouri; if you build along it, you will eventually be flooded and destroyed or bypassed. The flood plain in Missouri is immense, often ten miles or more across, and here the River itself, when glimpsed through the treeline or at a state boat access, is massively broad and rapidly moving, even in July. There are places in east central Missouri, however, where the River flows through narrower reaches and the bluffs are several hundred feet high. Even in those places the River has moved over time, leaving its banks to carve new channels, perhaps on the other side of the bluffs. Entire towns exist only as names on the older maps. The Journals repeatedly talk about banks caving in while Lewis and

Clark watched, and new bars being formed before their eyes. This was especially dangerous, because the current was so strong that it was impossible to make progress in the main stream. It was necessary to look for calm water on one side of the river or the other and move forward there, but of course, it was in just such shallows that falling banks and snags or sawyers were most likely to be found. How those men must have suffered in the humid, breathless heat of a Missouri summer, poling or rowing or pulling the keelboat upstream against the current by means of the cordelle attached to the mast, while thrashing through the undergrowth or slipping in the mud, all the while beating off clouds of mosquitoes and gnats. Adding to the physical discomforts were the uncertainties of the world around them, constantly in flux and with potential destruction at every turn. You catch a hint of this even in a modern vehicle on the tightly curving, narrow two-lane road which parallels the River.

Also paralleling the River is the Katy Trail, a biking and hiking path starting at St. Charles and running to the western Missouri town of Sedalia. This is on the railbed of the old Missouri-Kansas-Texas Railroad, which has become a state park ten to twelve feet wide and 185 miles long and is the longest of the "rails to trails" conversions in the nation. It gets used; about 300,000 to 400,000 people per year hike or bike along part or all of it, and on weekends one party is rarely out of sight of another. Small towns along the trail that were in the process of disappearing have been rejuvenated by the need for bike rentals, food and drink, and bed-and-breakfasts. I have even spotted wineries right along the path, where one may pause from the act of enjoying the scenic delights of the Missouri Valley to sample a native Chardonnay. The Katy Trail was even featured in the Travel Section of the Sunday *New York Times* not long ago, so it has clearly arrived as a civilized way to spend some time.[10]

Along the way on the south bank there is the quaint hill town of Hermann, which was founded in 1836 by the German Settlement Society of Philadelphia to keep German traditions alive in the New World. And so it does today, with a fine museum of German-American life and almost continuous German festivals all summer long into a month of Octoberfesten. It immediately became a center for grape growing and wine making, which continues to this day (after a pause, we are piously told, for the years of Prohibition). At the turn of the century, Stone Hill Winery here billed itself as the third largest in the world. The varieties I tried from three different wineries, in town, Seyvals and Reislings, were not bad but struck me as overpriced. Still, there was the novelty of it all to consider. Not much farther on, a few miles beyond the mouth of the Osage River, once considered the boundary of the West, is Jefferson City, its stately domed capitol building on bluffs overlooking the River, its grounds formally and gracefully landscaped—bustling small city of 35,000 whose one industry appears to be government. The city of Columbia, a half-hour or so due north, the site of the University of Missouri, seems to have absorbed most of the metropolitan functions of the area, so that shopping and entertainment are at a minimum in Jefferson City. But it seems a pleasant place to live, and no state I know of has a more serene and lovely governmental center.

At this point the River makes a turn northward before again heading west at Boonville, where there once had been a major ford, since the Santa Fe Trail crossed the River here to the now vanished town of Franklin. Boonville is no tourist town. There is no association with Daniel, and besides, all such interest has been soaked up at the homestead. It is a Midwest working town, even though the shoe factory is boarded up and the ornate old railroad station no longer has any tracks leading to it. But Boonville, unprepossessing as it is, has very few vacant storefronts and remains the home of the Kemper Military School, a grim-looking campus with prison-like buildings, which nevertheless has a nationwide presence. I can remember as a boy seeing Kemper ads with pictures of well turned-out young men in their high-collared uniforms, the image of a competence and self-control far beyond my own. Up on the hill to the east of the downtown is an old, well-preserved residential district with trees arching over the streets. I have read somewhere that Boonville has over 90 buildings on the National Historic Register.

The flood of '93 took out the Missouri River bridge here, but it has been temporarily propped up while a new one is in the process of construction. The north side of the River has been scoured clean of all vegetation for the bridge rebuilding, but there probably wasn't much left anyway after the rush of the floodwaters. There is a temporary marker indicating the original site of the village of Franklin, which had been abandoned years before because of floods and rebuilt a mile or so further away from the River as New Franklin. The marker also indicates that the '93 flood swept away the earlier marker. But about twelve miles northwest along a roller-coaster road through small fields of pasture and wooded country is Boonslick State Park, untouched by floods, where the remains of a once-thriving salt manufacturing operation founded by members of the Boone family have been unearthed. From a considerable spring bubbling out of the ground in a small wooded ravine the salty water was elevated by a foot-powered paddlewheel to reach the level of a sluice constructed of logs. The sluice could pivot to direct the water to any one of several furnaces, which were long stone or brick enclosures with a chimney at one end and an opening for the fuel, at the other. The furnaces had indentations for large kettles; one of the furnaces apparently held thirty such kettles, but most were smaller than this. The salt thus produced by evaporation was removed with paddles and placed on pallets to dry and was then ready to be shipped out. In spite of the necessity of salt for everyone—settlers, Indians, wagon trains alike—the operation did not turn much of a profit, and after a couple of decades of operation it closed down in the 1840's. Some of the early operators were the same men who opened up the Santa Fe Trail, a much more profitable venture, which also brought back from the Southwest the breed of mules used in westward expansion. But even if salt did not make fortunes, the area became thickly settled with farms. One commentator remarked that it seemed that all of Kentucky and Tennessee had emptied out to come here (why have Kentucky and Tennessee become associated with the dregs of humanity in this period, the Western equivalent of the Irish on the East Coast?). Now, even on a Sunday afternoon in early summer, I had the place all to myself, except for the bugs.

Across the River but not visible from the salt lick is the town of Arrow Rock and the rock itself, the site of the Missouri ferry for the wagon trains west along the Santa Fe Trail. To get there today it is necessary to double back to Boonville. Signs indicate the site of a state park, which turns out to be highly developed. Leaving the parking lot, I was surprised by ornate brick pillars with brass carriage lanterns supporting the portico of the Arrow Rock Visitor Center. This houses interesting displays of life on the Missouri frontier, but it also serves as the entrance to a veritable Disneyland tourist center, the restored Arrow Rock Village, where log cabins and pioneer structures have been metamorphosed into ice cream stands and souvenir shops. There is a substantial log inn here as well. These show-me folks have found good ways to rip off tourists bored with the wonders of nature and needing a rest from the long drive on the Interstate. Lewis and Clark mention the Arrow Rock, but I was too weary and disgusted to bother to look for the real thing amid the fakery.

The surrounding country is full of corn and soy beans with very little sign of human habitation along the road, which carries the now-familiar Lewis and Clark Trail markers, silhouettes of two men, one with a tricorn hat pointing westward, the other with a coon-skin cap, leaning on his rifle, also studying the country ahead. Nearby are small towns with names like Prairie Home and Pleasant Green and Pilot Grove, names William Clark himself might have given such places. It does not take long to arrive at the Kansas City metropolitan area, again far too bewildering and conflicting to dwell on. It is undoubtedly true that each major city has its own character and flavor, in spite of all the contemporary pressures against this—chain hotels, restaurants, theatres, malls which remain the same wherever the traveler goes. But it requires dedication and time to ferret out such individuality, and, frankly, it's not worth the effort to me unless I am planning on staying awhile.

But I had to include one part of the metropolitan region in my travels. Lewis and Clark paused for several days at the juncture of the Kansas and Missouri Rivers, speculating on what a good location it was for a fort and a trading post, and they even explored up the Kansas for some distance. But it was the town of Independence that interested me. Situated just downstream from the great turn to the north made by the Missouri, Independence has a rich past, which includes its role as major outfitter for the western wagon trains and the turbulence of the Mormon years. Here, the Mormon revelation said, was the site of the Garden of Eden, upon which was to be built "the chief city of the Western Hemisphere" (which turned out to be Kansas City). It didn't quite work out that way, since the Mormons projected an image of ominous violence wherever they went, and this was almost invariably countered with actual violence. Driven out of the Independence area, many of them moved to a location about fifty miles north to found a town they called Far West, the exact spot where Cain had killed Abel, said Joseph Smith, and where almost continuous raiding and killing went on, until the Governor sent the militia to drive the Mormons from the state. They left, some like Joseph Smith escaping from jail to do so, but Smith ended up murdered at their new city in Illinois named Nauvoo.[11] Today testimony of their presence in Independence is found in a new Temple near the downtown area, which has a steeple of gleaming aluminum that looks like the horn of a unicorn projecting hundreds of feet into the air.

Once you get past the detritus of modern life which surrounds all towns, the auto repair franchises, the package stores, the abandoned railroad facilities, you hit upon the older section, a step back in time to the unpretentious but comfortable Victorian houses that are found in many Midwestern towns today. McCullough's biography of Harry Truman provides a good sense of this environment.[12] The house that became the residence of Harry and Bess was actually Bess's family home, which at one time contained four generations of Wallaces and Trumans. It stands much as it was, although a metal fence has been added to ward off the fools who persisted in breaking off pieces of the woodwork as momentos. The citizens of Independence volunteered to surprise the Trumans when they returned from Washington for good in 1953 by painting and repairing it. I sometimes think of Harry Truman as a latter-day embodiment of the spirit of Lewis and Clark, navigating as he did each step of the intricate journey that took him from the farm to world leadership with a genuineness and honesty about him, all the while remembering where he came from and what he stood for. The magnificent Truman Library complex sits at the edge of the town closest to the Missouri, like the man, not interfering with the life of Independence, but playing an ongoing part in it.

Along the stretch of the Missouri north of Kansas City some hilly locations begin to appear on both sides of the river (yes, there are hills in the state of Kansas!). Taking back roads on one trip, I crossed the River north of Kansas City, past prosperous-looking farms with comfortable houses set well back from the road. In front of one was a bronze-like statue of a beef steer, a signal that I was entering cattle country, which one does not leave until crossing the Cascade Mountains in Oregon. But first I wanted to visit the town of Leavenworth, site of the equally famous army encampment and federal prison. The town itself was not much to see, but the base—that was an entirely different matter. In one form or another Fort Leavenworth has been here since 1827, at first to protect the Santa Fe trade and then later the settlers heading west. Today it has grown to become a unique combination of campus (it is home to the army's national staff college, where all line officers come to study war and peace, both now and in the future, and therefore is home to many of the Army's most thoughtful people), army base, and small city unto itself. I drove along its tree-shaded boulevards, busy with traffic at most hours of the day, past miles of dormitories, stores, social service offices, theatres, and athletic fields, towards the Missouri where the oldest buildings stand, imposing Victorian structures bearing the names of Grant, Sheridan and Sherman. Grant Hall has a clock tower visible for miles up and down the River. The house-like buildings closest to the River look like officers' quarters, and each has a well-tended sign on the lawn bearing the date of its construction. There were no guns or tanks or bombs visible to raise the testosterone level. There weren't even very many uniformed soldiers visible, apart from the dozen or so men and women taking runs along the walkways and looking incredibly fit. I noticed that almost everyone walking or driving by (women excepted) wore crew cuts, so it wasn't hard to remember where I was.

The federal penitentiary is next door to the base and visible from it. What started out as a stockade for AWOL soldiers on western duty has graduated to become a massive institution well known in fact and legend as home to all kinds of desperados convicted of federal crimes. It does not look at all like a place that could be scornfully referred to as a "country club," like Lewisburg in Pennsylvania or Danbury in Connecticut. This is the real thing. It is vast. There are outbuildings all over the place, some looking quite mysterious, some clearly animal barns. The main building looms up over every other structure in sight, with those many long, narrow windows several stories high that admits some light to the levels of the cellblocks. What makes Leavenworth different from other prisons, apart from its size, is the large, imposing dome that sits perched on top of those windows. Even though it does allow more light to enter, it is meant not to be functional but symbolic. A sense of solidity and self-importance and even moral authority is conveyed by this classical feature, for the dome seems to place the building and all that goes on within as above reproach, insurance that justice will be respected.

A few miles further up the road I smelled gas and thought my van must have sprung a leak. But I eventually figured out what I smelled was the odor of herbicide-fungicide-fertilizer being sprayed on the fields. The highway is well traveled in the springtime by open-bed semis carrying fertilizer and seed. In the midst of this rich agricultural region is the small town of Atcheson, known for its inclusion in the full name of the Santa Fe Railroad (the "Atcheson, Topeka, and the Santa Fe" for those not familiar with the Johnny Mercer song of a few decades ago) and the birthplace of Amelia Ehrhart. I once saw a picture of her family home and tucked it away as a stereotype of a Kansas farmhouse. Wrong again! It sits on probably the most desirable location in town on the highest point overlooking the Missouri. The views are spectacular from the long verandah across the front of the house. What must have been the dining room has tall windows that make it look like a chapel. But this isn't the only fine home in the area; not only the row facing the river, but several blocks back are filled with comfortable, well-maintained houses on immaculately-kept streets. So much money with so few visible sources must mean it has been inherited, and that, I suspect, from the heyday of the railroad. At any rate, such vestiges of nineteenth-century living are well worth viewing.

It is possible at St. Joseph to look down on the River from the highway and, if you're lucky, see a casino-gambling sternwheeler under full steam. By the time the Iowa line is reached, though, the world has flattened out in ways that differ subtly from anything further east. The western thirty to fifty miles of the state drain toward the Missouri, not the Mississippi, and the level of fertility that we associate with Iowa lessens. There is nowhere near so much rich topsoil because the level of rainfall has begun to fall. There are very few towns within a mile or so of the riverbank, and irrigation rigs begin to appear, which indicate that we are on the farthest edge of the humid east. There is a band of unusual land formation paralleling the River, known as the Loess Hills, composed of a strange soil found nowhere else in the country and left uncultivated, but these hills have little effect on the overall landscape, which now shares more with Nebraska and Kansas than it does with Missouri and Illinois. The real West is nearby. And before the Omaha-Council Bluffs area, there is the mouth of the storied Platte, the route of the trails west and the dividing line between what is known as the upper and the lower Missouri (when writers toss around that phrase "upper Missouri" this is what they mean).[13]

Before reaching the Platte, though, there is a town worth becoming acquainted with, Nebraska City. Although some of its promotional literature tries to associate the town with Lewis and Clark (Clark did report that its bluffs would make a good site for a fort, but he was always making that remark), we know that all they did was sweat and struggle their way past it during that sweltering July. But within a few decades a settlement was begun here, first as the original site of Fort Kearny in 1846 (it was shortly moved to the Platte), built to protect those setting out on the Oregon Trail. Later it was where the only wooden house between the Missouri and the Rockies was to be found, later still as the site of the Otoe County Courthouse, the first public building in the Territory and still in regular use. It became the home of the newlywed Mortons in 1855, where Julius, from Upstate New York via Michigan, and his bride Carrie, from Maine also via Michigan, came, leaving immediately after their wedding in Detroit. Julius edited the local newspaper, and together they planned and built their first home on the shortgrass prairie and began to landscape the area, especially finding a need for the trees they were accustomed to in the East. The family grew, the house grew, and the plantings grew as well, and Morton began to spread his convictions about the virtue of tree planting. He hit upon an Arbor Day as a legal holiday to encourage the virtue and importance of trees, and apparently this was an idea whose time had come. On the very first Arbor Day in 1872 in Nebraska over a million trees were planted. Since then, of course, Arbor Day has become firmly entrenched among the civic holidays celebrated mainly by school children. Morton went on to become Secretary of Agriculture in Cleveland's second administration and his house underwent successive rebuilding, until it has grown into a 52-room mansion now in the possession of the Nebraska State Parks Commission. It is surrounded by a splendid

Arboretum containing examples of every tree and plant grown in the state, and houses a modern conference center and lodge built by the National Arbor Day Foundation, headquartered here, for use by individuals as well as large groups.

Like many towns in the West, and befitting its Arbor Day heritage, Nebraska City takes especially good care of its trees, where the boughs almost meet over the residential streets and frame a large collection of interesting old houses. One such house is home to the Old Freighters Museum, another contains the Otoe County Museum of Memories, still another houses the Wildwood Period House and Gallery (supposedly named for the utterance of the wife of the banker who built it in 1869: "You don't really expect me to live in these wild woods, do you?"— apparent testimony to the early success of Morton's tree planting). The town also gets good mileage out of what it calls "John Brown's Cave," where one of those killed at Harper's Ferry once lived and scooped out a cellar for fugitive slaves from Missouri to hide in until they could be ferried over to Iowa and freedom. John Brown himself apparently visited the cabin over the cave but did not spend much time here. The local economy for this community of six to seven thousand people is based on the usual services to agriculture, but in addition has some industry; a plant producing gas meters employs about 600 people, and two unionized shops, one a woolen mill, the other a meat processing plant employ a total of 500 more. Until 1945 it was home to the Kregel Windmill Factory, which produced wind machines famous all over the plains under the brand name Eli. And an innovative man named John Bouleware, who operated a successful ferry business, once built the world's first pontoon bridge here. Looking as if it zigzagged across the Missouri, it was supported by small boats and opened at the point of its vee to allow river traffic to pass by. It lasted, however, only two years, broken up by ice jams. Another innovation at Nebraska City was Major Joseph Brown's steam wagon, to be manufactured here to haul freight to Denver and other points west. He had the prototype shipped from

New York and tested it on what even today is known as Steam Wagon Road. It made it about six miles from town before breaking down, and, for whatever reason, repairs were never made. Today the prosperity of the downtown commercial district relies on the presence of a factory outlet mall, small when measured by the standards of a city but in considerable demand in the middle of the prairie. And, as in other towns we will look at later, there are all kinds of celebrations here which are testimony to the town's energy, primarily a three-day Arbor Day Festival in the spring and an Applejack weekend in the fall, which includes the Grand Prix of go-carting, water-barrel fights, a scarecrow contest, apple pie-baking contest, an Apple Bowl college football game with the crowning of a Little Miss Applejack. The celebrations continue into October with Living History events at Arbor Lodge State Park; in recent years this has involved a Civil War battle reenactment.

Thirty miles up the road (and the River, which plays a remarkably small part in the lives of towns in this part of the world) is the village of Plattsmouth, which, as its name implies, began life with a natural advantage. But even though the populations of the two towns are about the same, Plattsmouth has fallen behind Nebraska City in prosperity, as a comparison of each town's downtown shopping mall suggests. Plattsmouth's is in a gutted courthouse building and cries out for more tenants, whereas Nebraska City's is busy and full. While there are some attractive small homes on the hill above the business section with well-tended flowerbeds brightening the street, they reflect a less affluent and energetic community, even though Plattsmouth is almost on the edge of the Omaha metropolitan area and undoubtedly has residents who make that daily commute. Even the Platte has betrayed the town by having moved its mouth several miles up the Missouri since the town was built.

During that July the Corps of Discovery passed the site of today's Lewis & Clark State Park, west of Onawa, Iowa, on a crescent-shaped lake that was then the channel of the Missouri. When I once stopped here, I was amazed to find in the water of Blue Lake a full-sized replica of the Lewis and Clark keelboat tied up at a dock. No one was around the park, so I had no idea what the keelboat was doing there. A year or so later, I dropped in again to learn more and found that this time I was not alone. Craftspeople dressed in buckskin and calico were setting up booths. A craft show, I thought, good. But the park was full of teepees and lodges made of hides ranged in no apparent order, and people dressed in costumes like those of the craftspeople gathered around pits in the ground, most of the men hunkered down, (the sod carefully placed to one side) where meat (I later learned it was mostly buffalo meat) was sizzling on spits or grills. Full beards and flowing hair for men seemed to be the dominant fashion, although there were some shorthaired, middle-aged folk and children sprinkled in the crowd. Every kind of vehicle from psychedelic busses of the 60's to Lincoln Town Cars was arranged in the parking area behind the teepees. I went down to the dock, through sounds of friendly greetings of "Howdy, Hoss" and "Hey, Buck," (apparently the standard form of address at such gatherings, not a case of mistaken identity). There a group of young men were swarming over the keelboat, which was badly listing to port. They were running a pump. Vandals had pulled loose some of the caulking during the night, I learned, and it would take about another hour to repair the damage.

I had figured out what was going on by now. I had not entered a time warp but had stumbled on a black-powder rendezvous combined with a celebration of Lewis and Clark's passage. Thousands of people—they prefer to be called "buckskinners"—engage in this hobby, but this was my first encounter with them, and it took a period of time to become adjusted. I had visited "living museums" where guides dressed up in period costume and answered visitors' questions as if they really were the characters they masqueraded as: "Maw and me, we wuz talkin' about that busted fence jus' last night." But this was a quantum leap. There were several hundred people here and I seemed to be the only tourist. They were spending a weekend full of activities, including crafts, a black-powder shoot, lectures, discussions, and films about the Lewis and Clark Expedition. They were here to take boat rides in the keelboat (when it was again seaworthy), dance and play music, and generally have the good times that occur when like-minded people get together. I have learned since that this kind of thing goes on all over the country, but especially in the west. In my part of upstate New York bluegrass festivals and reenactments of Revolutionary War skirmishes may serve the same function, but I had paid little attention to them. People come from many miles away to participate in these reenactments; there was one person there, I learned, from Oregon, who had come just for this celebration.

The weekend was sponsored by the Onawa Chamber of Commerce and the Iowa State Department of Natural Resources, and two other groups, the Friends of Discovery, volunteers from the area who built and maintained the keelboat and the pirogues, and the Discovery Corps, who serve as the camp color guard, and participated in planning the festivities. But a young man named John Adams seemed to be the one everyone turned to with problems, and it was he I was ushered to in order to learn what was going on. He bore the title "Booshway," and we never did get around to defining that, but I suspect it is a corruption of the term "bourgeois'" used by the French trappers, I seem to remember, to denote the head of a post. John appeared to be a vigorous, athletic-looking leader, possessing a remarkably fine full beard and hair long enough to start down his shoulders where an authentic set of buckskin garments took over. He also had the slightly abstracted, far-away look in the eye of the genuine enthusiast. He makes his living during the summer, he told me, by teaching history and nature in the State Park and during the rest of the year by giving lectures, talks, courses, on the Missouri, the history of the Plains, or Lewis and Clark, whatever people want to hear about. He has run the Missouri from Yankton to here in six days in a 30-foot boat modeled on Lewis and Clark's white pirogue, which he built himself. He spoke with animation about the attempt to find a landing site with the river at flood, darkness coming on, and drifting logs rushing along out in the channel. He took the same boat up the Platte for a documentary film made by Nebraska Public Television. He is fulfilling a childhood dream by living the way he does, he told me.

These festivals began in 1985, when a fellow from Council Bluffs named Butch Bouvier presented a carved model of Lewis and Clark's keelboat to the park. Local people thought it would be a great idea to build a full-sized replica, and this proved to be the focus needed for an annual celebration. The hull was launched at the 1987 festival, in the presence of the governor of Iowa, who took a hand in the construction. The mast and cabin were completed for the 1989 festival, and the weekend has been getting bigger and better ever since. There were about eighty camps here today, he said, a total of some 250 people, not counting the population of the town of Onowa, which hosted several events. Well-known Lewis and Clark scholars, such as Gary Moulton, have given presentations, and V. Strode Hinds, one of the founders of the Lewis and Clark Trail Heritage Foundation, has been present at every festival. Robin Williams (the filmmaker, not the actor) was on hand at the 1994 festival to film the doings for the 900 Club.

Adams became eloquent when he spoke of the insights he has gained into the lives of the explorers by sailing the keelboat on Blue Lake. He knows that the breezes in this part of the river valley are prevailingly from the southeast in the summer, so the sail could have been used often on this stretch of the river, even if only for ten minutes or so at a time, since after a bend in the river the trees would get in the way. Still, it would have been worth the effort to give the men a rest from poling, which meant manhandling 25-foot poles, pushing against the bottom, walking the length of the craft on narrow catwalks, lifting the poles, walking to the bow, then repeating the whole maneuver. Rowing would have been done rarely, he thinks, only out in the channel, which they would avoid whenever possible, because it was there they would catch the current. Towing would be the last resort, the towrope or cordelle attached to the mast, where it would give maximum directional stability (if attached to the bow it would tend to pull the boat under, whereas the mast served as a kind of pivot), the men strung along the shore or, more often, pulling in the shallows, their feet sinking in the sand or mud, tripping over rocks, fighting brush and insects. He has brought the keelboat through some narrow twists and turns using the cordelle. He explained how small things can make a big difference on the treacherous river. One year, for example, the women of the encampment sewed pennants to be placed as decoration in the boat's rigging. When the boat was on the lake under sail a sudden brief storm came up and the pennants jammed the pulleys so that the sailors couldn't get the sail down. In a flash the boat's career was just about ended. Remember, Lewis and Clark weren't even aware that a keelboat on the river had to be loaded bow down when they started, so they had to learn everything about river navigation on the job, so to speak, where one error could end the expedition. So did the Onawa sailors.

The white pirogue was finished in 1990 and had been in the water since then. The red pirogue was finished but remained on its trailer, because there are many things wrong with it, Adams claims, in terms of its authenticity. This boat has a permanent folding mast, like the Mackinaw boats of the Ohio River, and he is sure the original's mast was a removable affair, put in place only occasionally. He thinks the pirogues were probably double-ended, one of them most likely a dugout, although he has no hard evidence for this. The tasks of exploring the tributaries, picking up game left on banks by the hunters, and locating the stragglers on the shores would be best accomplished by a craft with the flexibility of a dugout. He was sure all the boats used a steering oar rather than a tiller, in order to gain the responsiveness the river requires. The pirogues would have been paddled, not rowed. The Frenchmen who manned them are described as singing all the time, a good indication they were setting a rhythm for stroking. The white pirogue is also on its trailer at present because it leaks.

All the time Adams was offering bits of boat lore he was constantly interrupted by people coming to him with problems about accommodations or setups or jurisdictional disputes. He handled all these matters coolly and with decisiveness, without losing track of where he was in his discourse. An impressive performance, which must have embodied the aplomb of Lewis and Clark themselves. And he had a fund of information larger than the boats alone. When I asked him whether the town of Onawa was so far back from the river because of the fear of floods, he smiled and mentioned that in Minona County there were at least two towns platted but never built. Those townsites are now under water. The river, in other words, didn't seem to interfere with town planners, for better or for worse. Far more likely, he thinks, Onawa's location had more to do with the desire of the railroad for a straight-line right-of-way north from Council Bluffs. He knows from studying maps of 1863 that at one time the river ran through what today is the Lake, and it is often possible to read a former course of the river from scouring marks it leaves, at least until the next movement wipes out those marks. I found all this fascinating but had to leave and couldn't stay for the next day's festivities, not even for the promise of a buffalo burger dinner. Adams offered to round up a crew and take me out on the keelboat, word having come in that it was now seaworthy, but I didn't want him to go to all that trouble. In retrospect, it seems he was looking for an excuse to take a short cruise, and I would have done him a favor by accepting the offer.

Thus far along the journey, the visible world differed primarily in degree, not in kind, from what the explorers were accustomed to. They were just beginning to encounter unfamiliar behaviors in the River, but so far nothing that could not be met with decisive responses, if order and discipline were strictly maintained. Such relative familiarity would last only a short while longer. The fecundity of the landscape would soon change with the aridity and the approaching lateness of the season. The fragility of human life will be underscored, as one of their number will die. Entering the upper Missouri meant a New World for them in several ways.

1   Henry C. Hart, *The Dark Missouri* (Madison, University of Wisconsin Press, 1957), pp.8–9.

2   Rufus Terral, *The Missouri Valley: Land of Drouth, Flood, and Promise* (New Haven, Yale University Press, pp.84–85.

3   Terral, p.84.

4   Sue Schneider, *Old St. Charles* (Tucson, Patrice Press, 1993) p. 96. This obscure little book has proved to be remarkably useful.

5   Betty Burnett, ed., *The Flood of 1993: Stories from a Midwestern Disaster* (Tucson, Patrice Press, 1994), p. 68.

6   Burnett, pp.130–131; p.22.

7   Schneider, p. 24.

8   Schneider, p.39.

9   Schneider, pp.17–22.

10 "Wheeling Along Where Trains Once Ran," *The New York Times,* 28 Sept. 1997, TR8.

11 Wallace Stegner, *The Gathering of Zion: The Story of the Mormon Trail* (New York, McGraw-Hill, 1971), pp. 17–24.

12 David McCullough, *Truman* (New York, Simon & Schuster, 1992), pp.39–65.

13 Terral, p. 110.

CHAPTER 5

The Way to Siouxland

...This Prarie is Covered with Grass of 10 or 12 inches in hight, Soil of good quality &,...Still further back at the distance of about a mile the Countrey rises about 80 or 90 feet higher, and is one Continual Plain as fur as Can be Seen, from the *Bluff* on the 2nd. Rise imediately above our Camp, the most butifull prospect of the River up & Down and the Countrey opsd. Prosented it Self which I ever beheld; the River meandering the open and butifull Plains, interspursed with Groves of timber, and each point Covered with tall timber, Such as willow Cotton Sun Mulberry, Elm, Sucamore, Lynn & ash....

Clark, July 30, 1804 (*Journals,* II, 430)

By now the Corps of Discovery was experiencing the full extent of a midwestern summer. There was blistering heat accompanied by high humidity, mosquitoes, and other pests. Violent swings in the weather brought moments of extreme danger, as unexpected storms threatened the boats. The banks of the River were continually caving in before their eyes. In addition, their diet consisted almost solely of protein, 8,000 calories a day of it, from meat, game and fish (although Clark from time to time would send York overboard to collect cress, and the captains, at least, seemed partial to fruit picked along the way), so that skin eruptions began to cause discomfort—and worse. Modern habits of sanitation were probably unknown (and bathing in the Big Muddy would be an unsatisfactory business at best), and their clothing was probably crusted with perspiration, which would lead to further irritation. Many of the men were also showing signs of digestive and respiratory ailments. On the day of the above entry, Clark includes the following observation: "Sergt. Floyd verry unwell a bad Cold &c." in his field notes. Within a month Floyd would be dead, the victim of a ruptured appendix, and the only member of the expedition to die along the way. Nevertheless, as Clark's repeated expressions of wonder and beauty indicate, they were entering a strange new world as they progressed upriver. The fecundity of the land is mentioned over and over, the variety of fruit and vegetation, the plentiful turkey and geese, the huge and numerous fish, the deer and elk, and even though they had not yet seen them, signs of countless buffalo. Clark does not engage in scientific enumeration of the species but instead celebrates them by repeating their names in a litany of praise at the fullness of the environment. Surely, they were entering the "Garden of the West" that the geographers had promised.

On August 20, as the expedition was approaching the site of today's Sioux City, Charles Floyd died, the first American soldier to give his life west of the Mississippi. All of today's accounts are quick to reassure us that no medical treatment of the day could have saved him, since, appendicitis, the rupture of the appendix, and consequent peritonitis weren't even recognized until the 1820's, and the first successful surgical treatment came in 1884. The Rush's pills the captains gave Floyd for "Beliose Chorlick" probably hastened his death, but undoubtedly would have been proscribed by Dr. Rush himself. Another common treatment of the day would have been to bleed the patient, which would have done no good, either.[1]

We gain special insight into Clark's character by comparing his journal entry with his field notes for the day. First, the journal entry:

> Sergeant Floyd much weaker and no better. Made Mr. Fauforn the interpreter a fiew presents, and the Indians a Canister of whisky we Set out under a gentle breeze from the S.E. and proceeded on verry well—Serjeant Floyd as bad as he can be no pulse & nothing will stay a moment on his Stomach or bowels—Passed two Islands on the S.S. and at first Bl;uff on the S.S. Serj.' Floyd Died with a great deel of Composure, before his death he Said to me "I am going away" [I] want You to write me a letter"—We buried him on the top of the bluff 1/2 Miles below a Small river to which we Gave his name, he was buried with The Honors of War much lamented; a Seeder post with the (1) name Sergt. C. Floyd dies here 20th of August 1804 was fixed at the head of His grave—This Man at all time gave us proofs of his firmness and Deturmined resolution to doe Service to his Countery and honor to himself after paying all the honor to our Dececed brother we Camped in the mouth of *floyds* river about 30 yards wide, a butifull evening.
>
> (*Journals*, II, 495)

Clark, as usual tries to convey the flow of the day by including matters other than the central one, and he gives us something of his concern for Floyd's fading condition. Floyd's moving last words provide an authentic starkness. The presentation of the circumstances of his burial would satisfy any court of inquiry to follow. The one-sentence eulogy celebrates his qualities as a soldier, which were among the best in the Corps, since he was the first to be appointed sergeant back at Wood River. In the final line the party's campsite is given as "Floyd's River," which now objectifies the

man and his honors. Clark's feeling for his comrade is evident but carefully under control, as befits a commanding officer.

But the field notes tell a different and more personally affecting
story. The presents to the interpreter and the Indians are gotten out
of the way first. Then Clark tells us "I am Dull & heavy been up the
greater Part of last night with Serjt. Floyd, who is a[s] bad as he can
be to live the [motion?] of his bowels having changed &c. &c. is the
Cause of his violent attack &c. &c." Never, I think, have ampersands
been more expressive than this. After including the day's course,
almost as if to locate the event in space as well as time, Clark
continues: "we Came [to] make a warm bath for Serjt. Floyd hopeing
it would brace him a little, before we could get him in to his bath he
expired, with a great deel of composure, having said to me before his
death that he was going away and wished me to write a letter—."
Floyd's last words are not quoted directly, but are spoken to Clark
and presumably heard by him alone. We also learn that the bluff was
given Floyd's name, as well as the river (both bear the name today),
and that Lewis read the formal funeral service, which in the journal
entry had been suggested only by the passive voice. This draws Lewis
into the somber event as well, and thereby enlarges the scope of what
has occurred. Clark's initial version of the eulogy also differs in one
significant respect: instead of the characteristics of the ideal soldier,
we hear that Floyd "had at All times given us proofs of his
impatiality Sincurity to ourselves and good will to Serve his
Countrey." Not "firmness" and "Deturmined resolution" but the
more personal qualities of "Sincurity" and "good will." Clark reveals
himself as genuinely grieving over the loss of a friend (perhaps a
distant relative, but we're not sure) before he notes the casualty of a
non-commissioned officer, and in so doing bespeaks the depths of
his emotions. The two entries also display his firm rhetorical

control, his ability to differentiate what language is appropriate for its specific purposes.

——————————

Today the approximate site of Floyd's burial place is marked by a monument visible for many miles, a 100-foot-high Egyptian obelisk made of white stone and rising from a 125-foot-high bluff overlooking the Missouri at the south edge of Sioux City. Through the efforts of local groups the Monument was designated a Registered National Historic Landmark in 1960, and bears the honor of being the very first such landmark so designated. The view from the hill is a spectacular wind-swept panorama of parts of three states, the entire valley, the metropolitan area, and the swift River, which here is narrower than usual. When the Corps of Discovery returned from the Pacific, they discovered that the grave had been partially uncovered, either by animals or marauding Indians. They filled it in and replaced the cedar marker. But fifty years later, in 1857, the River had undermined much of the bluff, and Floyd's grave was again disturbed, this time his remains scattered over the hillside. Most of the skeleton was recovered part way down the slope, the skull almost to the water's edge. The forearms were never found. The townspeople reburied Floyd, this time about 200 yards east of the original site, to reduce risk of destruction by further erosion. Over time the marker was whittled away by souvenir hunters, and the grass over the grave was trampled down by cattle. When Floyd's Journal was published in 1894, he was once again remembered and disinterred, to be placed in a more fitting grave. The remains were identified as his by the absence of the arms. A local lawyer inscribed his skull with his name, so that he would not be misplaced again, and he was reburied with a marble slab as a marker. Then a locally initiated fund-raising effort began, which, matched by grants from the State of Iowa, the federal government helped to finance the building of an imposing memorial. On the anniversary of Floyd's death in 1900 the cornerstone for the present monument was laid.[2]

There are other memorials to Sergeant Floyd. There is a Floyd Golf Course and a Floyd softball complex. There is a Floyd Boulevard, paralleling the Floyd River, which enters the Missouri just east of the downtown business area (the Missouri makes a sharp bend to the west at the city, so that Nebraska is due south of Iowa at this point). Until the Floyd River was "channelized," a word used to describe flood control efforts such as dikes, dredging, and straightening, it regularly overflowed, destroying residences of many of the city's poor. Today there are almost no residences along the River and little chance of flooding. In addition to being the home of extensive railroad freight yards, and probably because of them, the valley of the Floyd has become the industrial center of the city. Along the tracks are found the Sioux Tools plant, huge grain elevators and feed storage bins, and weirdly shaped places which smoke all the time, indicating that they are producing chemicals, mostly for agriculture. Then there are the acres and acres of stock pens, today mostly empty.

Sioux City's industry was built on its meatpacking plants. At one time the Big Four—Armour, Swift, Cudahy, and Wilson, as well as Morrell and Rath—all had beef and/or pork butchering operations here, so that Sioux City ranked behind only Chicago and Kansas City as a meat-producing center.[3] I spoke with one man who fondly remembers his father taking him to the stockyards when he was a boy to view the colorful spectacle of the thousands of cattle and the teeming crowds of buyers bidding on each lot of animals. In those days the market, not the buyer, set prices. The packing plants employed workers from all over the world and paid them handsomely for heavy, sometimes brutal "man's" work. Today along these tracks only Morrell is left in the city itself (IBP is across the River—more about that later), where it used to be possible to run the animals directly from the railroad cars that brought them here into the slaughterhouse. One 13-acre pen area is still covered with a steel roof, the largest ever in the country when it opened in 1975. Why the animals required a steel roof I do not know, maybe to prevent them from catching a cold before they stepped onto the conveyor belt to the slaughter line. The plants used to steam and smoke twenty-four hours a day—and smell. As one resident said, "It used to stink to beat high hell, but that was the smell of money." Jobs in the packinghouses were all unionized and they paid well. But it was, and remains, a tough industry, and labor wars were common, some involving violence and the occasional mobilizing of the state militia to calm things down. And the work became less steady as downturn in demand or temporary surpluses could result in layoffs. Today young people say they don't want to work in the remaining plants, even though jobs are tight in the area. So the packers recruit out-of-state, especially among immigrants, claims the manager of the State's Department of Employment Services office, and the wages are still good in comparison with other jobs available.

A vivid moment in the history of the city's meatpacking days occurred on December 14, 1949, when at 11:30 in the morning the Swift Number Two Building exploded in a blinding flash. Although there was little fire except a blaze from a ruptured gas main on the street, the plant immediately took on the appearance of a bombed-out ruin, reminding residents of pictures of World War II damage. Even though it was lunch hour for many who had left the building, twenty-two people were killed and 97 injured. The medical facilities of the city were stretched to the limit. Private cars, even beer trucks, were pressed into service as ambulances. There was a strong possibility of another explosion, since no one knew what had caused the first one. To this day no one can be certain, although the story is that several employees remembered smelling gas the day before. Anxiety ran high, even though the sight of a street littered with wieners and cold cuts provided a touch of comedy. Swift paid claims brought by the injured and the families of the dead, but blame was never legally assessed. It is hard to find current residents who want to talk about the incident, even though the memory of the disaster is still buried in their pasts.[4]

The shell of the four-story Swift plant (packing houses in the old days were built vertically, so that gravity could do some of the work, such as draining blood and moving carcasses) has been turned into a mini-mall, K.D. Station, containing restaurants, bowling lanes, a miniature golf course, and a model railroad museum. All through the thick stone walls of the gloomy corridors are imbedded bits and pieces of the building's former life—gears, scales, hooks, clubs, carts, and the like—objects which survived the explosion. When it rains really hard in Sioux City, I am told, blood sometimes seeps from the walls. Still, here are found the best margaritas in town, so people keep coming. I once stopped at the model railroad museum, which had a huge layout with hundreds of cars, engines, and miniature buildings. The elderly attendant ran a few trains for me, since I was the only visitor, but he didn't seem much interested in discussing the real railroads of the city and how they put an end to the riverboat trade almost overnight.

The city was first laid out in 1848 by an entrepreneur from Illinois named William Thompson, who called it Thompsonville. Among the first settlers was a French-Canadian trader with his Sioux wives and their father, Chief War Eagle, who was helpful to European settlers in the area. War Eagle's grave is located at the other end of town from Floyd's, on a bluff overlooking the confluence of the Missouri and the Big Sioux Rivers. In his honor the town was renamed Sioux City in 1857, and at that time became a frequent destination for riverboats, including the famous steamboat *Yellowstone* on its maiden voyage. The peak of traffic occurred in the 1870's and 1880's. Even today an occasional barge appears on the River, but within a decade of the town's founding the railroad came through and cut into the river trade because it was more reliable in winter, cheaper, and able to pick up and deliver more conveniently. And there was plenty to haul; the area was becoming the center of a burgeoning agricultural region, which if not as fertile as the more humid area to the east, nevertheless produced vast quantities of foodstuffs. The trains still run. I counted five mainlines radiating out from the City.

Another monument to Floyd can be found in dry-dock in the beautifully landscaped and maintained park along the riverfront, an easy walk from the downtown area. The town's tourist information center is housed in a resplendent riverboat named the *Sergeant Floyd*. It is about 140 feet in length and was used by the Corps of Engineers from the 1930's through the 70's to move workers, equipment, and supplies for the building of the dams and channel improvements along the Missouri, and to set navigational buoys along the channel. After the construction on the Missouri was completed, she became a floating bicentennial exhibit on inland and Gulf Coast waterways, celebrating the contributions of the Corps of Engineers. Then she was decommissioned and moored at St. Louis, where efforts to transform her into a floating museum were unsuccessful. As with Floyd's Monument, the people of the city seized an opportunity to enhance their area and brought her here to serve as a Welcome Center and a museum of river history. The brightly painted exterior and gleaming interior serve both ends admirably. Piles of *Sioux Bee* honey and *Jolly Time* popcorn (local products) greet the visitor, who then moves through gangways with display cases containing photographs and memorabilia illustrating riverboating along the Missouri.

But most arresting are the models of riverboats, from their very beginnings to modern times, built to scale, highly detailed, appropriately painted, and even, when required, weathered. I was so taken with their quality on my first visit that I asked the young man attending the desk if he was the Blair Chicoine identified in the cases as the modelmaker. He was and seemed to be pleased that I had remarked on his work. He has proved to be a mine of information, for he is a genuine enthusiast about the River and, since he is a native, knowledgeable about the city as well. He collects a paycheck as Director of the Center, but his vocation is building custom models on commission; on one of my visits he showed me a mostly completed model of the Lewis and Clark red pirogue, which was weathered so perfectly that it would pass for being 200 years old. When I asked about the full-sized replicas at Onawa, he offered the grudging respect of the professional, although he thought he had spotted a few minor inaccuracies there.

Probably no one knows more about the Lewis and Clark boats than Blair. Here are some nuggets I picked up. Contrary to those who think of the Ohio Valley boatbuilders as crude and unskilled, he believes that the builders who crossed the Alleghenies were genuine craftsmen, who tailored their designs to new realities, especially the shallowness of the water and the variety of obstacles the boats encountered. And the materials they had to work with also differed; the timber available was often less workable and elegant that what was used by eastern builders, and there was a greater need to conserve materials. Boats on western waters had fewer curved pieces, but fewer were needed, and the boats were not as sturdy because strength was not as relevant as in ocean-going vessels. Although he didn't want to commit himself, Blair thinks that the expedition's keelboat design may have come from Jefferson himself, because there are enough idiosyncrasies to differentiate it from the standard keelboat design. And he wonders if Clark's retrofitting at Wood River, so that the locker lids could be raised to provide protection from arrows or bullets, wasn't also due to Jefferson. All attempts to recreate the Lewis and Clark boats come from journal entries and Clark's one drawing in the Journals. But once the fundamental design of the riverboat became established with the horizontal piston engine and the rod-and-turnbuckle construction (it was actually possible to adjust the amount of "whip" or flexibility in a riverboat to better cope with river conditions by loosening the turnbuckles), the proportions were set. It is possible to build an entire boat to scale, Blair says, with very few measurements, some of which come from builders' plans, others from photographs, still others from rule-of-thumb, such as the mast will be angled one-half-inch to the foot, the funnel likewise, and so on. The best source has been insurance company documents, which often provide careful measurements. Blair uses all these methods in his modeling, and he remarked on the contemporary publications for model enthusiasts as well, which sometimes provide plans and suggestions.

Just down the way from the *Sergeant Floyd* is another example of a riverboat, the modern casino boat *Belle of Sioux City*. This boat is a fraud. The stacks fold down and are for show only, the real exhausts from the diesels that propel it porting from the stern. And the stern-wheeler isn't a sternwheeler; modern screws drive the ship on the water, and the rear paddlewheel is powered by an electric motor for show alone. But it does float, and from time to time it cruises the River with its complement of gamblers. Even at dock and at noon on a weekday crowds can be found here. I once wandered through and observed the faces and the body language of the players, most of whom were either elderly or quite young. Everyone seemed to work at being cool, even a gray-haired dowager who collected a pile of quarters from a slot machine in her hat as I passed. I saw a craps player on a run, but no one would guess it by his expression or his understated wind-up with the dice. The poker players just looked bored, and those at the blackjack table were glum, since the house seemed on a roll. The atmosphere on this day, in sum, was neither unwholesome, as some opponents of gambling fear, nor, apparently, was anyone having very much fun, as others believe. It seemed like a job. Unlike other state-run operations which channel gambling profits directly into the general budget, Iowa, I learned, sets aside a percentage of the take for a non-profit corporation, which, in turn, makes grants to localities for education and historic preservation. Money for the Welcome Center's project with schoolchildren was funded this way. Maybe those who gamble are viewing their activity not as enjoyment, then, but as philanthropy.

Both riverboats have as their setting a well-maintained park stretching from the *Floyd* almost to the Big Sioux River. There is a full marina at one end. In season the plantings of annuals are spectacular, and there is also a carefully tended rose garden. Joggers are seen at all hours of the day, and pets, invariably on leashes, also enjoy their turn around the circle (Iowans are indefatigably law-abiding, so the dogs are tended). In the middle of the park is a good-sized modern structure with a raised floor, open sides and arched roof of some translucent material. This puzzled me, since it wouldn't serve well as a band shell or a stage, since all its sides were open. It turns out to be a dancing pavilion and is used often in the summertime for all sorts of dancing, from square-dancing to down-and-dirty (the latter hard to imagine amid the roses). Weddings are regularly held here as well. The townspeople speak of it with a good deal of affection. The Riverfront Park is separated from the commercial area by the interstate highway (which has pedestrian bridges over it) the approaches to the bridges to Nebraska, which contain, according to a local map, "the two most stupid highway intersections in the State of Iowa." Like most Midwestern towns, the downtown area sprawls out, not so much up, since real estate is more readily available. A prime lot next to the bridge is known as Ski Sioux City, because it is reserved for dumping the snow from streets and parking lots in the winter.

On first impression the center of the city appears functional rather than aesthetically pleasing. Much of its commercial architecture dates from the period when square was good and no-nonsense was better. But there is a fine old Civic Auditorium of yellow brick with art deco ornamentation—ears of corn friezes and profiles of Indian chiefs and such. Better still it remains in constant use. A few blocks away is the modern Convention Center with chastely modern white arches, a building highly functional for trade shows, ice-skating, basketball games, and the like. There is a mirror-glass mini-skyscraper which houses the headquarters of the Terra International Corp. (agricultural chemicals) standing next to the Badgerow Building, a twenties structure with an imaginative frieze running around its crown. An entire six-block area running from one major department store, Younkers, to another, J.C. Penney's, is connected by "skyways," aerial walkways designed to protect shoppers from the weather, and, incidentally, to encourage downtown shopping in the face of competition from the outlying mall. On the edge of the downtown area looms the Marian Health Center, two large clinic and hospital buildings, also joined by skyways to doctors' offices and parking ramps; these are probably the largest buildings in town. Tying the area together are the plantings. Sioux City is very big on flowers.

It also celebrates the arts. The Sioux City Art Center is a new structure that shows taste and economy while it provides a good setting for works of art. I once visited there during its annual juried exhibition, an event that has been going on for over a half century. I found the collection of fifty-some artists on display from all over the upper Midwest to be interesting, if not mind-boggling. The juror, a museum director from Florida, found, to my taste, the murkiest and most pretentious works to honor, all the way from a painting displaying how Mother shaped my values and made me a mess, to an indistinct rendition of female body parts, to the discovery that crutches could be mounted on canvas and carry "symbolic meaning." Fortunately, from my point of view, the Museum lightened the miasma with its purchase awards, which were at least full of light and clarity and even sometimes of humor. But I noticed that there were no local entrants and asked if that meant there was no exhibition-quality work being done in town. I couldn't read the expression on the face of the docent I put this question to, but I thought I saw a small grim smile, as if I had hit a sore spot. She assured me that local artists were alive and well and that I could get a sense of what was happening locally at a gallery down the street. But there was a powerful midwestern rainstorm in progress, and it was all I could do to make it to my van without drowning.

Another downtown building worthy of notice is the Woodbury County Courthouse stuffed into a block with a bank, a parking ramp, and the Gothic-towered City Hall. The exterior is unremarkable yellow brick with borders of ornamental frieze, popular in Sioux City, but the

interior turns out to be a revelation. The central area has huge murals—
Romans receiving justice from the gods, pastoral peace and plenty, and
the like. But the dome was what drew my attention. Its long strips of
muted yellow, cream, and light blue glass created elongated geometric
patterns and provided a subdued, peaceful light. I first visited the building at the end of a lunch hour when crowds were gathering outside the
courtrooms upstairs, but everyone behaved calmly under the influence
of that light. I learned later that the architect for the building was
George Grant Elmslie, a colleague of Frank Lloyd Wright and Louis
Sullivan at one time in his life, and one of the creators of the Prairie
School of architecture along with them. The town makes little fuss
about its Courthouse, and one of the best things about it was that it was
a working building and not a monument.

This is a refreshing aspect of the community. In spite of the Chamber
of Commerce's attempt to push something called the "Sioux City way,"
there is a quiet, unspoken pride in the simple beauty of the place, which
manifests itself in the care with which the streets, the parks, the buildings, and private homes are maintained. While no paradise, Sioux City
strikes me as more alive, in the sense that it is a functioning, organic
whole. It is not problem-free, but there is a spirit and self-confidence
found here that is refreshing to one coming from the tired, decaying
small cities of the east. I spent so much time here because it was the first
place that revealed to me a tone and attitude I was to find further along
the Trail.

And there is plenty of comfort here as well. The tree-shaded streets
are filled with modest and not-so-modest homes, which nevertheless
rarely call attention to themselves. Except, that is, for one suburban
neighborhood across the Big Sioux, where expensive homes (for this
part of the world) occupy curving drives built around an Arnold
Palmer-designed golf course, and where eventually an upscale shopping
center is to be integrated into the neighborhood. But even this small
touch of ostentation (the subject of derisive eyebrow-raising even by

some of the town's professional people, who could afford it) was muted in comparison with the standards of the suburban world further east, as if there was something not quite proper in displaying one's good fortune. Far more representative are the plain but obviously well lived in homes on street after street framed in arching shade trees. And I even spotted a 20's-style small apartment building with a kosher grocery on the ground floor, like many I had seen growing up in Detroit.

But some older dwellings were built to call attention to themselves, like the Pierce Mansion, a gaudy Romanesque-style pink stone mansion built in the 90's, which today, after nine prior owners, has become the home of the city's Public Museum. It contains good collections of local history displays, Native American artifacts, and natural history exhibits. The Director, however, told me that they are running out of space and are looking for a new home. Among the displays was a collection of glass photographic plates recovered from an itinerant photographer, who had made up a book of photos of the town's mansions and had sold it to the owners. The plates prove that there was a fierce competition to build a grander house than one's neighbor, even if that meant bordering on the grotesque. Some of these places are still standing and make a fine tour to commemorate the "vanity of human wishes." Mr. Pierce himself provides a case study. A real estate developer, who also built a cable car line and the electric plant to power it, his grandiose home was to aid in boosting the development of the city's North Side. But within nine years his fortune was swept away, starting with the Panic of '93, and he found it necessary to raffle off the place, selling 40,000 tickets at a dollar apiece. But these few mansions are exceptions, just as the town's irritating habit of tearing up its streets and creating improbable detours only serves to underscore the general orderliness. This is best shown in the many parks, not only on the waterfront (there is an even bigger riverfront park farther south, called Chautaqua Park, which is used for the summer celebration called "River-Cade", and one larger yet serving as a greenbelt). They come in all shapes, from

Grandview Park in the north end, with a bandshell, the site of summer-time concerts, to a large park in the south end with a variety of athletic fields, and in between several pocket-sized parks commemorating local figures, as well as War Eagle and Leif Erikson.

Another form of civic celebration took place in the past and tells us something about the people who settled here. At the Museum there were a few photographs of places called Corn Palaces. During the late 1880's, after a series of abundant harvests, someone—to this day no one knows who—suggested the appropriateness of a public festival of thanksgiving. Civic leaders were quick to see the commercial as well as the spiritual possibilities and held a special meeting, where it was pointed out that Ottumwa had its Coal Palace, St. Paul its Ice Palace, why not a Corn Palace for Sioux City? It was an idea whose time had come. Within a week the plans were drawn for a crude 100x100 wooden frame covered with rough timber and wire, to which could be affixed the appropriate decorations. It was to have a hundred-foot-high tower with a cupola, arched windows, and a flying buttress decorated with colored grain. Within a week a grand structure (it had grown to 210x185) was thrown up in the downtown area by 46 men and ten teams using 300,000 board feet of lumber, 500 pounds of wire, 500 pounds of carpet tacks, 15,000 bushels of corn, and 3500 yards of colored cloth. It was a great success, the marvel of the Midwest, and President Cleveland and his bride even interrupted their honeymoon to pay a visit. The Palace brought in much more income than was spent in its construction.

After the celebration it was torn down, but rebuilt annually until 1891, larger and more ornate each year. By now it was drawing trainloads of spectators (and businessmen) from as far away as Boston. The tower had grown to a 160-foot-high spire, and one year the dome had a map of Iowa made of grain on its top, so that visitors could not help but be reminded of where these marvels were occurring. But bad weather that fall cut attendance, so that for the first time it was a financial loss. Moreover, the

Panic of 1893 was just around the corner, and civic spirit was no longer running so high. So that was the last Corn Palace in Sioux City. The town of Mitchell, however, in the center of South Dakota and only twelve years old, adopted the idea, and its permanent Corn Palace stands today as a busy tourist attraction on the upper plains.[5]

On one visit to the area I parked my van at a campsite in Stone State Park not far from Briar Cliff College. Although on the edge of the city, it seems a completely isolated spot in the Loess Hills, with a steep, winding drive to the camping area at the summit that kept me in second gear all the way. There are many long vistas to be seen from this drive, so that it is hard to imagine we are on the edge of the Great Plains. When I first drove in, not a person was in sight and I anticipated a peaceful evening. But when I returned after a tour of the city, I discovered that about a dozen carloads of young men, women, and children had pulled into an adjoining circle. With extensive experience of state park campgrounds in the east, I suspected an orgy, or at the very least a blowout, so I prepared for the worst as bedtime approached, rolling up windows and stuffing my head into my sleeping bag. I never heard a peep from them. They apparently belonged to a prayer group or a camp meeting, or some such organization that practiced vows of silence. In all my years of camping I have never encountered their like before or since.

I like to "collect" colleges, so I thought it might be interesting to get a look at Sioux City's two four-year colleges, Morningside and Briar Cliff. Since the former is the older of the two, I looked for it first. The town, remember, is almost bisected by the industrial flats along the Floyd River, and Morningside is on the south side of that division. When people are determined to lay out their streets in a north-south, east-west grid, but find rivers or hills in the way, all hell can break loose, and that happened in Sioux City. There is limited access from one end of the town to the other. I finally caught on to the fact that those white spaces on the map were really impassable hills, and then I eventually found the College. It is a yellow-brick sort of place tucked into a city neighborhood, which suggests schools in much larger cities. It appears to be thriving (unlike some other colleges not too far away), and is weathering the financial storms faced by small liberal arts colleges today. And the neighborhood surrounding it has a distinct "collegetown" flavor.

Briar Cliff was just as difficult to reach but for very different reasons: it is located on an isolated hilltop at the north end of town. Access is limited to streets with names like Pinewood and Plum Creek Road. The setting is remarkable, the architecture somewhat depressing square brick functional. It remained unspoken, but I got the impression in town that Briar Cliff had something of a higher social standing, even if I heard no assessment of educational quality. But today the College recruits students from the Vietnamese, Laotian, and Mexican populations drawn to Sioux City by jobs in the meatpacking industry. The President, Sister Margaret Wick, remarks that "We've been educating first-generation college students,...and now they've done so well that their children are ready for Notre Dame."[6] Briar Cliff is valued by the community and seems to be filling a necessary role.

I once enjoyed a morning's discussion about the area with Blair, a Briar Cliff graduate, and V. Strode Hinds, a retired oral surgeon, on the bridge of the riverboat *Sergeant Floyd*. Hinds is an Iowa native, who went to the State University and taught there for four years before coming to Sioux City, where he has lived since 1958. A trim man with white crew-cut hair, something of a lantern jaw, and shrewd eyes that don't miss much, he seems to know everything about the town. When, for example, Blair began to explain the name of the Badgerow Building as an anagram of the partners that built it, Strode jumped in to point out that it was in fact a family name, the daughter married into the X family, who built the building and named it after her, etc., etc. He has been involved with the Lewis and Clark Trail Heritage Foundation from the very beginning and served as one of its first presidents. The organization began, he explained, with the efforts of a local man, J.N. ("Ding") Darling, who left

Sioux City for the *Des Moines Register* and a measure of fame as a political cartoonist. Darling was an enthusiast for wild and scenic river protection and hoped that the Missouri could be protected from development. He persuaded an Iowa congressman in the mid-60's to introduce legislation for a federal commission to look into preservation. The bill passed, and one of the commission's recommendations was the formation of private groups to promote awareness of the region's history and to work for preservation. The L&CTHF (as it is affectionately known) was one result. From the beginning the Foundation has appealed to a broad spectrum of people, from those whose interest is recreational, geographical, or historical. Sometimes its annual meetings have sessions that test and increase detailed information of the Trail and the Journals, much, I imagine, as the Baker Street Irregulars pore over the corpus of Sherlock Holmes.

I got a glimpse of how many of those enthusiasts are out on the Trail, since most, it seems, check in with Strode as they pass Sioux City. Dayton Duncan, who had written *Out West*, a fine account of life along the Trail in the mid-80's, was now writing scripts for Ken Burns, the documentary filmmaker, and Lewis and Clark figured prominently in plans for their then-upcoming television productions. William Least Heat Moon, the creator of a best seller a few years ago about travel along the secondary roads of the country, was headed up the Missouri by boat, with a trailer following him to handle the portages around the dams. His work has recently been published. From the bridge of the tugboat Blair and Strode spotted logs coming downstream and chuckled to think how Moon was going to handle those. Strode reeled off the names of a dozen or so people he knew who were writing about the Lewis and Clark experience, including Stephen Ambrose, whose history of the Expedition has since become a bombshell bestseller. I got the impression Strode was gently warning me, in case my motive was to cash in on the L&C industry that appeared to be developing as we

approached the Bicentennial in 2004. I was properly humbled. I still am,
even though Strode has since died and I am writing these pages anyway.

I raised questions about the local economy, since I hadn't yet determined whether Sioux City was a boomtown, a declining town, or a
town in transition from meatpacking to services. In the back of my
mind was a visit to Gateway Computers, the large and highly successful
direct mail marketer of personal computers, located across the Big
Sioux in South Dakota but in fact part of the Sioux City area. Over 1400
employees were working there, and it was good fun to see entire semis
painted with the immediately recognizable spotted black-and-white
cow logo, each filled with hundreds of the black-and-white boxed computers. Gateway resulted from a local teenager, who worked in his
garage repairing computers for a Texas firm. He saw that he could
assemble his own machines to the buyers' specifications, did so, and by
a combination of market, savvy, quality merchandise at reasonable
prices, and good timing, caught the wave in computer use to become
one of the most successful of all computer producers. But Strode
pointed out that Gateway has created mainly low-skill, low-wage jobs
with very few local spin-offs, although one firm has developed sophis-
ticated computer technology to check for flaws in huge conduits and
has offices all around the world. Basically, Strode maintained, Sioux
City remains a small city with an agriculturally based economy, typified
by the cooperative called Sioux Bee that markets honey gathered from
many producers. This kind of economy brings along a special benefit:
farmers learn to deal with booms and busts by not overspending on
speculative ventures in the good years and by maintaining their equilibrium during the bad years. They are accustomed, as Strode puts it, to
reading the economy. During this visit Sioux City's unemployment rate
was about 5 per cent, but no one seemed very exercised that this was too
high or too low.

I wondered whether young people left and did not return. Many of
the brightest do leave, as might be expected, but a surprising proportion,

I learned, come back at a later period in their lives. Twenty years ago the college-bound escaped to the University of Nebraska, the closest major university, or to Ames and Iowa State, or maybe to the University of South Dakota at Vermillion just up the road. But today there seems to be greater diversity, with Missouri, Iowa, and even Yale mentioned as destinations for local students. A long time ago I attended Grinnell College in central Iowa, and I can remember only two or three of my contemporaries from this part of the state. But today Grinnell is an option as well. I also asked whether recruiting medical people was a problem and received an emphatic "no." The two medical centers here see themselves as state-of-the-art. Problems occur only when physicians' wives are not brought into the process at an early stage. Sometimes the adjustment to small-town midwestern life proves to be too difficult, and the family will leave after about two years. But for those who remain life can be comfortable, relatively safe and predictable, and full of a certain level of activity and fun. There must be more softball diamonds per inhabitant than any town in America, and the summer's schedule is packed with all forms of activity.

In some ways Sioux City's transformation from working-class meatpacking center to white-collar service provider parallels what occurred in Pittsburgh. Both cities, after a relatively short period of turmoil, became metamorphosed into new creations without totally severing ties with the past. The reminder of Sioux City's past is still very much in evidence. The largest single employer in the area, IBP, Inc., is across the river in Dakota City, Nebraska. Originally founded in 1960 with a $300,000 loan from the Small Business Administration (!), Iowa Beef Packers, as it was then known, embodied an entirely new approach to the economics of producing and marketing meat. It bought or built low, single-floor, highly automated facilities at the site of feedlots to avoid the costs of transportation, and then divided carcasses into particular cuts, vacuum-packed them, and individually boxed the cuts, thereby avoiding the shipping of fat and bone and minimizing the labor involved in placing meat in supermarkets. The firm grew rapidly, especially in places like Iowa, Nebraska, Kansas, and Texas, where union shops had been outlawed.[7] This "butcher-friendly" idea was so successful that virtually overnight the old traditional slaughterhouses of Sioux City were made obsolete. Within two years Armour closed its doors, idling 1200 workers, and Swift was not far behind, after some nasty labor-management quarrels. The revolution was hardly bloodless. Violence flared up with every attempted contract renewal. IBP was shut down four times by strikes between 1969 and 1984, and it imported strikebreakers, which guaranteed trouble. In the 1970's one of IBP's founders was convicted of conspiring with a Mafia figure to bribe IBP's way into New York City supermarkets, and there was another scandal in the 80's when the Federal Trade Commission reported a too-cozy relationship between IBP and the government employees hired to regulate it.[8] But the changes in the industry were irreversible, and as an indication of this, it is noteworthy that even the great Chicago Union Stockyards closed in 1970 for lack of business. By 1980 19 of the top 20 supermarket chains in the nation were using boxed beef, and five of them used it exclusively.[9] Today, IBP is not only the leading producer of boxed beef, but it has taken the lead in the pork market as well (Sioux City packers had switched mainly to pork in the early 1980's) and has moved into specialty meats and ancillary products, such as gelatin and tallow. Part of the huge facility at Dakota City is a tannery, which makes its presence powerfully felt when the wind is from the west.

I once paid a visit to the IBP international headquarters (the name change came when beef was no longer its reason for being and Iowa was no longer its main location) to get the story, as I thought of it, of the drama of labor-management relations in the industry. The building, a sleek, no-nonsense structure, is separated a goodly distance from the tannery for obvious reasons. And once past the regimented parking lot (with very few spaces for visitors, apparently they don't expect many), I entered a richly appointed lobby with a face as glossy as the firm's annual report. But the unsmiling receptionist was not at all glad to hear that I wanted to interview someone about labor relations. After an unseemly bit of whining on my part, she finally placed a call upstairs to the Public Relations Office, and asked me to wait without offering me a seat. Indeed, there were no seats. A period of time passed, and finally a non-committal young man in a good suit appeared, quizzed me carefully as to what I intended to do with any information he gave me, handed me a fact sheet and some publicity releases, and intended to leave it at that. When I brought up the matter of labor friction in what I thought to be a diplomatic and non-threatening way, he looked at me with narrowed eyes and coldly stated that 12,000 of their 30,000 employees at 22 different locations were unionized, and that each contract negotiation had been marked by strikes. Period. End of interview.

One of the reasons for an interest in meatpacking has to do with the shadow of violence it has cast over the city's image. In the town of Le Mars, a half-hour to the northeast, I learned that there are some residents who to this day will not come to Sioux City, because they view it as a potentially violent place. This is similar to many upstate New Yorkers have towards New York City. To gain another perspective on the city, I looked up a college classmate of mine in Le Mars, who for years published the local newspaper. Le Mars itself is worthy of attention. On the road into town there is a billboard proclaiming "Le Mars—Ice Cream Capital of the World." The Governor of the State had made it official. It turns out that the Wells family, through shrewd business sense, had built their dairy into an international organization, making ice cream and other dairy products under hundreds of different brand names, reserving the best stuff for their own "Blue Bunny" label. Milk comes in from all over the midwest via tanker trucks and railway cars, and the town's second largest industry is trucking. I had hoped to learn how the French had made it to western Iowa, but it turns out Le Mars isn't a French word after all. It was founded as a railroad junction, and as the railroads pushed further west creating settlement after settlement, they began to run out of names. So here the initials of the first names of railroad executives' wives were arranged to form a likely sounding word. Undoubtedly, Le Mars is preferable to Sarmel or Relams.

There are good stories about the early days of Le Mars. A wealthy Englishman bought land in the area, since other English investors were striking it rich in the cattle industry. But this man had grander ideas; he hit upon how useful it would be to teach young second or third sons of the gentry, who did not care for a life in the military or the church, to become farmers, and so he founded an agricultural college at Le Mars. The squires came because they had little choice, but matters did not turn out quite as planned. They had little interest in farming, but they immediately established two saloons, which they called the House of Lords and the House of Commons. Both stayed in session around the clock, to the dismay of their professors. But even the legislative life can pall after awhile. A full-fledged rebellion was brewing until the young gentlemen discovered the Sioux horses made superb polo ponies. With a diligence heretofore undisplayed, they practiced and trained, and since they found themselves at a rail junction, they were able to travel virtually anywhere on the continent for competition. They were so good that they defeated the reigning world champion polo team and were then able to call themselves world champions. The agricultural college never gained such distinction and soon withered away, which meant that the checks were no longer forthcoming, so the team vanished as well. But Le Mars had its moment in the arena of international sport.[10]

The former Westmar College here, unrelated to the agricultural debacle, provides another interesting story. Founded by the Evangelical Church in 1890, it remained a viable enterprise until the Evangelicals merged with the United Brethren Church in the 50's. Later the EUB Church merged with the Methodists. But the Methodists already supported four other colleges in Iowa, one of them, Morningside, just down the road. Almost overnight Westmar was undercut, not primarily by the loss of money (not much of this was directly coming from the churches), but by the loss of a path for student recruitment, private support, and a source of leadership. It appeared that the College would close. But about this time a Japanese industrialist, who, together with his family, wholly owned a college in Tokyo, was looking to build a network of colleges in this country as part of a plan to familiarize Japanese students with America and its ways. It was also a moneymaking proposition. Since many students in Japan could not find a place in college there, they could be charged $1000 to take a placement exam and then $25,000 per year for tuition. He bought the College, along with other places, such as Loretto Heights College in Denver, and he renamed this one Teikyo-Westmar University, with the stipulation that up to 50 percent of its enrollment be provided by him, that is, from Japan (a better arrangement than in Denver, where 100% of the students eventually came from Japan). Faculty members were not happy, nor was the conservative community, especially when the industrialist set up his own president and turned over financial operations to a Chicago lawyer with a reputation sullied by his local arrest on drunken driving charges. The headaches proved to be too much for the Japanese industrialist, who found a buyer for the School in California. But alarmed by rumors that the state was about to buy the campus for a prison, and warned that the school was about to lose its accreditation, the city of Le Mars passed a bond issue to buy the campus itself (nine of ten residents voted for it). It has since leased it back to a new administration, headed by a former lineman for the San Francisco 49ers.[11] Colleges don't die easily.

I thought I could get some of my questions about the area answered by going to a luncheon meeting of the local Lions Club. This was a new and somewhat threatening experience for me: would I be expected to roar? As it turned out, there was no roaring, only a tail-twisting yowl and a twenty-five cent fine from everybody for not knowing an obscure point of Lionism. I sat next to a couple of farmers, who apparently thought my question about the size of the average farm hereabouts was hilarious. "A lot bigger than it used to be," they chuckled. "Used to be able to start with a quarter acre," added another. A pastor across the table took pity on me and noted that one of his parishioners and his family farmed 10,000 acres. Because the soil fertility here can't compare to the eastern two-thirds of Iowa, there is more reliance on animal raising, especially hogs, and growing the corn and grain to feed them. I had noticed flooded fields and asked if farmers around here tiled their fields for drainage; not many, was the answer, except where the land was flat, but even these fields weren't draining because the level of the ground water was so high. I saw few dairying operations and wondered where Wells got its milk. Not from us, they said, mainly from Wisconsin and Minnesota. Farming is a serious business these days, I heard over and over again, and no one can make it that isn't a careful businessman. Farmers must learn how to deal with banks, seed and equipment dealers, and they must relate to a wide variety of corporations, national and international, to develop markets. Farms in this part of the world are still family-owned and operated; they are incorporated but not conglomerates. The price of corn today is about what it was twenty years ago, so continuing productivity is required just to stand still. When lunch broke up, the farmers were sobered by the discussion, which is apparently a recurring one, and no laughing matter. And I had gained a new perspective on them and their lives, just as Lewis and Clark were becoming aware of the New World around them.

1   Moulton provides a summary of medical opinion (*Journals*, II, 496n.)

2   Much of this material is from Roy E. Appleman, *Lewis and Clark: Historic Places Associated with their Transcontinental Exploration (1804–1806)*, (Washington, U.S. Department of Interior, National Park Service, 1975, repr. St. Louis, 1993), pp.285–287.

3   Jimmy M. Skaggs, *Prime Cut: Livestock Raising and Meatpacking in the United States, 1607–1983* (College Station, Texas A&M Press, 1986), p.189.

4 Information on the Swift disaster was found in a file of newspaper clippings from the *Sioux City Journal,* especially a feature article from July 25, 1954. These clippings were provided for my use at the Sioux City Public Museum by its Archivist Grace Linden.

5 Julie Goodson, "Sioux City's Corn Palaces," *Sioux City Journal,* March 28, 1971, found in the aforementioned clippings.

6 "Small Iowa Schools Getting Creative in Efforts to Attract Students," *The New York Times,* Sunday, June 22, 1997, p.10.

7 Skaggs, pp.190–193.

8 Skaggs, p.204.

9 Skaggs, p. 194.

10 This story was told to me by Carter Pitts, former publisher of the LeMars newspaper.

11 "Small Iowa Schools Getting Creative," p. 10.

Chapter 6

Spirit Devil Dances with Wolves

In a northerley direction from the mouth of this Creek [the Vermilion River] in an imence Plain a high Hill is Situated, and appears of a Conic form and by the different nations of Indians in this quarter is Suppose to be the residence of Deavels. that they are in human form with remarkable large heads and about 18 Inches high, that they are Very watchfull, and are arm'd with Sharp arrows with which they Can Kill at a great distance; they are Said to Kill all persons who are So hardy as to attempt to approach the hill; they State that tradition informs them that many Indians have Suffered by those little people and among others three *Mahar* men fell a Sacrefise to their murceyless fury not many years Since—

Clark, August 24, 1804 (*Journals*, II, 505)

The Corps of Discovery was entering the short grass high prairies. They had viewed the coyote and the prairie dog for the first time. They had concluded talks with the first of the Native Americans they were to encounter. There was also a change in the very tone of voice in which they embody their experience. While Clark will continue to remark on the beauty and fecundity of his surroundings, Floyd had died and two days later Lewis had almost died of some kind of mineral poisoning when he inhaled fumes and tasted what Clark suspected to be arsenic. The Teton Sioux, of sinister reputation, were nearby, as indicated by the frequent prairie fires, probably a signal system. Now, we find, even the spirit world, in the shape of tiny demons, has intruded as a potential danger. The expedition had coped with all kinds of physical difficulties, with courts-martial, and a funeral, but this was the first time that these men of the Enlightenment had to directly confront the supernatural.

They must have taken the tale as potentially significant, or at any rate, worthy of careful examination. On an extremely hot day eleven of them, plus Seaman, Lewis' dog—a formidable party if all they were pursuing was a joke—hiked the eight or so miles from the Missouri up the Vermillion and cross-country to the hill. Seaman was so exhausted and thirsty that he had to be sent back to the River, and Lewis, still weak from the purging pills after his poisoning, wasn't in much better shape. Even York fell behind, too fat, Clark claimed, for a fast walk. What they found on arriving at the hill was a perfect cone about seventy feet high rising from a plain totally flat as far as the eye could see. Once again, the differences between the two versions of this episode are instructive. In the field notes Clark stresses the mysteriousness of the great flock of birds hovering around the top of the mound, which flew away when the party climbed to the top. The reason then became apparent: the birds had been feeding on thousands of flying ants, which landed on the men and, Clark says, "bit me verry Shart [sharp?] On the neck." (*Journals*, III, 7) Hardly an ordinary day on the prairies! But there were no eighteen-inch-high devils, no permanent casualties, and a rational explanation for everything. In the revised version there is nothing of the exhaustion of anyone but Seaman, no wonder surrounding the cloud of birds, and the ants do not bite. The insects, Clark reasons, have been driven to the leeward side of the mound by the prairie wind, where the birds know enough to gather to eat them. Upon careful examination, the "earth and loos pebbles and other Substances of which it was Composed" correlate exactly with the composition of the riverbank, from which Clark concludes that the hill is "*most probably* (italics mine) the production of nature." Is this the caution of a scientist, or is there still some question in Clark's mind? At any rate, the birds and bugs are, he thinks, "a Suffient proof to produce in the Savage mind a Confident belief of all the properties which they ascribe it." (*Journals*, III, 10-11) He is right back with the Enlightenment attitude of superiority over the "savages." We need to watch this characteristic pattern of simultaneous interest in and skepticism about Indians' views throughout the journey, for it will become highly significant as the expedition moves further away from the settled world.

Spirit Mound, as it is known today, was noteworthy for two reasons. Once the party climbed it, they were rewarded with the first glimpse of what we will never see—thousands of buffalo feeding on the prairie to the horizon. Paradoxically, it is one of the few places we can stand exactly where Lewis and Clark did (if we get the owner's permission) and know that, while all around has changed, the hill is still there. It is located due north of Vermillion, the site of the State University and the first location of the territorial courts in 1861. On the highway from Sioux City there are small signs advertising the presence in Vermillion of the "Shrine to Music Museum." When I first saw these I assumed that a museum on the prairies would consist of hokey objects like double-belled euphoniums and washboards in various keys. Such an attitude spoke multitudes about how easterners like myself tend to appropriate all pretensions of culture to themselves. The Museum is on the campus of the University, itself not a very attractive place, and the "Shrine" occupies what appears to be an old Carnegie-style library building. Inside is a stunning revelation. There are seven galleries, each tastefully set up around a separate theme, such as ethnomusical study of Native American instruments or exotic instruments of the non-Western world. Another gallery explores the treasures of nineteenth-century European folk instruments. Yet another spotlights nineteenth-century American keyboard instruments—early pianos and melodeons and reed organs for home and church use, including a functioning pipe organ which is one of the first built in America. But even more surprising are the rooms displaying treasures of European instrument making. There are magnificently ornamented, inlaid, and painted pianofortes, clavichords, harpsichords, and pianos from all over Europe; there are medieval and renaissance instruments, including a lute made entirely of ivory. Most amazing of all, there is an entire room of stringed instruments by Stradivari, Guarneri, and the Amatis, one of the greatest collections of its kind in the world. The core of the Museum comes from one man, Arne B. Larson, who, according to his son Andre, the curator, was a congenital collector: "He kept everything!" he said. Started in 1973, the Museum has grown from the original Larson collection by buying other collections, as the money became available. Andre went back to school to earn his Ph.D. in order to develop and administer the Museum. And, yes, there is an exhibit of band instruments and a memorial to Yankton's answer to Spike Jones' musical spoofing, Stan Fritz. But this is a small price to pay for helping to bring in funds to develop the collection. Today, the Museum is operated by the University. It is used in teaching and research, and the auditorium within the building serves to provide concerts for the community, many of them utilizing the instruments in the collections. The existence of this musical center in the Dakotas strikes some of us as being as unusual as the Spirit Mound.

As a university town Vermillion is prosperous in a non-ostentatious way, with comfort predominating over glitter. Elms, genuine elms, long gone from the East, arch over streets of large frame houses, many with porches wrapped around them, where matrons in Land's End-style fashions proclaim that faculty members and their families live here. Vermillion and Yankton, some twenty-five miles apart, have parallel histories: both grew from trading posts founded after the Treaty with the Yankton Sioux allowed settlers to buy land the Sioux claimed they did not need (the Yanktons were not unanimous on this matter; one faction, led by a man named Smutty Bear, opposed the sale). But Yankton had connections. The first traders to set up for business were D. M. Frost and John B.S.Todd, and Todd was from Springfield, Illinois, where the well-known Todd family included President Lincoln's wife. Frost and Todd got a territorial charter for a town in 1862, although they kept their residence in Sioux City, and they organized the New York Colony, a hundred families from central New York, thirty of whom made it to Yankton by 1864. Todd ran for Congress against a candidate from Vermillion, and won, and of the several towns vying for the official capital of the Dakota Territory (which included today's North Dakota and parts of Montana, Idaho, Wyoming, and Nebraska) Yankton, naturally, was the choice, to be known as the "Mother City of the Dakotas." Vermillion was promised a university, which didn't happen for twenty years or so, Bon Homme got the penitentiary. By 1866 thirty-six steamboats either stopped or sailed past Yankton; ten years later it became the staging point for miners headed for the Black Hills gold rush. But political dominance had to yield to reality. By 1883 Bismarck had become the territorial capital, and Pierre was named the new capital for the south, even though there was nothing there but a fort (and the suspicion lurked that it was made the capital so that land speculators could profit). As many as eighteen trains a day were dumping settlers at Huron to the east, and they fanned out toward the Missouri to their new land claims. In 1891 Pierre won an election to become the state capital.

Some questioned the honesty of the election. Vermillion faded into the background, where it has quietly done well for itself.[1]

The road to Yankton from Vermillion has interesting signs, too. One small town proclaims itself as the "Hay Capital of the World," but a few miles further on another raises a sign saying "Hay Capital of the Universe." We are within the arena of Western hyperbole, which has itself become a tradition, one well exploited by Mark Twain, for instance. Yankton is on the Missouri near the confluence with the James, a river whose valley is fifty to seventy-five miles wide and is referred to as "the longest unnavigable river in the world."[2] More hyperbole. It runs almost from the Canadian border, and it takes three weeks for water to travel the length of the state. I have crossed the James in flood season when it was a lake five or six miles wide, with only the highway about the level of the water, and it seemed to take more than a little body English to keep my van from plunging into the water. There is a story about the Missouri, which occurred to me as I crossed the James. It is about a man coming upstream in a boat and spotting a tent pitched in what looked like the midst of the water. In front of it was a man fishing. Then from some distance away came a dog trotting towards the fisherman, his feet making little splashes, as if he was walking on water. But both man and dog knew perfectly well where the sandbar began and ended and were making the most of their own little world, knowing that maybe tomorrow or the next day or in a few weeks their refuge would be gone. I hoped that if I left the highway I could find such a bar to land on and could drive right on, out of the river.

Yankton is a busy town of twelve or thirteen thousand people, which provides goods and services for the lower James Valley, as well as some light industry. The two largest employers are a state mental health facility and Sacred Heart Hospital, and there is a college, Mount Marty, and a former college, which houses a federal minimum-security prison. The edge of town is cluttered with farming supply places and repair garages. Downtown is a district from the 1880's, which is listed in the National

Registry of Historic Sites. The town's main commerce is divided between a no-nonsense downtown area and a busy modern strip out on the north side. The bars have video lottery machines with instant payoffs—or not. People I talked with do not believe legalized gambling has done much for the economy, since the money spent on gambling is not spent elsewhere. And unlike Iowa, where funds are earmarked for historic preservation and education, South Dakota's definition of "preservation" can include filling potholes, so I gathered.

The one nationally known Yankton enterprise is the Gurney Seed and Nursery Company, whose catalog and mail-order ads appear all over the nation. The shipping facilities and retail outlet are to be found near the center of downtown next to the River, and the store looks like most other garden outlets, except that one entire section is filled with hundreds of little brown paper bags, with each variety of seed the Company carries in its catalog. When I asked Ernie Meyers, the customer representative, whether the seeds were produced locally, he told me that each one needs to be grown apart from other varieties that would cross-fertilize it, and so the best locations for seed production were individual valleys in the Colorado mountains. The Company was started by a retired Civil War veteran who moved in 1866 from Iowa to northeastern Nebraska with his new bride to develop a timber claim there. Charles Gurney, known as "the Colonel," went into business supplying model orchards and windbreaks to the homesteaders. He was so successful that he sent his son D.B. to Yankton to expand the business, where he set up close to the present location (in what is reported to have been at one time a house of ill repute), adding a greenhouse, a flower shop, a confectionery, and a restaurant. In spite of the bad economy of the 1890's on the prairies, the firm of C.W. Gurney and Son survived and prospered through drought, depression, and tornadoes. D.B. and his four brothers carried the business into the twentieth century, working with plant breeders at the state agricultural college to develop new seed and plant varieties. D.B. became a patron of the town as well, leading the drive to construct the unusual double-deck bridge to Nebraska and founding the first radio station in town, which became known throughout the prairie states (radio travels a long way out here) as "The Voice of the House of Gurney." Lawrence Welk, a North Dakota boy from near the South Dakota border, began his radio career in the studios on the top floor of the nursery. Before that time, the radio station broadcast from the front parlor of the Gurney home on Pine Street, which is still standing. D.B. died in 1943, but the business is still carried on by the family.[3]

Fine old homes are scattered throughout Yankton, some of them extending back to the 1870's, and a walking tour of the historic district has been organized. Once again, the leveling character of the Midwest is evident here; there were no "exclusive" neighborhoods in town until the rise of the suburbs after World War II created age-graded and income-graded areas. Mansions can be next door to modest bungalows. Many "firsts" are represented in Yankton, among them Christ Church Episcopal, the Mother Church of the Dakotas, and the AME Church, dating from 1885, the oldest Black church in the Territory. On the west side of the town is the Hospital and the College, together with a Benedictine Center and Convent that gave rise to both. The is also a park containing the Dakota Territorial Museum, which has, among other exhibits, replicas of the original legislative building and the governor's office, a 1900 hotel bedroom containing a dresser from the room where General and Mrs. Custer stayed (his encampment at one time was just north of town), a Missouri riverboat, two gondolas from Venice, a one-room school house, a Burlington Northern Caboose, a blacksmith shop, a 1925 American LaFrance fire engine, and a replica of the Deadwood saloon where Wild Bill Hickock was shot by Jack McCall, who was brought to Yankton for trial and hanging. He was hanged two miles north of town and buried in an unmarked grave, so that he is not in the Museum. It is remarkably thorough for a small-town museum. The sense of history is alive and well in many places on the plains.

In what was virtually the exact center of the town, before the Territory became a state, the campus of Yankton College was laid out. It is no longer a college but instead serves as a federal prison camp. Although the College closed in the 1980's, it still maintains an office to deal with the ongoing need for transcripts and other unfinished business. At present it is located in the basement of a downtown mini-mall carved out of what had once been the J. C. Penney store. When I paid a visit the Registrar and one clerk, together with a volunteer named Don Rasmussen, formerly the Dean of Students until his job was eliminated in the 1970's, were at work on the details for a student reunion coming up soon. Don was glad to tell me the College's story. The founder and first president, a man named Joseph Ward, was also instrumental in South Dakota statehood, and together with his friend and member of the first Board of Trustees, General Beadle, is in the national Capitol's rotunda as South Dakota's two representatives in the statue gallery. The school was supported by New England Congregationalists, like so many other colleges in the Midwest, and, as was their habit, they never supplied much in the way of funds. But they sent students from the East, and for many years the College was more than a regional institution with more than mere pretensions to culture. Its music conservatory was a distinguished one, and Shakespeare's plays were performed annually from the teens of the present century. The sciences were also a special strength, even without extensive equipment, and Yankton grads did well in graduate studies everywhere. The first chemist hired on the Manhattan Project, I was told, was a Yankton grad. More Rhodes Scholars were produced in the 30's proportionally than any other college in the Midwest. This was not a cow college.

What happened? With an enrollment of about 650 in the mid-sixties and projections of 1000 for the future, things looked rosy, but as the number of college-age students began to decline, so did Yankton's share. Young people in the 60's and 70's were not noted for seeking the peace and quiet of the high plains. Enrollment dropped dramatically to the mid-300 level and never increased very much after that. Mergers with other colleges were explored, but nothing ever came of this, no one seemed interested. Finally, in November 1984, the Board of Trustees voted to close the doors at the end of that term. Although it was obvious that there were serious problems, even the President, who had arrived from Connecticut only that fall, had no advance warning, nor did the faculty, which had been there longer. There would be no winter term. That was it. A member of the Board, a local businessman, was appointed to tidy up outstanding affairs.

Maintenance on the buildings had been deferred for some time, and there the campus stood, in the middle of town, soon to be a decaying eyesore. No buyers could be found, and the residents of the neighborhood were becoming restless. Local congressmen were enlisted in the search for someone to take over the buildings, and finally this approach got results. According to Rasmussen, then-Senator Pressler put the College in touch with the Justice Department, which had been looking for a site in the upper Midwest for a correctional facility. Government representatives took a look, liked what they saw, and negotiations began. When word got out, as it will in a small town, there was an immediate uproar—a prison in our residential neighborhood? The town's reputation would suffer, property values would plunge, and, worst of all, no man, woman, or child would be safe! In what was to become a model way of defusing the situation, the future warden kept the community informed every step of the process, answered their objections, calmed their fears, and persuaded them to become part of the decision-making process. Today townspeople look on the prison grounds as the safest place in town. Two full-time horticulturists are on the staff, and there is no shortage of gardening manpower, so the grounds are a showplace. Open houses are held every month, and prisoners are used in community projects. While a prisoner has walked away from time to time, there have been no permanent escapes. And of course the prison provides a hefty payroll. Far from being an embarrassment, Yanktonians now look on the facility with pride. Even in libertarian South Dakota, it seems, there are examples of successful government intervention.

There are still funds left over from the government's purchase of the campus to pay for the relocation of the College's ongoing office, and there are plans to place it to a new building on the edge of town. Rasmussen wonders if there will be enough room. He showed me the archives, and never, I'm sure, has a college's life been so thoroughly documented. They have just published a directory that includes every student who ever attended Yankton. Photographs abound, even glass plates, about 200 of them, as far back as the turn of the century, displaying the outdoor theatre, the observatory, and early graduating classes. Every official meeting of the Board, the faculty, the student government, every copy of the student newspaper and yearbook, every athletic award, literally everything seems to be here. And the College's official history was last published in 1962. There is a book waiting to be written in these archives.

The level of activity in Yankton is astonishing. It seems incomprehensible that a town of this size can sustain so many civic events. There are Czech Festivals and Danish Festivals and Fur Trader and Haying celebrations. There are craft shows and quilt shows and flea markets galore. There appears to be a sizeable artists' colony, and there is a Lewis and Clark repertory theatre and a Lewis and Clark Living History presentation, as well as band concerts, orchestra concerts, and string quartets. There are several rodeos, tournaments in horseshoes, archery, duck-shooting, volleyball, softball, as well as—always—fishing, of course. And in October there is a Dacotah Territorial Reunion and a Cowboy Poets' Festival. But the town's biggest celebrations are reserved Riverboat Days in August, where over 100,000 people come for a week of dancing, parading, a tractor pull, mud volleyball, arm wrestling, road racing, a golf tournament, and a rodeo, as well as a good-sized craft fair and foods of all varieties.Where do all these people come from? For those in this part of the world, it is nothing to travel two hundred miles for a good time. It is hard work to enjoy oneself to this extent, but the energy it takes to survive South Dakota's brutal winters and searing summers must carry over into the ability to play this hard as well.

There is another example of governmental intervention in the area, the Gavins Point Dam. Indeed, the waters behind and around the Dam, including the twenty-eight-mile-long, forty-five-feet-deep Lewis and Clark Lake and Lake Yankton (actually within the Dam area) are the greatest drawing cards in Yankton, where well over two million visitors come annually for the camping, the boating, and the fishing. Fishing, especially, is serious business. Fish Days begin to be celebrated in June and go on all summer, culminating with the Bass Tournament after Labor Day. At the Dam there is an aquarium of all fish species found in the area, including the pallid sturgeon, for which there has been no documented natural reproduction in the area for over ten years. Naturally enough, then, there is an "Endangered Species Building," as well as a hatchery that releases thousands of little fish each year into the Lake to keep all fishermen happy. We're talking big catches here, too, not fish stories. To qualify as a South Dakota Trophy Angler, which is everyone's goal, there must be documented, as a minimum, a largemouth bass of five pounds, a catfish of fifteen pounds, a lake trout of ten pounds, a walleye of eight pounds, a muskie of twenty-five pounds, or a paddlefish of fifty pounds (the state record is 120 pounds, 12 ounces).

The paddlefish, or spoonbill, is one of the more remarkable creatures of these waters, and not only because of size. A boneless prehistoric monster of sorts with a huge protuberance of a lip that looks, yes, like a paddle, this fish "inhales" its food from the river bottom and so must be snagged since it doesn't bite. The season is strictly regulated to one month in the autumn, and when a specified number have been snagged, the season ends. One fish per season is allowed to each person. I don't see how dragging for a creature which then puts up no fight can be much entertainment, but then I'm no fisherman, preferring when I have fished to do so for dinner only. Nevertheless, thousands appear in

October for the privilege of snagging one of "lusus naturae," and having one's picture taken next to it.

The Dam is really big, about a mile and a half long and about seventy-five feet in height. But it is the smallest in the system of Missouri dams, which run up into Montana at Fort Peck. All but the Fort Peck Dam are the result of something called the Pick-Sloan Plan, which has an interesting history. In 1942 and 1943 the Missouri went on flooding rampages so serious that Congress felt it necessary to get involved. Two separate and competing branches of government came up with programs that were each designed primarily to aggrandize the originating agency. Col. Lewis Pick, then a division engineer at the Omaha Office of the Army Corps of Engineers, was assigned the problem, and came up in a matter of months with a proposal for a series of major dams on the Missouri, hundreds of minor dams on feeder streams, and a series of levees below Sioux City, which, together with some channel improvement, would provide flood control, increased navigation, and some hydro power production to help foot the bills. These were, of course, the major tasks of the Corps of Engineers, the kinds of jobs they were designed to do. If the Corps were put in charge, their budget would be guaranteed for years. But the Pick Plan was hotly opposed by the Bureau of Reclamation, ostensibly because it was feared that it would have too great an impact on the lower Missouri Basin by lowering the water level and hence interfering with navigation. This, at any rate, was the rationale for developing a second proposal to Congress, this one from William Glenn Sloan, an assistant engineer in the Billings, Montana, office of the Bureau. This plan emphasized irrigation and reclamation of unusable lands for farming, and also included some power production. The battle was joined, with railroads and Western governors and congressmen supporting the Sloan Plan, because it would bring greater farm production, happier farmers, and busier railroads. But industrialists and Easterners got behind the Pick Plan, which would, it was believed, stop interruptions to the economy caused by flooding and would provide an alternative means of transportation to the railroads to prevent them from raising freight rates. The conflict between agriculture and industry seemed irreconcilable.

What was the result? True to the enduring instincts of politicians not to irritate powerful constituents, Congress adopted *both* plans, almost without alteration, in the Flood Control Act of 1944, a "shameless, loveless shotgun wedding," as it was called at the time.[4] Between 1946, when construction began on the Garrison and Fort Randall Dams, and 1963, when the generator switches were thrown at the Big Bend Dam below Pierre, hundreds of millions of dollars were invested in turning the Missouri into a "chain of lakes." Gavins Point is the smallest and has the primary function of controlling the flow on the open river all the way to St. Louis. In times of heavy rainfall when upriver reservoirs fill up, Lewis and Clark Lake offers the opportunity to hold the surplus. About a hundred or so miles upstream Fort Randall creates the good-sized Lake Francis Case and produces ten times the electricity of Gavins Point. But the biggies are further upstream—Big Bend meets peak demand for power in the entire Missouri Basin and creates Lake Sharpe, three times the size of Lewis and Clark Lake; Oahe, above Pierre, generates the largest supply of electricity on the River with six of the biggest generators in the world when they were installed, and creates Lake Oahe, a huge body of water extending over 230 miles, as far as Bismarck. Finally, Garrison, north of Bismarck, which was the largest structure of its kind in the world when it was built, impounds Missouri waters in Lake Sakakawea (notice the spelling), the largest man-made lake in the country, 178 miles long, all the way to Williston and the confluence of the Yellowstone, averaging two to three miles in width and at its broadest six miles wide. If fishing is avidly pursued at Gavins Point, at Lake Sakakawea it is a religion, perhaps the dominant religion.

In the forty or fifty years the dams have been in existence, it is possible to measure their achievements against the claims originally made for them. First of all, power production has been beyond expectations.

But a visitor to the dams notices a curious phenomenon—the power lines head mainly to the east, the southwest, and the south, to Minneapolis and to Denver and to Omaha and Kansas City, not primarily to the region where the power is produced.[5] There has been little industrial development and little cost reduction in electricity in the area. Navigation on the Missouri has dwindled to a fraction of what had been projected, even though the channel can support more of it. Pick-Sloan was designed for five million annual tons of traffic, whereas actual tonnage today is not much over one million tons. Navigation has become the "Army's bad joke," since millions were spent to deepen the channel to twelve feet only to find that, as the lakes rose to their planned levels, there wasn't enough water in the river to fill the new channel.[6] The dams provide the capacity for massive irrigation, but only about ten percent of the original planned irrigation features have been put into practice, primarily because the farm commodities best grown in the region—wheat and other grains—have been in oversupply, so that further production isn't needed.

Nebraska has benefited the most from irrigation, but Montana, for example, has lost to the lakes seven times the acreage it has gained from irrigation.[7] Remember that the land lost in the creation of the lakes was bottomland, the most fertile and best-watered farmland available in the region. I once asked a state trooper (who had pulled me over for speeding in the flat lands near Aberdeen) whether there was irrigation around here, and he replied, somewhat grumpily, it seemed to me, that this was too far from the Missouri. But that had been the point of planned irrigation. Recreation was incidental to the original Plan, but here there have been huge successes. Water sports, hunting, and fishing have become primary industries in the Dakotas. But another unanticipated result has been increasing federal presence. The Missouri is managed as if it were a federal river. The Corps of Engineers ensures navigability, the Bureau of Reclamation determines the flow through the federal reservoirs, the Western Area Power Administration markets the electricity produced, the

Fish and Wildlife Service safeguards threatened species, the EPA monitors water quality, the Bureau of Land Management safeguards river flow through wild and scenic portions, the Departments of Interior and Justice try to insure that Native American water needs and the needs of federal agencies are met.[8] In a part of the country where "government" is a suspect word, more and more of the River has become "federalized," in an ironic twist not appreciated by everyone.

But there is another chapter to the story of the dams, the story of their impact on Native Americans. Vine Deloria, Jr. tells about his great-grandfather, a noted medicine man among the Yankton Sioux, who, when his time was approaching, asked to be buried where an arrow shot high up in the air would land. It came down in the hills far from the river bottomland where the tribe lived. This was an unusual request, since the custom was to place the dead in the large cottonwoods along the river. "Bury me in a hole six feet deep, covered with a nice thick layer of rocks. Bury me in the manner of the whites because I want to sleep in peace when I go into the ground." When the Fort Randall Dam was built, the waters by the tribal burial place came up over the tallest trees, and within fifteen feet of the medicine man's rocky tomb. But it was never flooded and even after seventy-five years his magic was still good.[9]

The Pick-Sloan Plan was, without doubt, Deloria claims, "the single most destructive act ever perpetuated on any tribe in the United States."[10] Pick-Sloan affected twenty-three different reservations, with the Crow Creek, Lower Brule, and Ft. Berthold residents suffering the most. Larger reservations were more able to hold their grazing lands intact, even if they lost most of their bottomlands. The first two lost almost all their usable land, and Ft. Berthold was chopped into five pieces which made communication virtually impossible. Although existing treaty rights provided that land could not be taken from these reservations without consent, none of the tribes was consulted prior to the enactment of the Plan. Lake Oahe took over 160,000 acres of land from the Standing Rock and Cheyenne River reservations, 105,000 acres of it bottomland, with 90% of the timber and 60% to 75% of the grazing land, dislocating 325 families, about 30% of the population. Lake Sakakawea took 152,000 acres of Fort Berthold and 94% of agricultural land, dislocating 80% of the residents. Electrical production has not helped Native Americans, since not enough jobs were created to enable them to afford electricity, and what irrigation there was required a capital outlay not possible for most of them. At one point the Sioux tried to participate in the recreation boom by building Chief Gall Resort, across from Mobridge. The Resort consisted of a restaurant, a 56-unit motel, a conference center, a campground, a museum, and a restored Indian village. But it never succeeded, in part because of inadequate capitalization, in part because of the strong anti-Indian feeling in the area.[11] The damage to the people flooded out by the Government's blind insistence on spending money on itself belongs in the list of outrages alongside Wounded Knee.

The highway west from Yankton soon peters out and secondary roads take over through the Yankton Sioux Reservation. Once this Reservation encompassed the entire southeast quarter of the state, a triangle from present-day Pierre to Brookings, to Sioux City, with the Missouri as one side. But the Yankton Sioux were persuaded to sell off land they did not "need," and unlike the Teton Sioux who decided not to sell, they found themselves by 1895 in a very reduced space, today's reservation, which is a rhomboid of about twenty by thirty miles. Maybe they were right to sell; I saw no one out and about until I reached the Fort Randall Dam, and even there a chain bars the way to the Visitor Center, as if it offered things of value only during the height of the tourist season. On an earlier trip I had been to the Visitor Center, a model of Big Dam Propaganda. One person was mowing the hay growing between the fences and the road. There is a quaint law in South Dakota, which says that if the owner of the adjacent fields does not take this marginal crop within ten days of its ripening, it is available to anyone who wishes to harvest it. Just upstream from the dam two roads begin, SD 1804 going up the east bank and 1806 the west bank. This provides a mild but pleasant shock of recognition for a Lewis and Clark enthusiast, since these are the dates of the journey out and the journey back. I crossed over the dam to follow 1806 for a way and found myself in a lunar landscape known as the Manganese Hills, where black veins pop out of barren, stony, wind-swept ridges paralleling the river all the way to Chamberlain. It is hard to tell if the bluffs are tailings from mining operations that have passed on or whether they are natural formations. I later learned it is the latter. These hills are no longer mined, since it is apparently cheaper to get one's manganese from Siberia or South Africa than it is to pick it up in South Dakota.

The Interstate meets the River at Chamberlain, the largest settlement in the area, although that isn't saying much. Yet the River is impressive from the bridges high over it here, spanning the bluffs, and the town provides a kind of oasis for travelers, who can restock and refuel. Once when camping nearby I had a catfish dinner at a Chamberlain restaurant but almost drowned in the grease. Further up the road at Big Bend Dam on the Crow Creek Reservation I crossed over to 1804 and wondered how far it wouldl take me (the answer is all the way past Pierre and Bismarck and Williston to the Montana line). The country above Chamberlain and the interstate is even more sparsely settled. One of the small pleasures of travelling the byroads of Iowa is that you can almost always glimpse several farms, and often the water towers and grain elevators of more than one town are visible at any point. It is companionable country. But here the settlements have thinned out, and it is unusual to see even one inhabited dwelling. The country is changing, and it has an eerie kind of attractiveness. Near the river the land breaks into low, bare, undulating hills that look like waves. It is interesting how often nautical images are appropriate to the prairie, over a thousand miles from any ocean. In the fields occasional irrigation rigs stand idle, but soon even they disappear. I glanced apprehensively at my gas gauge; there was no place for miles and miles to fill up. A common response on the part of early settlers coming from the forests of Minnesota to this vast treeless plain was stark terror, and I began to understand the reality of agoraphobia myself. But the "wide open spaces" of the Great Plains are just beginning.

In fact, Pierre, at the center of the state, is a better place than most to serve as the gateway to another world. It is an absurdly small town to be a state capital, along with Dover, Delaware, the smallest, the size of Yankton, although it seems nowhere near as busy, and in fact it seems barely to make a dent at all in the face of all that surrounding space. Sioux Falls, the state's largest city, looks to Minneapolis, and Rapid City, the second largest, looks to Denver, but Pierre (pronounced "Peer") looks only to the open sky and treeless plain. There are only ten bridges across the Missouri in the entire state, including the roads on the tops of dams, and there seem to be fewer connections than that. John Steinbeck once remarked on the lack of a transition between east and west at Bismarck: "The two sides of the river might as well be a thousand miles apart."[12] But what is found at Pierre is different. It is the transition from a non-place (South Dakota barely exists in the consciousness of most Americans) to a definitely remembered place, The West, as known to the imaginations of moviegoers all over the world. Sparse rainfall becomes sporadic rainfall; Pierre has recorded one and a half inches of rain in a half-hour, over ten percent of the average year's precipitation.[13] Farming becomes less and less possible and gives way to grazing. We begin to recognize the landscape of the Great Plains, land of the buffalo "where the deer and the antelope play," and the Sioux repeatedly bite the dust.

Towards the end of that first September, as the expedition approached the confluence of the Missouri and the Bad Rivers, the site of present-day Pierre, apprehension was growing over the anticipated meeting with the Teton Sioux. Their reputation for harassing traders, thieving, and obstructing movement upriver had often proved to be a reality, and their number and fierceness as warriors was also well attested. Up to this time not one of the St. Louis merchants had been able to get past them. The first council with the Oto and Missouri a month earlier had been anything but a shining success. Lewis and Clark had given speeches on how the Great Father in Washington was going to look after his children if they only would live peacefully with their neighbors and trade with Americans, not the British or the French, and they distributed presents supposed to appeal to the primitive nature. But the tribes knew how to "yes" an adversary into stupefaction, and while they remained impassive, they could not have been happy with the beads, face paints, medals, and certificates which were handed out; they wanted whiskey and guns, or at the very least trade goods needed for a better life. As James Ronda points out, the misunderstandings and confusions resulting from this meeting should have been a warning of the difficulties ahead.[14] This first test of diplomatic skill, the establishing of good relations with Native Americans, Jefferson's most important priority after finding the Northwest Passage, was not passed with distinction. The world of the tribes was far more complex than anyone in the East had anticipated, and at this point in their experience it was an open question as to whether the explorers had the ability to adjust to it and succeed. They were coping well with the new physical environment, but they were less secure in adjusting to a succession of new and unfamiliar societies.

Tuesday, September 25, through Friday, September 28, were among the most dramatic days of the entire expedition. The Journals tell the story well. This period displays some of the greatest strengths and weaknesses of Lewis and Clark, and it has played a significant part in the shaping of our relationship with the Sioux ever since. To tell the story of these days in detail would be redundant; the Journals do it best. But in brief, events went like this. After the first long-awaited encounter, three of the Teton Sioux chiefs came on board the keelboat. Gifts were exchanged, and the chiefs were given a tour of the keelboat. Lewis and Clark offered them a taste of their whiskey, which they proved to be very fond of, and after finishing their quarter-glass apiece, they "sucked the bottle after it was out." Clark then took them back to the shore in one of the pirogues. The second chief, known as The Partisan, pretended to be drunk, so Clark believed, "as a Cloake for his rascally intentions" (the field notes call it his "vilenous intintious") (*Journals*, III, 113). He verbally assaulted Clark, saying that since he had not received presents of sufficient quantity and quality, he would not allow the expedition to continue. At the same time, several of the braves grabbed the pirogue's cable and another put his arm around the mast, in effect holding Clark captive. Clark lost his temper; the field notes indicate that he was not only insulted but in danger of being personally injured, whereas the later version says, "his justures were of Such a personal nature I felt my Self Compeled to Draw my Sword," as if a Virginia gentleman's honor was being called into question (*Journals*, III, 112, 113). That Clark was losing control was indicated by the uncharacteristic taunt that he had more medicine on board his boat than would kill twenty such nations in one day (attested by the journals of both Gass and Ordway although not included by Clark; he was apparently not proud of this outburst).[15] On board the keelboat Lewis saw Clark's drawn sword, heard his commands, and, expecting the worst, ordered the entire company to arms. The cargo hatches went up to provide a breastwork for protection, and the keelboat bristled with arms. Black Buffalo, the elder Sioux chief, defused the crisis situation quickly, by ordering the warriors away from the anchor rope. Nevertheless, Clark on shore, with only five of his men with cocked muskets, confronted the mass of warriors whose bows were strung and drawn at point blank range. But just at this moment the other pirogue with twelve soldiers arrived from downriver, changing the odds. The Sioux warriors relaxed their bowstrings and withdrew. Clark offered his hand to the chiefs, but it was refused. On second thought two of the chiefs waded out to the pirogue as it was returning to the keelboat and were taken on board for the night at their request, whether to guarantee a peaceful evening or to keep in contact with the explorers, no one was sure. So ended the action of the first day. Whether in grim irony or not, Clark comments that the island where they anchored that night, about a mile upstream, they named "bad humered Island as we were in a bad humer" (*Journals*, III, 114).

The second day was peaceful by comparison, although the crew had to learn to live with the eyes of hundreds of watchers on the banks constantly focussed on them. The chiefs began to practice their usual hospitality, but everyone remained wary. Lewis and Clark spent so long in feasting, speeches, ceremonial smoking, and observing the dancing and singing late into the night that they asked to be excused because they were sleepy. Clark's observations of the people and their customs were acute, almost as if there were not life-and-death issues around him, and he even tried to instruct the Sioux at one point on maintaining peace with their neighbors instead of taking captives, such as the group of Omaha women and boys he saw bound at the Sioux camp. But Thursday once again brought crisis. "The Bank as usial lined with Sioux" (it sounds as if Clark feels he has lived this way for years), Clark suspected treachery from those on board, especially after the Omaha prisoners, to whom he had offered small presents, warned that the expedition was to be stopped from going upriver and robbed (*Journals*, III, 121). The Sioux were tense as well. After another evening of feasting and dancing, trouble flared up, when Clark's pirogue hit the keelboat's anchor cable by accident as he returned, and the cable snapped. Clark had to shout loudly for all hands to be up and at the oars to stabilize the keelboat, so that it would remain safe in the current, but the sound of his voice immediately mobilized two hundred braves ready for battle! It appeared that the chiefs had issued the order, believing that the Omaha were about to attack, and Lewis and Clark were acting as their agents. Both sides remained alert all night. By this time Clark saw The Partisan, whom he calls "a Double Spoken man," to be the villain, and seems to sense that there was a conflict for authority with Black Buffalo, so that on the next day when The Partisan demanded tobacco as the price for allowing them to proceed, he was first refused, although tobacco was given to Black Buffalo. At this point Clark took a slow-burning fuse from the gunner in charge of the swivel cannon, ready to fire it; Ordway's journal tells us was loaded with sixteen musket balls, while the two smaller swivel guns were loaded with buckshot, whereupon Black Buffalo gave his tobacco to the warriors holding the keelboat's bow rope, took the rope himself, and handed it to the boatsman (*Journals*, IX, 68). Almost by way of apology, it seems, for losing his aplomb, Clark sheepishly says, "I am Verry unwelle for want of Sleep" (*Journals*, III, 125). And the next day they succeeded in running through the gauntlet and were on their way to the Arikara villages.

Depending upon one's point of view, Lewis and Clark had heroically faced down the criminally inclined Sioux by means of their bravery and superior firepower, or they had permanently alienated the one tribe they were specifically instructed to placate, and had failed in their mission to open the Missouri to American trade. But what were the alternatives? What would it have taken to satisfy the Sioux? More time? A greater quantity of gifts? Guns, maybe? A broader knowledge of the complexity of Sioux clans and rivalries? Would the Sioux have attacked on that first day with their women and children present? Why did the Tetons suspect Lewis and Clark were acting on behalf of the Omaha? What did they know and what should they have suspected about rivalries and relations among the Sioux families and factions? A substantial part of their problem, as Ronda points out, was that the Native Americans saw Lewis and Clark as traders, more powerful and numerous and with a bigger boat, but no different in kind from other traders, whereas Lewis and Clark, believed they were diplomats and explorers, preparing the way for future traders and establishing the preconditions, which were to be peace with neighboring tribes and acknowledgement of American sovereignty.[16] The goods they distributed were only to be viewed as tokens of their sincerity. But the Sioux and the Oto and the Missouri had absolutely no conception of an explorer as an agent of a nation, since nothing in their experience corresponded to this. Certainly the Yankton Sioux chiefs, who parlayed with the expedition at Calumet Bluff, next to the site of today's Gavins Point Dam, agreed that peace and trade were good things, even though they did not understand these abstractions in the way Lewis and Clark did. But the politeness of the Yankton chiefs obscured these differences, and allowed the Americans to think their first encounter with the Sioux was a complete success, their diplomacy vindicated. They were so confident of their ability to win over the Tetons upriver that they foolishly left the expedition's one Sioux speaker with the Yankton to help organize a visit of their chiefs to Washington. This self-deception was fostered by their desire. They ignored the prophetic warning of Half Man, who told them about the Teton: "Those nations above will not open their ears, and you cannot I fear open them" (*Journals*, III, 30).

Even Pierre's history has a peculiarly ghostly quality to it. We know something of it from the accounts of the Verendrye expeditions of the 1730's and 1740's, when they arrived at the junction of the Missouri and the Bad Rivers in their quest for the Western Sea. As French explorers apparently are fond of doing, they left a plate of lead buried in the ground near the site of today's Pierre (remember those lead plates the Frenchmen buried along the Ohio?), which schoolchildren unearthed in 1913 (celebrating Arbor Day, perhaps).[17] They may or they may not have glimpsed the Black Hills, but they found little to detain them at Pierre. The traders of the American Fur Company built a post here, even though the furs were still a long way off, and eventually it got named after the member of the Chouteau family who financed the enterprise, but Fort Pierre never really prospered. The famous steamship *Yellowstone* made it up the river as far as the Fort on its maiden voyage in 1831 but was stopped by low water. Eventually, though, riverboats did stop there to unload supplies for the Indian wars and the Black Hills gold rush of the 70's, but that period of activity was brief, too. When a power struggle for the capital of the Dakota Territory was waged in the 80's, Pierre served as the compromise between the adherents of Yankton and Bismarck, even though there was apparently little there but the fort. This insubstantial quality carries over into the present. Residents have put together a driving tour of historic homes, but most of them are from this century and those that are older are not distinguished by much but their age.

The domed State Capitol sits on extensive grounds overlooking the Missouri, but it doesn't exude the bustle or self-importance of most capitols. When I stopped there on a weekday once, there was very little traffic in and out, and the parking lot had plenty of spaces, even some available under the shade of the well-tended trees. There is a small lake beside the Capitol, which is formed by a gushing artesian well, which brings up so much natural gas that the fountain can be lit. The Building itself is constructed of a soft stone (sandstone, I think), certainly not marble or granite, and the dome is painted a deep brown. I entered a foyer, up long, windswept steps and entered another world. In addition to the usual statues of personified abstractions such as Wisdom and Perseverance, I found myself in the same kind of subdued light I found at the Courthouse in Sioux City, created by stained glass rectangles of soft yellow, blue, green and brown. The dimness contrasted strongly with the glare of the sunlight outside, but the hues inevitably reminded one of the prairie environment, here tamed and muted. The corridors leading to executive and legislative offices contained portraits of each governor and display case containing replicas of the inauguration gowns of each of the governors' wives. The Governor's mansion nearby is an 18-room ranch house. Little in the sun-and wind-swept streets surrounding the Capitol suggests that this is the nerve center for an entire state.

Behind the Capitol is the state cultural center, a striking building dug into the side of a hill, its curved facade showing only earth toned stone and dark glass. It is meant, I think, to suggest something of the sod dwellings of homesteaders and the earth lodges of the Missouri River tribes. The exhibits inside are strong on geology, ornithology, and flora and fauna, but not so informative when it comes to human history. One of the largest exhibits dealt with entertainers from South Dakota. There was considerable space devoted to the history of Hollywood movies, even when it had little to do with South Dakota. Apparently the staff, at least, has been starstruck ever since *Dances With Wolves* was filmed in South Dakota. The State's most illustrious citizen, Sitting Bull, isn't even represented substantively, even though his story is a natural one for such a museum, and I could find nothing at all on Crazy Horse, its greatest resident, even if he was born elsewhere. The Registrar told me the sad story of fundraising in a state that has little tradition of public philanthropy and, for that matter, not very much cash. I was moved to make a silent vow that, if the opportunity presented itself, I would help to find funding for this fine museum space.

There is vitality here, as is often found in a community which serves as the supply and market base for a farming area, even if the state government is a small contributor to its prosperity. South Dakota is an active agricultural producer, among the leaders in rye, flaxseed, durum wheat, and hay production, but almost all of this lies in the eastern and southeastern parts of the state. Most of farm income in this part of the state comes from livestock, the remnant of the great cattle bonanza of the 1880's. Because of the Indian wars through the 70's, South Dakota was the last place on the Great Plains to get grazing herds, and so there is less of the cowboy culture here than in, say, Kansas or Nebraska. But the cattle raisers did finally come to take advantage of free land. There were stories in the English press, like the one about the serving girl who put $150 of her wages into fifteen head of cattle, let them graze free on the range for ten years, and then sold them plus their progeny for $25,000.[18] The Dakotas had become a favorite international investment. And pasturage on the central and northern plains was among the richest in the world, if those large and indeterminate areas of South Dakota soil contaminated by selenium could be avoided. Such soil is poisonous to humans and animals but absorbed readily by plants, which, if eaten by grazing cattle cause "alkali disease," which emaciated the animals, which then lost their hair and frequently their hooves, and infected anyone who ate their meat.[19] But for a decade much money was made, until the winter of 1885–86, when ferocious blizzards killed off three-quarters of the herds and the most of the business. Cattle are again found here today but on a much reduced scale, mainly because of overgrazing, which has depleted the buffalo grass and other nutritious plants, leaving only the less nutritious, so that as cattle eat over more and more territory, they literally create a desert.[20] The lack of moisture is harder on short grasses than taller prairie grasses, too, and attempts to cultivate buffalo grass have been slow in coming, mainly because of the difficulty of gathering and germinating its seed. The land holdings for individual ranchers have to grow in acreage to support the same size of herd, and this in a time of declining beef consumption. It is little wonder that the population of the countryside is declining, while that of the towns is increasing. And huge greedy corporations have little or nothing to do with it; the bonanza farms of the past century were subject to the same natural disasters of drought and flood as the little guy, and they disappeared as well.

Although it is not the accepted form to stop one's narrative to advertise another's book, I need to acknowledge my appreciation of the work of Ian Frazier in his *Great Plains,* published in 1989. But there are reasons. Frazier's book is hardly unknown; indeed, it is hailed as a modern classic. It is the result of extensive research and close familiarity with the region. Frazier criss-crossed the region to the tune of about 25,000 miles and even lived there for awhile. It is gripping storytelling, funny in places, but fundamentally serious, an elegy for a vanishing world which has come for him to embody the death of the imagination in America. The final paragraph of the book pulls together the stories, places, and ideas he has been working with:

> Now, when I have trouble getting to sleep, I sometimes imagine that my bed is on the back of a flatbed pickup truck driving across the Great Plains.... The back of this truck has sides but no top. I can see the stars. The air is cool. The truck will go nonstop for nine hours through the night. At first the road is a straight as a laser—State Highway 8, in North Dakota, say—where nothing seems to move except the wheels under me and the smell of run-over skunks fading in and out in my nose. Then the road twists to follow a river valley, and cottonwood leaves pass above, and someone has been cutting hay, and the air is like the inside of a spice cabinet. Then suddenly the wheels rumble on the wooden planks of a one-lane bridge across the River That Scolds at All the Others. Ever since the Great   Plains   were   first called a desert, people have gone a long way toward turning them   into one. The Great Plains which I cross in my sleep are bigger than any name people give them. They are enormous, bountiful, unfenced, empty of buildings, full of names and stories. They extend beyond the frame of the photograph. Their hills are hipped, like a woman asleep under a sheet. Their rivers rhyme. Their rows of grain strum past. Their draws hold springwater and wood and game and grass like sugar in the hollow of a hand. They are the place where Crazy Horse will always remain uncaptured. They are the lodge of Crazy Horse.[21]

This is heady stuff, and today seems to be the dominant tone when dealing with this country, nostalgia for that which is gone forever, a fecundity and an innocence no longer recoverable. Certainly this is a sympathetic point of view, well supportable by a consideration of history. But I find that this is not my primary response to the Plains. For me the vastness produces an almost mystical sense of life, not death, and an intimation that new possibilities, not for economic growth or population increase, but for recognition of the self and its inmost concerns, lie just around the next turn in the road or just over the horizon.

The hundred-mile trip from Pierre to Mobridge seems to take all day, after the obligatory visit to the next dam. This one is Oahe, six miles north of Pierre, with a lake behind it that has a coastline equal that of California or the Pacific shore or some such meaningless statistic. Mobridge is a bustling town across the river from the Standing Rock Reservation, and there is evidence of Indian activity in the downtown section. There is also much fishing. But most noteworthy about the Mobridge area are the two monuments on windswept points across the river a few miles apart from each other. One is to Sacagawea, and is pockmarked with buckshot and barren of ornamentation. The other is to Sitting Bull, supposedly marking his grave. It is a new monument since my first visit, a kind of abstract likeness in a pinkish stone, which faces south toward the land of his birth on the Grand River. Around the base of the statue I found what I can only describe as a double-row necklace made of bits of colored cloth interspersed with herbs and dried leaves. This is in stark contrast to the broken beer bottles, fast food debris, and general garbage strewn around the site. Two cultures leave evidence of their presence. Down the road is a shiny new casino run by the Standing Rock Reservation. This is fitting, for Sitting Bull, who joined the Buffalo Bill Wild West Show for a year, not for the money—he didn't see much—but for the opportunity to study the white man, symbolically has an opportunity to see plenty of him.

There is a good story about Sitting Bull's grave. After the ignominious defeat at Little Big Horn, the army ruthlessly pursued the Sioux. Crazy

Horse and his remaining band surrendered a year later, while Sitting Bull took his tribe into Canada. But in 1881 the situation had cooled down enough so that he was persuaded to bring his people back to reservation life in order to avoid starvation. At this same time a new movement was sweeping through the defeated and dispirited Sioux. From out of Nevada came word that the Son of God was once again on earth in the form of an Indian named Wovoka, or maybe Jack Wilson, who preached that he had come to save the Indians alone. The time was at hand when the buffalo would return, the white men disappear, and all the dead Indians would come back to life. This Messiah taught the Ghost Dance, which was to be performed in special shirts that would deflect the white man's bullets. Sitting Bull became a kind of high priest of the movement, and the first major Ghost Dance was held at his Pine Ridge encampment in October, 1890, and went on and on until the participants would enter a hypnotic trance and supposedly view the spirits of the dead. Although Wovoka had preached patience and non-violence, panic among the whites grew to the point where they expected apocalyptic warfare. And they got it, or rather created it. In December Sitting Bull was to be arrested, in order to cut off the threat of violence. In the process of the bungled arrest, Sitting Bull, his son, and six other Sioux were killed. The rest of the Sioux fled. Two weeks later the fugitives surrendered unconditionally under a flag of truce halfway across the state and were herded into a camp on Wounded Knee Creek. A medicine man named Yellow Bird raised a fist in defiance and promised that the guns of the nearly 500 soldiers could not harm them because of the Sioux' sacred shirts, but his gesture was apparently taken as a signal to open fire, so the soldiers panicked, and in a matter of minutes they slaughtered 200 to 300, two-thirds of them women and children. As one of the squaws lay dying, she was reported to have torn at her shirt, saying, "Take it off. It was no good after all." Thirty-one soldiers died, most from their own bullets, and eighteen received the Congressional Medal of Honor "for distinguished conduct." Sitting Bull was taken to Fort Yates in North Dakota, where he was buried.[22]

Or was he? Ten years later a photographer dug up his skeleton for a picture and the bone he removed and donated to the North Dakota Historical Society turned out to be the femur of a young woman. There is the possibility that the Sioux secretly took Sitting Bull's body and buried it elsewhere to avoid just such a desecration. In the 1950's Clarence Grey Eagle requested that the bones be brought "back home," to where Sitting Bull had been born, on the Grand River. When North Dakota refused to consider this, Grey Eagle accompanied by some friends and a Mobridge mortician (a nice touch) went to Fort Yates and at five in the morning dug up Sitting Bull or whoever, took the remains to the site of the present monument, and buried them under twenty tons of concrete. No issue in North-South Dakota relations has ever occasioned such heat. In 1954 Karl Mundt of South Dakota eulogized Sitting Bull on the Senate floor and said that since he had made his reputation in South Dakota, North Dakota should not have him back. Senator Wild Bill Langer of North Dakota insisted that Sitting Bull's bones had been scattered over North Dakota and that the Mobridge monument was a fraud, apparently on the grounds that if we can't commercialize him, no one will.[23] There the matter stands: the deflation of a religious movement borne out of desperation and the sordid brutalizing of a great leader. Only after the power of the Sioux, both physical and spiritual, was gone could we begin to sentimentalize and exude sympathy for them and make works of art like *The End of the Trail* and *Dances with Wolves* so popular. The Spirit Devils may have taken their revenge in unexpected ways, not with their arrows but by trivializing our perceptions.

1 Much of this material comes from Herbert S. Schell, *History of South Dakota* (Lincoln, University of Nebraska Press, 3rd ed., 1988 [1984]), pp.208–228.

2 Schell, p.8.

3 Bob Karolevitz, "House of Gurney is Yankton Landmark," *Yankton Daily Press and Dakotan,* Monday, May 22, 1995, p.4.

4 John E. Thorson, *River of Promise, River of Peril: The Politics of Managing the Missouri River* (Lawrence, University of Kansas Press, 1994), pp. 60–81.

5 Thorson, p.76.

6 Michael L. Lawson, *Damned Indians: The Pick-Sloan Plan and the Missouri River Sioux, 1944–1980* (Norman, University of Oklahoma Press, 1982), p.187.

7 Thorson, p.81.

8 Thorson, pp.113–114.

9 Found as the "Preface" to Lawson, pp.xii–xiii.

10 Lawson, p.14.

11 Lawson, pp.45–59;184–188.

12 Thorson. P.27.

13 Terral, p.139.

14 James P. Ronda, *Lewis and Clark Among the Indians* (Lincoln, University of Nebraska Press, 1984), p.23. This book should be required reading for anyone with an interest in the West.

15 Ordway (*Journals,* IX, 68) quotes Clark as saying, "He could have them all destroy'd as it were in a moment." The line cited comes from the version in Gass's Journal (*Journals,* X, 45). Clark himself says only "I felt my Self warm" (*Journals,* III, 113).

16 Ronda, p.26.

17 Schell, pp.26ff.

18 John Milton, *South Dakota: A Bicentennial History* (New York, W.W.Norton, 1977), p. 106.

19 Schell, p.8.

20 Bob Karolevitz, "House of Gurney is Yankton Landmark," *Yankton Daily Press and Dakotan,* Monday, May 22, 1995, p.4.

21 John E. Thorson, *River of Promise, River of Peril: The Politics of Managing the Missouri River* (Lawrence, University of Kansas Press, 1994), pp. 60–81.

22 Thorson, p.76.

23 Michael L. Lawson, *Damned Indians: The Pick-Sloan Plan and the Missouri River Sioux, 1944–1980* (Norman, University of Oklahoma Press, 1982), p.187.

24 Thorson, p.81.

25 Thorson, pp.113–114.

26 Found as the "Preface" to Lawson, pp.xii–xiii.

27 Lawson, p.14.

28 Lawson, pp.45–59;184–188.

29 Thorson. P.27.

30 Terral, p.139.

31 James P. Ronda, *Lewis and Clark Among the Indians* (Lincoln, University of Nebraska Press, 1984), p.23. This book should be required reading for anyone with an interest in the West.

32 Ordway (*Journals*, IX, 68) quotes Clark as saying, "He could have them all destroy'd as it were in a moment." The line cited comes from the version in Gass's Journal (*Journals*, X, 45). Clark himself says only "I felt my Self warm" (*Journals*, III, 113).

33 Ronda, p.26.

34 Terral, p.26.

35 Terral, p.56.

36 Ian Frazier, *Great Plains* (New York, Penguin, 1989), p.214.

37 The story has been told often, with individual variations. Here I have referred primarily to Robert G. Athearn, *High Country Empire: The High Plains and Rockies* (Lincoln, University of Nebraska Press, 1960), pp.123–125, as well as Frazier, pp. 41–43 and Dayton Duncan, *Out West: American Journey Along the Lewis and Clark Trail* (New York, Viking Penguin, 1987), pp.170–175.

38 This remarkable episode is described in Milton, p.132.

CHAPTER 7

Talking Stone to Yellowstone

Set out early a fine morning the wind from the N.W. after brackfast I walked on Shore with the Indian Chief & Interpreters, Saw Buffalow Elk and Great numbers of Goats [antelope] in large gangues...those Animals winter in the Black mountains...and this is about the Season they Cross from the East of the Missouris to go to that Mountain, they return in the Spring and pass the Missourie in Great numbers.... This Chief tells me of a number of their Treditions about Turtles, Snakes, &c. and the power of a perticiler Rock or cave on the next river which informs of everr thing none of those I think worth while mentioning—

Clark, October 17, 1804 (*Journals*, III, 180)

In his matter-of-fact tone Clark is detailing wonders reported by the chief never before noted down or, apparently, shared with a white man. The spectacle of mass migrations of deer, antelope, and buffalo as they swam or waded across the Missouri must have been a powerful reminder of the richness of the plains. And it will be vaster than they suppose. Clark makes it sound as if the "Black Mountains" are just over the horizon, when in fact they are 150 miles away and several hundred miles from the Rockies. The day before Lewis, in his return to journal-writing, had remarked on a bird he had found in a state of suspended animation: "I run my penknife into it's body under the wing and completely distroyed it's lungs and heart—yet it lived upwards of two hours." A few days later he will describe in a laconic tone how a crewmember shot a grizzly but was chased so persistently by the wounded beast that he dropped his tomahawk and gun. Then the same crewman shot a buffalo cow and broke her thigh but she was nevertheless able to pursue him until he hid in a ravine. Animals are not behaving the way they are supposed to.

Clark seems genuinely interested in the traditions about the natural world told to him by the Arikara chief. He is more specific in his journal than in the field notes, where he simply states that the chief told him "maney extroadenary Stories." We don't learn the stories about turtles or snakes, but he at least mentions them, and four months later we will hear of the Indian faith in medicine stones: "They have great confidence in this Stone and Say that it informs them of every thing which is to happen, & visit it every Spring & Sometimes in the Summer—." He continues:

> They haveing arrived at the Stone give it Smoke and proceed to the wood at some distance to Sleep the next morning to return to the Stone, and find marks white & raised on the Stone representing the piece or war which they are to meet with, and other changes, which they are to meet" This Stone has a leavel Surface of about 20 feet in Surcumfrance, thick and pores," and no doubt has Some mineral qualities effected by the Sun. The Big Bellies have a Stone to which they ascribe nearly the same Virtues.
>
> (*Journals*, III, 299).

There is a difference here from the treatment of the eighteen-inch devils at Spirit Mound six weeks earlier, no archness directed at the irrationality of the Indians, even though they will continue to be addressed as children. Lewis and Clark are still men of the Enlightenment. Note the quotation marks Clark uses to make sure these statements are properly attributed to the chief. But they are *experiencing* things far beyond what reason has led them to accept, and so the irrational grows closer than ever before. Earlier in the week Clark reports stories the chiefs tell him about a man, woman, and dog turned to stone. The woman held a bunch of grapes, and Clark notices that "we obsd. A greater quantity of fine grapes than I ever Saw at one place" (*Journals*, III, 169).

As in the case of the Sioux, Lewis and Clark persisted in misunderstanding the political situation among the Arikaras, Hidatsas, and Mandans. Concentrating on their primary aim of creating peace among the tribes, so that trade could be carried on by American citizens, they believed that the Sioux nomadic hunters exploited the River farming tribes. It was only logical, they thought, to form alliances against the Sioux, withholding trade until the latter learned to behave more peacefully. But such a view vastly oversimplified the nature of tribal relationships. Clark rightly saw that the Arikaras, together with the Hidatsas and the Mandans, were the "gardners for the Soues," but failed to note that the three peoples gained in the exchanges and were not exploited but, in fact, were shrewder bargainers than the Sioux. For their agricultural surplus they received a wide variety of goods from the west and southwest. Occasional raids furnished outlets for the high spirits of younger men and enabled qualities of bravery and judgment to be displayed, so that leaders could emerge. And in times of war against those outside the trading system, the two tribes would cooperate. In the explorers' face-to-face encounters with the Arikara chiefs, the Indians' innate politeness predominated; they agreed that peace was good and claimed to be astonished that Lewis and Clark would think they would try to stop their voyage up the River. But they also indicated that the price to be paid for becoming part of the American trade network, the end of trade with the Sioux, was too high, especially since the American trade connection was so far nothing but promises.[1] The needles and combs and mirrors and cocked hats and braided jackets passed out by Lewis and Clark struck them as paltry and insulting. And the alcohol that had been so well received elsewhere was refused here, with the comment that those whites who gave Indians alcohol were not friends but only interested in seeing them act like fools.[2] It was clear that the two parties had different perceptions of political reality, and of the two the Arikara one was the more realistic. But they, too, had their blind spots. They were amazed by Clark's man York, who impressed them as a spirit creature, even though he got carried away with all the attention; at one point he called down Clark's displeasure as he playfully chased the children and threatened to eat them (*Journals*, III, 157). One of Arikaras later reported that they saw Lewis and Clark as on a special vision quest (the idea of exploration for its own sake was inconceivable), where they were to overcome obstacles, such as an awesome beast without a mouth who ate by "breathing the smoke of the meat through the nose," and a "troop of Amazons who kill all their male children, pulverize their genitals and conceive again by the injection of the powder obtained."[3] What impressed the Arikaras most was not the words or the gifts brought by the Corps of Discovery, but the power of their objects, such as the sextant and the magnet and phosphorus. Lewis and Clark believed their diplomacy was a complete success, while the Arikaras had deep reservations about them and were not yet willing to trust them completely.

As one crosses the border from South to North Dakota there is no sudden transformation, as there is from the east to west across the Missouri. The Red River, which forms the eastern boundary of North

Dakota, flows in the "wrong" direction, north, and waters one of the great agricultural regions of the world. It has been compared to the Nile Valley. To the west the growing aridity stretches to the Badlands, a bizarre and twisted nightmare of erosion and exposed rock where almost nothing grows ("there, gentlemen, is hell with the lights puts out," as it has somewhat melodramatically been described).[4] But coming north along the Missouri there is only an increasing sense of soaring altitude and spaciousness, with the same undulating swells along the watercourses, interrupted by vast treeless flatlands. Bird songs can occasionally be heard, in spite of the road noise. There are no other sounds except the sibilance of the ever-present wind.

Contrary to preconceptions gained primarily from TV weatherpersons trying, I suspect, to console us because of our rotten eastern weather, North Dakota does not get all that much snow, less total snow than any state where the January temperatures average below freezing. But the blizzards are real, the result of snow with low moisture content driven by ferocious winds and creating those famous drifts often twenty feet high. People have died from suffocation in those drifts, and once in 1966 an entire passenger train was lost in snowdrifts for several days on the same stretch of track where General Custer had been marooned 90 years earlier.[5] The summer heat can be equally inhospitable to human existence. In one 12-month period in 1936 extremes of temperatures were recorded from 121 to -60 degrees. I can't agree with Bernard DeVoto, when he talks about "the northern quality that is so hard to define, an absence rather than a presence of something. A premonition of winter at the crest of summer."[6] It's simpler than this, and anyone who has experienced the blast-furnace heat of midsummer would love to feel that premonition. There are precious few transitions. Clark noted that frosts had arrived in early October with snow before the end of the month. There are a handful of beautiful days of autumn but virtually no spring. The tired jokes about the Dakotas run like this: "I missed summer; I overslept," or "ten months of winter and two months of hard sledding." But the sunsets are remarkable year-round, and the special tones of earth and sky have always captivated the painterly eye. Sundogs or perihelia, the illusion of multiple suns that occur only at high latitudes, furnish a special treat.[7] Even breathing in the high plains air is different. There is a sensation of being "up," higher than ever before, as latitude kicks in. In fact, the plains are not usually level; they are constantly tilting towards the Rockies, as one heads west.

In spite of rich grain and corn growing areas to the east, the Missouri Plateau stands on the edge the short-grass plains, which are suitable primarily for grazing because of erratic rainfall and inhospitable soil. The salvation of the northern plain is that it receives three-quarters of its meager annual moisture during the growing season, but even so, western North Dakota offers a precarious toehold on an agricultural livelihood. Mostly, it is cattle country, with hazards to animals such as blizzards and frequent droughts. But just east of the River fields of wheat, small grains, and sunflowers, grown for their oil and their seeds, seem to thrive. North Dakota is the nation's leading producer of barley. We are not in corporate farming country, no Green Giant or ConAgra signs in evidence. Nevertheless, in order to make a go of it individual holdings must be over 1000 acres. Six sections or 3840 acres is just about the right size for a farm here. On those rare occasions when humans are visible in such vast fields, it is the habit to wave and make eye contact, just as road protocol provides for a brief hand salute to every oncoming vehicle (usually women alone in their cars don't do this; maybe it's a guy thing).

The story of the settlement of this inhospitable land, told well at the North Dakota Heritage Center in Bismarck is a saga of ignorance, courage, and misery. Lured by the reality of cheap land and the myths of fertility offered by the colorful pictures and prose the of railroad brochures, and conned by the pseudo-science of the time, which purported to prove that "rain follows the plow," immigrants from Europe during the 1870's and 80's began to settle on what appeared by their standards to be munificent homesteads of 160 acres. Their lives were wretched. Busting through the tough and tangled grasses of the prairie sod was unimaginably difficult, not like the tall grass prairies further east and south, and on top of the extremes of weather and frequent prairie fires, there were the insect plagues. Mosquitoes descended in clouds (they sometimes still do), and periodically crickets and grasshoppers appeared in Biblical proportions, leaving total destruction of all growing things in their wake. One year it was reported that they were so bad they ate the binder twine on the sheaves of grain, destroyed clothing, and gnawed the handles of farm tools.[8] There was virtually no wood available for building houses or for heating and cooking fires, only the fallen trees that the rivers brought downstream during spring floods. Their first dwellings looked like dollhouses made mostly from the packing cases their goods were transported in. Perhaps worst of all was the isolation, the separation enforced by distance from one's neighbors through the long winters, during which visiting others was often impossible, and the constant work sunup to sundown in the summer which left no time or energy for sociability.

When the banks or merchants foreclosed on the loans, farmers could collect buffalo bones from the plains for about $6 to $12 a ton.[9] These would be shipped east for use in filtering sugar, making fertilizer, or for manufacturing china. More often they went to work on the bonanza farms. Large-scale farming had already been pioneered in California, but only in North Dakota did holdings of 12,000 acres come to be farmed under the supervision of one man. Rapid advances in farm technology helped, and often-new machinery was tested here before going on the market. The Fargo agency of the McCormick Machinery Co. was the firm's most profitable. Sometimes the manufacturer had an agent permanently stationed at a single bonanza farm. In 1885 a man named Dalrymple managing 32,000 acres for absentee owners (they were mostly all absentee owners) employed 600 men at planting and 800 at harvest. These seasonal workers, known as "hoboes" or "tramps", were essential to man the 200 gang plows, 200 reapers, 30 steam threshers, and 400 teams of horses in Dalrymple's inventory. Bunyanesque stories emerged from these operations. It was said that Dalrymple and a plowman headed in a northwesterly direction one morning and plowed in a straight line for two days. When they stopped for the second night Dalrymple asked whether the plowman thought they had gone far enough; the response was "I hope you don't go any further or we may never get back." One report in the Fargo paper noted laconically that a man on one of the big farms started out in the spring and plowed a straight furrow until fall, whereupon he turned around and harvested his way home. Wheat was the essential crop, but potatoes began to be grown commercially, and the Great Northern bean, the "Yankee" bean, was first developed and grown here. Sugar beets were a staple for some time. But there was not enough diversity; size did not prevent the bonanza from falling prey to weather and insect damage, just as small holdings did. And the bonanza was even more susceptible to the most deadly peril of all, economic depression, so that when the bottom dropped out of the market in the late '80's (and periodically ever since), bonanzas went under as well.[10]

Still, the immigrants came, mostly Norwegians, but also Czechs, Poles, Finns, and Icelanders, as well as Scots, Irish, and a scattering of those from the eastern states looking for cheap land and a fresh start. No other state, however, had such close ties to Europe. One prominent group was especially interesting, the so-called German Russians. At one time Catherine the Great, herself German, offered German farmers free land, freedom of religion, no taxes for thirty years, and exemption from military service to settle the eastern half of her empire as a buffer against Asiatics. By 1770 tens of thousands fleeing unsettled conditions in their homeland had migrated to the lower Volga, and a later group of refugees from the Napoleonic wars encouraged by Alexander I came to the Black Sea region. These people never became assimilated and maintained their own communities, some Catholic, some Protestant, usually Lutheran and they rarely mixed, even with other Germans. By the 1870's, however, resentment against them within Russia reached the point where marauding gangs began attacking them, and authorities did little to stop the aggression. Politicians, as usual sensing what would enhance their popularity, rescinded the exemption from compulsory military service. It clearly was time to leave. Some settled in Kansas, others went to South Dakota, then moved permanently to North Dakota, where they came to form the second largest ethnic bloc. The family of Lawrence Welk, North Dakota's most famous citizen, was of this group, settling near the Missouri outside the town of Strasburg. He recalls in his autobiography that he spoke only German until he was twenty-one.[11]

Bismarck can be spotted from a long way off. Together with Mandan, just across the River, about 70,000 people live here, where the Heart River joins the Missouri from the west. Apart from a bluff or two on the west side of the river, where Fort McKeen once stood, built to protect the workers on the Northern Pacific in an early illustration of "corporate welfare," there seems little to recommend it over any other site for a settlement. But a look at the larger map clarifies why it is here; Bismarck is about as due west as possible from the major early population center of the Red River Valley, Fargo. And railroads love straight lines. Apart from being a minor fur trading post for a few years, it began life as a railroad town. The year before tracks reached the eastern bank of the Missouri, the town, then called Edwinton, was staked out. The name was soon changed to Bismarck, in the hope that Germany's Iron Chancellor might be willing to provide financial backing (an appeal to vanity that didn't work). Almost without pause the tracks were begun on the west bank at Mandan. Goods and people were ferried across the river, and when the Missouri froze hard, tracks were laid on the ice. By now gold had been discovered to the west in Montana, and the northern route was the quickest way to get there, so there was a special urgency to finish the transportation link. This was 1873, and the Sioux were not happy about the influx of people on their hunting grounds. So in order to guarantee the white man's right to trespass, an extensive new fort was built, Fort Abraham Lincoln, which had as its first commander Lt. Col. George Custer, with his Seventh Cavalry, consisting of 655 soldiers. Custer used Fort Lincoln as a base for his swift raids into Sioux territory. On one such expedition his men discovered gold in the Black Hills in the midst of the Sioux' most sacred grounds. It was from here three years later that Custer headed for the Little Big Horn. He and Libby also had a charming house built on the post, where he played with his pets and she felt privileged to stand over him as he wrote in his journals. The house today has been reconstructed, as his reputation has not, no matter how hard his fans, I almost said "groupies," have tried. Directly across the river from the Fort lay an area called Whiskey Point, which contained fifteen saloons and at least that many houses of prostitution. The entire area was swept away by a flood in 1874, which was seen by a few as an act of a moral God, but by most as a grievous loss.[12]

By 1878 Bismarck had only grown to a population of 1500, with 24 saloons for thirsty railroad workers and passengers, as well as whatever soldiers could make it across the river (the railroad bridge wasn't built until 1883). But Alexander McKenzie had arrived and was in the process of building his reputation as the shrewdest and richest man in the Territory. It was through his labyrinthine efforts that Bismarck was named the territorial capital in its struggle with Yankton and other claimants. To end the interminable conflict he had engineered a bill through the legislature that mandated a nine-member committee charged with naming a capital and that its selection was to be nondebateable and final. The committee was to meet in the acting capital, Yankton. But the local town fathers were furious over the implications of this bill (that Yankton was to have serious competition for the site of the capital), and they refused to allow such a meeting in town, even though by law such a meeting had to take place there. McKenzie gathered the committee members in Sioux City, loaded them on a train which arrived in Yankton at 5:00 a.m., and without getting off, they named Bismarck as the permanent capital. Then they turned back to Sioux City immediately, before anyone in authority in Yankton even knew they had been there. As one result, McKenzie controlled homestead grants of 11 million acres in what would become North Dakota, as well as a share of the railroad, and Bismarck began its growth, reaching a population of 5,032 in six years. Not coincidentally, McKenzie was the wealthiest man in the Dakotas even before they became states in 1889. It appears that in those days and in that time, making money could have a high entertainment value.[13]

Bismarck has proved to be a revelation to me. Too often in the east the name is something of a joke, a code word which summarizes all that is inhospitable about the northern plains—especially its weather and its remoteness. But this thriving place is no joke. Along with its setting amid the rolling hills and river bluffs, there is a palpable feeling of energy here. Its busy, sprawling modern downtown area contains tree-shaded areas near the Medical Center and newer, sun-drenched retail areas as well. To the west across the River is the town of Mandan, which appears to be, in part, a bedroom community. To the south are more retail "strips," a good-sized mall, many lower-cost housing neighborhoods, and plenty of remaining space. There is a United Tribes College, a thriving vocational and technical school for Native Americans, which is the site each year of a well-attended tribal festival. Out past the airport sits the University of Mary in rural isolation on its own beautiful river bluffs. It was founded as a four-year college for women by Roman Catholic nuns, but today is coed, although its emphasis is still on the "feminine" pursuits of nursing and teaching, as well as business administration.

It is the northern section of the city where most of the more comfortable residential areas are to be found, especially near the grassy and well-landscaped grounds of the State Capitol. This is a nineteen-story monolith built in 1934, after the original Greek-style building had burnt down. True to their agrarian roots, North Dakotans are quick to point out how inexpensive the prairie skyscraper was and how well constructed, even though the interior is a masterpiece of art deco architecture. Remember, we are in a part of the country where government is not the growth industry that it has become in Albany or Harrisburg, but when everything in the State government is in one place, even nineteen floors can be filled. As in Pierre, the building contains a corridor of honor, where pictures of famous state politicians and war heroes are to be found, as well as other celebrities. It was refreshing to see that no more fuss was made over Lawrence Welk than over the jazz singer Peggy Lee or the Zen-quoting basketball coach of the Los Angeles Lakers, Phil Jackson. Across the Capitol grounds, past a welcome cooling fountain, is to be found the Cultural Center, a well-run museum (if sparsely attended—on one visit I appeared to be the only visitor for about the first two hours) that tells the gripping and painful story of the first settlers in a highly graphic fashion. I have talked with some people in the Historical Society office there about sources for the history of Bismarck and was somewhat surprised to find that there don't seem to be very many. When I looked but did not find the section of the Museum dedicated to the state from 1942 onward, I was told that there hasn't been enough money available to mount these displays, even though there is a mountain of material in storage.

On a nearby bluff sits Bismarck State College, a two-year institution that seems to be bursting with the activity of conferences and workshops even during the summer. Education is viewed as highly important here, where any form of livelihood from the land requires a good deal of knowledge from agronomy to economics to zoology, and the institutions are here to support such needs. I also learned that the University of North Dakota maintains a Graduate Center downtown, which offered whatever courses and programs were found necessary for the area, and that these offerings were usually originated by those who wanted them. There was also a two-year vocational school somewhere in town that I have never caught up with. West of the Capitol is an area called Highland Acres, with comfortable houses and well-groomed lots; to the east were newer places and some apartment buildings, still spread over ample grounds, so that the impression was not of urban but of small-town living, even in comparison with a place like Sioux City.

In the northwest, beyond the Interstate and moving up the hills from the River is Bismarck's equivalent of the suburbs—winding streets, cul-de-sacs, and age-graded construction, a sizable community almost all of which has been built within the last ten years or so. There is still construction going on, including a dazzling white fenced compound which stretches down a hillside, undoubtedly what residents spoke of with raised eyebrow when they mentioned that a four-million dollar house was going up. Such ostentation, I gathered, is not popular here. Stretching along the River is a narrow floodplain called Pioneer Park, where the trees appear to be holding their own against repeated inundation, and a handsome riverboat called the *Lewis & Clark* is docked. The River is broad and the current powerful along this stretch, and the homes on the hilltops offering a view of it fetch premium prices. The scarcity of trees here is disconcerting to an easterner, but once this adjustment is made the beauty of long vistas becomes apparent.

This area was the site of one of the frontier's more tragic gold rush stories, the "Battle of Burnt Boat Creek." A party returning from the Montana gold fields, 21 men, one woman, and two children, had stopped upstream at Fort Berthold to buy supplies from the trader there and apparently imprudently boasted that they had taken $90,000 in dust out of Montana and that they were carrying it with them. Because a band of Indians had caused what was known as the Minnesota Massacre just the year before, the trader advised the party to wait until the heat died down before proceeding. But the travelers believed the trader wanted to delay them only in order to encourage them to spend more of their money, so they left the Fort. When they reached the mouth of Burnt Creek, near today's Pioneer Park, nervous and watchful, they encountered an Indian on the bank signaling to them. They interpreted this as a hostile act, fired upon him and killed him. The man had been a resident of a large Sioux village nearby, so an attack party was quickly mounted to retaliate for the murder. The travelers thought they were prepared. Their flatboat carried a small brass cannon, which they fired at the massed Sioux. Unfortunately, the cannon backfired, destroying the boat. Most of the travelers made it to a sand bar in the river, where they were easy targets for the Sioux. When the day had ended, all the members of the party, along with 40 Sioux were dead. The surviving Sioux found the gold dust and scattered it to the wind, believing it could only produce evil. When word of the tragedy reached the trader at Fort Berthold, he hired two local Indians to recover as much of the gold as possible, and they were successful in recovering about $70,000, which of course became the property of the trader.[14]

When driving through the city's suburban developments on a pleasant June Saturday, I expected to see people working on their lawns and gardens, but virtually nobody was visible, and I hypothesized that everyone was out fishing, which is even bigger here than in Yankton, if that is possible. When I asked one resident why there seemed to be so few flowers in people's yards, she attributed it to the dominant Scandinavian background of the residents, whose somewhat stark view of life left little room for flowers. Another resident had a simpler explanation—it was too early in the season, and annuals aren't really safe until late June or July. The people I have met in Bismarck are unfailingly interesting. Among others, I have encountered a local real estate broker who writes and lectures on wines, and a beer distributor who sponsors the local slow-pitch softball tournament and who has a master's degree in comparative literature, met his wife-to-be in France while studying there, and left a job teaching at a Colorado college to return to Bismarck. One of the best bookstores I have found for western materials and writers (apart from Powell's in Portland) is in the aforementioned mall in Bismarck, where one of the proprietors is starting her own publishing venture. Generalizations about the level of culture to be found here, then, are as risky as speculations about the vegetation.

I once spent an afternoon with a highly knowledgeable couple who filled me in on many aspects of Bismarck. They had come here from Minnesota via Helena, Montana, in 1972, brought to the area by the husband's job. They expected to stay three years, then move on, but after over 25 years are still here. It has been, they claim a satisfying place to raise a family and live in relative comfort. Bismarck has an active civic life, with its own symphony orchestra, local little theater, a good library, and healthy cultural and intellectual activities, including some large arts and crafts shows. The schools are good, the streets are safe, the neighborhoods comfortable. The people tend to be independent and share a work ethic, which enables them to be good community citizens, as well as dependable friends and neighbors. They seconded my intuitions about the level of energy among people here. The winters tend to be viewed as a challenge, and locals are fond of saying that they "keep out the riff-raff." Apart from state and local government, medical providers, and the public schools, the biggest employers are the power production centers, both in town and within an hour's commuting distance. North Dakota's state-owned bank, an institution I haven't encountered elsewhere, is also headquartered here.

When discussing the area, the subject of the decline of the Great Plains always comes up. Apart from Bismarck and Mandan, population in the state is decreasing, as food and energy production is maintained with fewer people each year. And industry has never taken root here. At one time the national defense provided a hefty payroll for North

Dakotans, since long-range missile emplacements and strategic air defense sites were found nearby. But these have declined. At a spot on the highway between Bismarck and Minot, I once spotted a group of barracks sitting on a suspicious rise in the otherwise flat prairie, an obvious underground missile site. On the hillside was a "For Sale" sign. In the late 80's a couple of academics from New Jersey named Popper looked at population decline in the entire region and recommended a plan to accelerate the trends by resettling those that remained and depopulating the Great Plains, so that once again the buffalo herds could take over. They would be easy to maintain since this was their native habitat, they would furnish cash from their meat, and jobs from the tourism growing up around hunting and watching them, and they would therefore build the region's economy. They called their plan "Buffalo Commons." Not so long ago they came out with a follow-up article which proclaimed that the Commons were in the process of being created even without governmental assistance at a rate even more rapid than they had foreseen.[15] Such a viewpoint naturally infuriates local residents, who quite properly see it as, at best, belittling their way of life and tending to make them and their wishes irrelevant, if not invisible.

As Senator Tom Daeschle puts it, the Poppers "took an element of truth and magnified it and created a distorted picture."[16] There are other alternatives to depopulation. Already, I learned, young people familiar with Bismarck are returning here to raise their families. I heard of one young woman, for example, who had been living in the Phoenix area, with a successful career developing software for health care facilities, but who was dissatisfied with urban life there. She was able to return and continue her career by telecommuting. The largest new employer in Bismarck is a firm hiring two to three hundred technicians to offer technical support for computer vendors; you may think you are dialing the manufacturer for help but instead you get a center in

Bismarck. So far high-tech jobs in the area amount to a mere trickle (and even computer support is not especially high paying). What Sen. Daeschle is looking for, value-added manufacturing for agricultural products, is only beginning, but it may well be a straw in the wind for a future at least as plausible as the Popper's depopulation. Large-scale growth is not possible, nor even desirable, for it would destroy the somewhat fragile environment that makes the region unique, but to me it is inconceivable that the dynamism and alertness of the residents will disappear.

As in Sioux City, the world of organized recreation is exhausting, even to read about. A fat booklet is published each year listing alphabetically the opportunities to engage and compete in activities from aerobics and archery to track and volleyball. Summertime brings such exertions to a frenzy of competition, with rodeos, marathons, river races, tournaments in soccer, softball, golf, baseball, tennis, and pistol-shooting and curling, some of which are also occasions for parades. There are plenty of musical events as well, with Concerts on the Prairie at Fort Lincoln, Fourth of July symphony concerts and pop concerts throughout the summer, brown bag in the Park noontime concerts, a Great Plains Jazz Festival, and a Folkfest and Polkafest. The United Tribes hold an International Pow-Wow for four days over Labor Day weekend. Nevertheless, there seems to be less of such communal fun than in Sioux City. The reason is of course the fishing on massive Lake Sakakawea, about a half-hour north of the city, where all kinds of fish are caught with all kinds of equipment and an entire fishing-related industry flourishes. And for another taste, the Standing Rock Casino, a highly successful tribal-run enterprise, offers luxurious gambling and sumptuous eating no further away than the Lake, but in the opposite direction. Although I would not push this too far, it is possible that the independent spirit that enables the Bismarck resident to survive the extremes of the climate leads to more individual leisure pursuits than civic ones. At any rate, this is still a very high-voltage community.

Just north of Bismarck is the first evidence of the unique lodges of the upper Missouri dwellers, a field of 43 depressions in the earth, the sites of the mounded homes of the Arikaras, the Mandans, and the Hidatsas. It is called Ward Earthlodge Village Historic Site, and one of the lodges has been reconstructed on this site of a former Mandan town. An airplane trip up the Missouri would reveal many more such circular depressions, especially about 60 miles north of Bismarck, near the Knife River, where today there is an excellent National Historic Site with a Visitor Center maintained by the National Park Service. Lewis and Clark came upon five villages here, and noted the remains of many other recently abandoned ones, starting at the Cannonball River. What they do not mention and perhaps were not yet aware of was that the populations of these settled areas had been decimated by smallpox, first encountered in the 1780's, when their populations were reduced by as much as 75%. The disease then recurred in 1801–02, just before the explorers got there.[17] Survivors from the various clans and villages clustered into the remaining few. We learn that the Arikaras were reduced from eighteen fairly large villages to three small ones. The Corps of Discovery found two Mandan settlements of the strangely shaped conical lodges on the Missouri and three Hidatsa villages up the Knife River at various distances from the Missouri. What they had arrived at was the trading center of the Great Plains, where the Mandans and Hidatsas presided over a vast network of trading relationships stretching into Canada and far out to the Rockies and the Spanish southwest, even though reduced in scope from pre-plague days. And the Missouri River tribes had far more experience in pursuing their trade interests than did the Americans. They had been the hub of such exchanges for centuries.

Lewis and Clark decided to spend the winter directly across the Missouri from the lower Mandan village on the west bank. To the amazement of the Mandans, who visited every day to watch the progress, the party built the kind of fort the army had accustomed them to, a triangular picket palisade enclosing the living and working quarters of the men—and women, by now, since the families of their French-Canadian interpreters were brought into what was known as Fort Mandan. The story of the growing commerce between the Corps of Discovery and the Mandans is an interesting one. The soldiers needed food to supplement the meager hunting during the winter months, and the Mandans needed repairs to their metal implements, such as hoes and pots and scrapers, which the forge at the fort could provide (later in the winter, all repairs being finished, the forge turned to the production of battle axes). A growing friendship based on increasing familiarity, however, never was allowed to cloud the central issue: Lewis and Clark kept trying to get commitments from the three tribes to conclude a once-for-all peace with each other and with the western tribes not yet encountered, such as the Blackfeet and the Shoshonis. And they worked to promote an alliance against the Sioux in return for promise of "most-favored-nation" treatment by the United States and her forthcoming merchants, who were to replace the Canadians as the primary supplier of trade goods. But the Mandans and Hidatsas were not totally convinced that the Americans could produce the needed goods—the trickle of presents they had seen thus far did not impress them—and they still could not understand how they were to gain by cutting off their best customers, the Sioux. But they were interested in absorbing any bit of energy or power the white men had brought, so they treasured the buttons or braid or implements they received for their cornmeal, a practice which, of course, Lewis and Clark took for a childlike delight in bric-a-brac. When the Corps of Discovery left in April, they had deceived themselves about the nature of their success, for while the Mandans were friendly, even gracious, they were still uncommitted to Lewis and Clark's brand of imperialism.

———————————

Today the Mandans and Hidatsas are better served by history at the Knife River Site than is the Corps of Discovery at the reconstruction of Ft. Mandan a few miles north of the town of Washburn. First of all, while both the Missouri and the Knife follow different courses than in 1804, the Historical Site is on an authentic original village location, whereas the reconstructed fort is at a convenient spot, probably ten miles below where it actually stood, now in the middle of the River (there are, however, efforts underway to promote an onshore site). Then, too, the Hidatsa village is lovingly reconstructed at the Visitor Center, with newly built lodges (we have a carpenter-eye view of their construction in the journal of Patrick Gass, which can be used as a blueprint), and nature trails where their gardens of foodstuffs and medicinal herbs are recreated. It is even possible to walk past their garbage heaps. Ft. Mandan is a flimsy cobbled-together version of a standard fort design. The gates are decorated with elk or antelope horns in "true" western fashion, and the "boat landing" is only a cleared area with pebbles—no place where a keelboat could be docked. I once trooped dutifully down the paths, past the beaver trees, peered into the living quarters, gazed out across the river, and got chewed up by the mosquitoes without ever receiving any vibrations that members of the expedition had been there before me. As a form of defiance, I refused to stop in the knick-knack shack that passed for a visitor center. I am sure, though, that things will change, as crowds of tourists will visit the area now that a handsome Lewis and Clark Interpretative Center has opened on the outskirts of the town of Washburn a short distance away. Funds have been made available for rebuilding the Fort for the Bicentennial celebration in 2005.

But surrounding both camps today is another feature of interest—power production. When I first visited the Knife River site in 1982 I took a photograph of the villages, and when I got home I found that the stacks of three power plants were visible on the horizon. I took that as an easy symbol of the ravages of time. But power production is, as they say, big business, around here literally as well as figuratively overshadowing the past. Two of these installations are on the west bank of the Missouri, the Stanton plant and the much larger Otis plant, which the ranger at the Knife River site called Glen Harold. When I asked where the coal came from, she told me that it was just dug anywhere on the property, but they were running out of coal and planned to end the mining within the year. What then? She wasn't sure but thought "it would mean an awful lot of trains." Sure enough, on my return trip I saw signs of digging right up to the plant itself. It is estimated that the state contains about one-quarter of the remaining coal in the country.[18] Farmers used to dig enough for their own use easily; the lignite, or "brown" coal, found in abundance in North Dakota, is mostly right beneath the surface in veins often twenty feet thick. Twenty miles west of here (draglines are visible on the horizon for much of the way) there is no concern about running out of coal at the Freedom mine, which supplies the adjacent Antelope Valley generating station and the first coal gasification facility in the nation at Beulah, right next door. The Great Plains Synfuels Plant sends the natural gas produced from coal directly into a pipeline supplying the eastern states, the equivalent of 26,000 barrels of oil a day, and in the process generates by-products such as anhydrous ammonia for fertilizer, liquid nitrogen, and phenol and naphtha, which fill the hundreds of tank cars on nearby sidings. Right across the road from this complex is a small rise where the entire operation can be viewed, and it is an imposing sight.

Over on the east bank is an operation of truly gigantic proportions, all the more so because it is directly on the highway and thus highly visible. About four miles north of the town of Washburn, a pleasant if sleepy place which has a small riverboat, apparently once a ferry, in a weedy park at riverside, lies the Coal Creek Generating Station, the largest lignite-fired power plant in the country. It is set back a mile or so from Highway 83 but is clearly visible from a long ways away. Across the highway is the Falkirk Mine, where four huge draglines are in evidence, the largest named "Chief Ironside", having a boom about the length of a football field and able to scoop up 105 cubic yards of earth in 90 seconds. The coal so snatched from the earth is sent over the highway on a four-mile-long conveyor belt, part of which (the part over the road) is enclosed in a giant tube, where it goes to a crusher and is then delivered directly to the electricity generators. We learn in a somewhat smug-sounding statement from the operator that there is enough coal in the area to keep the Coal Creek Station operating for its lifetime. Where is all this electricity going? When we read the press releases carefully and get past the pious claims about providing power to rural electric cooperatives, we find that the real cash customers are in the Twin Cities and Milwaukee. And while we're told that effective reclamation of mined lands is of "primary concern," with a commitment to a "quality environment which is and will be compatible with the spirit and desires of all the residents of North Dakota," the mine looks like the surface of the moon. Nevertheless, power is the name of the game, and it propels the non-farm economy of the region.[19]

And there is more of it, at the Garrison Dam a few miles further north. Garrison is the only big-time unit of the Pick-Sloan Plan in North Dakota, but it is massive, and Lake Sakakawea behind it is the largest man-made lake in the nation. We are told repeatedly that is a fisherman's paradise. To the rest of the Missouri Basin the high water of recent years brings dark thoughts of flooding; to those at Lake Sakakawea it means better fishing. The five generators at the Dam pro-duce enough electricity all by themselves to supply a city the size of Omaha. But the Lake has virtually destroyed the Fort Berthold Reservation, which shelters the few remaining members of the Arikara,

Hidatsa, and Mandan tribes, by cutting it in half and making the two sides of the Lake inaccessible to each other.[20] Nevertheless, the Tribal Headquarters at New Town, does its best by sporting an Affiliated Tribes Museum, a casino, and many businesses bearing signs that they are "native-owned." Lest we be too overcome with the vision of Native-American autonomy and success, we also read a message stenciled on the retaining wall beside some government-supplied housing: "Park in a line or no rations."

This may be a good time to settle the spelling of the name of the young woman (variously mentioned as from 15 to 17 years old) who accompanied her husband, the inept Charbonneau, on the expedition from the Mandan villages through the rest of the journey, after giving birth to a son in February of that winter. (As one wag has put it, this story has everything—a woman, a baby, a dog, and a Frenchman for everyone to laugh at.) Are we to call her Sacajawea, Sacagawea, or Sakakawea? Probably the most common spelling in literature on the subject is the middle one, but it is often pronounced with a soft "g" and therefore the rough equivalent of Shoshoni words meaning "boat launcher" or "boat pusher" (whatever that could mean to a tribe which lived high in the mountains). And she originally was a member of the Shoshoni or Snake tribe. But when a river, which flowed into the Musselshell, is to be named after her, Lewis writes, "this stream we called Sah-ca-gah-we-ah or bird woman's River, after our interpreter the Snake woman" (*Journals*, IV, 171). This etymology is correct if we assume that the name is a compound of two Hidatsa words. And she had been captured by and lived among the Hidatsas. Clark would later explain that in reporting on Indian vocabularies "great object was to make every letter sound." Add to this the fact that the Shoshonis were casual about names and often one individual would go by different names in different situations, and Lewis's pronunciation is highly plausible. We can more easily imagine someone being called "bird woman," too, whatever the direct reference might be. But the "Sakajawea" spelling has to go. That

first appeared in the edition of the Journals by Biddle, who never met
her and never heard her pronounce her own name. What, then, about
"Sakakawea," the preferred form in North Dakota? Apparently this was
synthesized from words found in a dictionary published by the
government in 1877, where the word for bird is "tsa-ka-ka." But the
compiler, a Dr. Matthews, points out that "Ts" is often changed to "G" in
this and other Indian languages, so he has no objection to the hard g
sound here. He also explains that there is no "j" included in the Hidatsa
alphabet.[21] North Dakotans apparently adopted their pronunciation to
be different and more completely accurate, but while there is still some
lingering scholarly controversy, they are not likely to be correct. Chalk
up another right decision for Lewis and Clark!

The northwest quadrant of the state is home to the Badlands, today
mostly incorporated in the Theodore Roosevelt National Park. After
miles and miles of grazing land (I remember once spotting a gigantic
steer on a butte about a hundred feet high and wondering if it was a
statue or a balloon, and if it was a statue how folks ever got it up there),
the occasional hay or wheat field, outcroppings of coal, or crazily
emerging bits and pieces of rock, it is a revelation to come upon those
swooping canyons with striated rock walls at least a thousand feet
deep, where all reception on the radio ceases.Along the highway are
side roads leading into genuine wilderness areas, but they are gravel
and perpetually dusty. And one town, barely a town, along the way
greets the traveler with a sign saying, "Welcome to the American
Outback." You can believe it.

An hour from Williston a new element is added—donkey rigs
pumping oil from the vast Williston Basin. From now on the landscape
is dotted as well with metal storage containers, flat tops for oil, pointy
tops for grain. Near the outskirts of Williston are piled up all the
detritus of the energy industry, the drills and pipe and strange-looking
machinery involved when plumbing the depths of the earth. The
downtown area is dominated by huge grain elevators next to the Great

Northern tracks. While it is not a large town, it is the only town in this part of the world. And I usually get turned around here, invariably ending up headed north to Canada some fifty miles away instead of east or west. Dazed by traffic or wide-open spaces, I guess. Thirty miles west is the confluence of the Missouri with the Yellowstone, where another of those seeming miracles will occur for the expedition on the way home. The main party with Clark had traveled down the Yellowstone from its source, while Lewis took a few men and explored the Marias Basin, and they arrive here within a few days of each other. At a viewpoint near the original site of Fort Buford, a windy grassy point (Fort Union down the road has been reconstructed, but there is nothing except a picnic area at Buford), I first noticed that the rocky hills along the Yellowstone were an unusual buff color, almost—yes—yellow! The name didn't require all that much of poetic fancy. The River brings into the Missouri a darker current, carrying mud to Big Muddy.

The expedition's first encounter with the Yellowstone was perfunctory. They explored its mouth, measured it, hunted along its banks, and rested for an evening with song and dance. Their progress thus far has been good, and their spirits were high. They were unaware of the agonies ahead.

1   Ronda's discussion of the intricacies of the Middle Missouri trade system, pp.48–56, is highly illuminating.

2   This phrasing comes from Biddle's rephrasing of Clark's *Journals* entry (History, I, 160). Clark says only "Those Indians are not fond of Licquer of any Kind" (Journals, II, 157).

3   Ronda, p.65, cites this material from *Tabeau's Narrative of Loisel's Expedition to the Upper Missouri*.

4   Terral, p.33.

5   Robert P. and Wynona Hutchette Wilkins, *North Dakota: A Bicentennial History* (New York, W.W.Norton, 1977), p.10; pp.15–16.

6   Wilkins, p.7–8.

7   Wilkins, pp.16–17.

8   Wilkins, p.13.

9   Milton, p.105.

10 Wilkins, pp.79–87. The rise and fall of the bonanza system merits a study by itself.

11 Wilkins, pp.60–68.

12 It is surprisingly difficult to find solid material on the history of Bismarck. Much of the above comes from an ephemeral work entitled *Bismarck and Mandan Visitors Guide*, March-August, 1994, pp.4–6. I was unable to get in touch with the editor to quiz her about her sources, and the North Dakota Historical Society has very little material on this topic.

13 *Visitors Guide*, p. 5.

14 *Visitors Guide*, p.36.

15 Deborah Epstein Popper and Frank J. Popper, "The Great Plains: From Dust to Dust," *Planning* (December, 1987), vol. 53, nos.12–18. I have not been able to locate the follow-up paper by the Poppers, but Mike Feinsilber, "Bring-Back-the-Bison Idea No Washout," Los Angeles Times, Sept. 18, 1994, pp. A–5, reports on it.

16 *Los Angeles Times*, p.5.

17 Ronda, p. 52.

18 Wilkins, p.183.

19 *Visitors Guide* to Sakakawea Country, 1994, p.37; pp.47–49.

20 Lawson. Pp.58–59, reports the grim statistics concerning the losses of the reservations along the Missouri. In the case of Ft. Berthold, for example, the Garrison dam took 152,360 acres, 94% of the Reservation's agricultural land. 80% of its families had to be relocated.

21 rving W. Anderson, "Sacajawea?—Sakakawea?—Sacagawea?: Spelling—Pronunciation—Meaning," We Proceeded On (the journal of the Lewis and Clark Trail Heritage Foundation), Summer, 1975, available on the Internet at *www.lewisandclark.org*. Most students accept Anderson's view.

Chapter 8

Montana: Land of Enchantment

Our vessels consisted of six small canoes, and two large perogues. This little fleet altho' not quite so rispectable as those of Columbus or Capt. Cook were still viewed by us with as much pleasure as those deservedly famed adventurers ever beheld theirs; and I dare say with as much anxiety for their safety and preservation. We were now about to penetrate a country at least two thousand miles in width, on which the foot of civillized man had never trodden; the good or evil it had in store for us was for experiment yet to determine, and these little vessells contained every article by which we were to expect to subsist or defend ourselves. However as this the state of mind in which we are, generally gives the colouring to events, when the immagination is suffered to wander into futurity, the picture which now presented itself to me was a most pleasing one. Entertaing (now) as I do, the most confident hope of succeading in a voyage which had formed a da[r]ling project of mine for the last ten years <of my life>,

I could but esteem this moment of my <our> departure among the most happy of my life.

Lewis, April 7th, 1805 (*Journals*, IV, 9–10)

As the expedition prepared to leave its winter quarters, Lewis presents the most memorable of the stocktaking passages thus far. He thinks of the Corps of Discovery in relation to the great explorers by way of contrasting his resources with theirs and, somewhat ironically yet proudly, dares to compare his exploits with theirs. One message coming through clearly is the relief at returning to the role of explorer after the difficult and often messy jobs of diplomat and trade envoy to peoples he only partly respected, understood, or even liked. (While Lewis is a careful observer of customs and appearances, as Jefferson had prescribed, we almost never get a sense that he sees them as adults worthy of serious attention as persons.) Four days later the party would get its last glimpse of other human beings for months. The keelboat, together with the band of soldiers and French boatmen, had departed for St. Louis, and with it has left the familiarity of its presence and the resources for defense it provided. Thirty-one men, a woman, a baby, and a dog were now alone on the seemingly endless high prairies, and Lewis looked forward to the simple pleasures of providing for survival with one's own resources, and, at the same time, confronted the uncertainty and precariousness of the situation with the thrills of both anticipation and apprehension. I can understand this; in bygone days, when I used to take groups of college students backpacking into wilderness areas of the Grand Canyon for a few days, it became my practice to sit on the Rim at sunrise the day before we hiked down into the Canyon to scare myself, partly with thoughts of what could go wrong, but more directly to confront the unknown.

But it is important to see how Lewis gets beyond this state of mind. This moment of uncertainty (by the way, where did that two-thousand-mile figure come from, when typically before this distances were underestimated?) provides the occasion for a generalization, or rather two of them, about human behavior. First (and least interesting) comes the statement that the future of the expedition, for "good or evil," is not only unknown but unknowable. It was for "experiment yet to determine," not theory or dogma. But the second is the more revealing: the human imagination, Lewis claims, gives its own coloring to events, so that, in a sense, the future can be controlled by the way one perceives it. If the mind-set that produces the first statement is the product of rational, scientific thought, the second could come straight out of Wordsworth ("the mind of man becomes/ A thousand times more beautiful than the earth/On which he dwells"). And this latter idea guides his thought at this moment, "among the most happy of my life," since his imagination transforms potential failure and death into "confident hope of succeeding." Another explanation could maintain that it is the Romantic shudder or "frisson," the thrill produced by danger that Lewis is expressing. In any event, the cool empirical testing of the future fades into the background before the passage has ended, and he embarks on a description of the sleeping arrangements on the way.

For the first nine days of the outward journey from Ft. Mandan they traveled in a northwesterly direction. From that point on until the junction with the Marias in June they went almost due west, deeper and deeper into arid country. April brought winds so strong that everyone got sore eyes from the blowing soil, and there were plenty of adventures to threaten life and limb (more about these later). By the end of the month the party had reached the confluence with the Yellowstone, which was celebrated by an evening of whiskey and fiddling, with everybody, Lewis tells us, in high spirits. They were entering yet another unfamiliar world, where the River was bounded by smoking bluffs of smoldering coal. Trees had almost vanished from the rolling plains, except in steep declivities where they had been protected from fires. The rich prairie grass was the object of seeming endless returning herds of buffalo, antelope, and deer, and the land provided a plentiful subsistence for the party.

At the same time, strange sights and activities were appearing everywhere: animals like the pocket gopher too elusive to be caught, birds like the gray brant that can't be shot, bighorn sheep which skip about where the marksmen can't take aim at them. There were frequent traces of Indians, such as old camps, lodgepoles, even a football floating downstream, but never an Indian, except for their dogs, which occasionally appear (we can only assume they also disappear, but we are never told what happens to them). Lewis almost stepped on a rattler poised to strike but killed it in the nick of time. Grizzlies, the fabled white bears that they had heard about from the tribes they encountered, at first left their huge tracks, then began to appear with some regularity, and they seemed to be almost magical in their refusal to die, even after they received many wounds. A buffalo calf followed Lewis around like a puppy, apparently terrified of Seaman, and another buffalo entered the camp at night and would have caused considerable mayhem if Seaman's barking had not diverted it. Seaman was bitten by a beaver and was just about given up for dead.

Two other episodes occurred to enliven the proceedings. The explorers often mentioned a peculiar quality of the soil along this stretch of the Missouri. No matter how heavily it might rain, Lewis tells us, moisture never penetrates deeper than two inches, so that the surface becomes gooey and treacherously slippery. At one point a soldier named Windsor slipped off the edge of one of these bluffs, with only his left arm and foot still holding on, and he cried out to Lewis (who earlier in the day had saved himself from a ninety-foot fall by the use of his espontoon, or walking stick), "God, God, Capt. What shall I do?" Lewis coolly coached him to remove his knife from his belt and dig a toehold, then talked him through removing his "mockersons" and moving along on his hands and knees until he found firm ground (*Journals*, IV, 262–263). Charging grizzlies are an understandable if frightening hazard, but when the very ground they walk on can not be trusted, then they are in a very foreign landscape indeed.

But an even greater hazard was posed by the white pirogue, which came to be regarded as jinxed. Less than a week out from Ft. Mandan a sudden squall had hit while the pirogue was under sail, and Charbonneau, of whom Lewis was later to say (charitably), "perhaps the most timid waterman in the world," was at the helm instead of the competent Cruzatte. Believing this to be the safest vessel, the captains had entrusted the medicines, navigation instruments, papers (presumably including the Journals), and the most valuable presents for Indians to it, and they had placed the non-swimmers here, together with Sacagawea and her baby as well. By means of some quick thinking Cruzatte had taken over and saved the boat before it capsized. But a month later, the same thing happened under similar circumstances— Charbonneau at the helm, a sudden storm, an incorrect movement of the tiller. But this time the pirogue went over, was stopped by its awning, and came upright again, filled with water within an inch of the gunwales. Charbonneau was on his knees praying, until Cruzatte threatened to shoot him unless he resumed his post at the tiller, and Cruzatte also organized a bailing party after the sail was taken down, so that they could row to safety. But as they maneuvered toward the shore many articles were floating overboard and in danger of being lost. Lewis's syntax is murky here, so that it sounds like there were either six or eight men in the boat at the time (*Journals*, IV, 1, 54). In fact, we learn elsewhere there was also a woman and a baby.

He and Clark were on shore together, an occurrence they were usually careful to avoid. When he saw the danger the pirogue was in, he threw down his gun and was unbuttoning his coat to swim to it, when he realized what a futile act this would be. The waves were high and the current strong, and the boat was three hundred yards away, so that "there was a hundred to one but what I should have paid the forfit of my life for the madness of my project." He adds, however, that "but this had the perogue been lost, I should have valued but little." Does he mean this? It makes for powerful self-dramatizing. But when we turn to Clark's less highly wrought account we learn of a detail Lewis had failed to mention, which undercut the need for a suicidal mission of salvage: "the articles which floated out was nearly all caught by the Squar who was in the rear" (*Journals,* IV, 154). To his credit, two days later Lewis sets the record straight about "the Indian woman" and ascribes to her "equal fortitude and resolution, with any person on-board at the time of the accedent" (*Journals,* IV, 157). Precisely what Sacagawea saved we do not know, but certainly some of the Journals and field notes and the paper on which to write future journals and field notes are likely possibilities. I find it curious and without easy explanation why Lewis does not mention her in the account of the accident, since she played such a vital role. But it is of a piece with his general treatment of Native Americans as less than responsible adults to fail to acknowledge at the time this act of heroism.

Not far past the confluence with the Yellowstone the westbound traveler enters the vastness of Montana, a state three times the size of Pennsylvania with about one-sixteenth the population. In an often-cited passage the poet Charles Olson once said: "I take SPACE to be the central fact to man born in America.... I spell it large because it comes large here. Large and without mercy." He must have been thinking of Montana. Its rivers head for three oceans: its mountains, some twenty-five ranges making up the Rockies are home to the Continental Divide. The high plains country of grasses and buttes, meandering streams, frequent rock outcroppings and occasional isolated mountains which comprise the eastern three-fifths of the state, seems to go on forever under the "Big Sky," a title from A. J. Guthrie, which fits so perfectly that "Big Sky Country" has become the State's motto. On the north side of the highway begins the Ft. Peck Reservation, mainly Sioux with some Assiniboines. When the Dawes Act allotted land to individuals, it also gave them the right to sell, and sell many did, so that no more than 25% of the Reservation remains today in Native American hands. This means that there is very little difference between the north and south sides of the road, reservation and non-reservation. There are occasional patches that are farmed but this is mostly rangeland, which means few signs of human habitation along the way. The small town of Wolf Point (population 2880) seems larger than it really is, because it is the only town in a very large area.

Apart from its spaciousness, Montana is different from most places in that it was settled mainly from west to east. After the mountain men had finished off the beaver (or the fashion for beaver hats had passed, whichever came first), the next white inhabitants were those drawn to the gold strikes in the 60's in Bannack (the first territorial capital, today a ghost town), Virginia City, and Last Chance Gulch, today's Helena. Then by the mid-70's when the Blackfeet, Gros Ventres, Assiniboines, and Sioux were all pushed north of the Missouri, and the Nez Perce were pursued to the Canadian border before surrendering to return to the reservation, the rich grass lands of the central part of the state were opened up for cattle herds to feed upon the most lush grasses the world had ever seen. In those days it grew a foot high, in places three feet, and would roll in the wind like waves on the sea. But overgrazing and the loss of the buffalo put an end to that. Blue bunch grass grows only from seed, and the buffalo's hoof had loosened the soil and planted the seed, but when cattle penned within fences ate it to the ground and sheep even cropped its roots and plows began to turn it under, blue bunch lost its vigor and began to disappear. Fortunes were quickly made as the railroads stretched out from the mining areas to take beef to markets, until the terrible winter of 1886-87, when blizzard after blizzard with temperatures to 55 degrees below zero decimated the herds. At the end of the winter, a foreman for a group of cattlemen in the Judith Basin was asked about the state of the animals. He took a postcard and in watercolors drew a gaunt steer with legs bowed and head down standing in a drift, with a patient coyote behind him waiting for the end. Below the drawing he printed "The Last of Five Thousand," and when this drawing was widely circulated, a career was born for the card's creator, Charlie Russell. The world of the cowboy did not end overnight, but it was radically reduced, as sheep, which can more easily survive the winters, began to replace cattle. Nobody romanticizes sheep.

Only then was the eastern part of Montana found to be of interest, and this to the homesteaders, called by the natives "honyockers" or "scissorbills"(the origin of both terms remains obscure), who came in vast numbers (for Montana), especially between 1909 and 1923. Three factors led to the "boom": the ongoing and increasing hunger for cheap land to call one's own; the accepted fiction that dry farming, deep plowing, intensive cultivation, and alternate years of summer fallow, could create a garden out of the desert (the notion that rain followed the plow was pretty well gone by this time); and the enthusiastic promotion of this country by the railroads, who owned much of the land along the right-of-way, and would earn more from real estate dealings than from shipping (although it didn't hurt the balance sheet to be able to fill freight cars headed west with homesteaders after they had brought cattle and grain east). Theodore Roosevelt's administration encouraged dry-country homesteading to relieve pressure on increasingly overcrowded cities, to feed the growing population, and to finance the completion of the railroad network. The high prophet of the movement, James J. Hill, railroad builder extraordinary, also apparently believed in his mission: "We must preserve jealously the right and possibility of free access to the soil, out of which grows not only all those things that make happy the heart of man and comfort his body, but those virtues by which only a nation can endure, and those influences that strengthen the soul. This is the safe-guard not only of national wealth but of national character. The man on the farm must be considered first of all in our policies because he is the keystone of our national arch."[1] Or perhaps his prose is more contrived than sincere, the product of an early specialist in public relations.

As long as the better-than-average rainfalls and heavy world demand for grain brought on by World War I held, the homesteaders prospered. But in 1917 a drought cycle began and by 1920 high winds set in as well, whipping away great clouds of topsoil loosened by the very worst form of cultivation for this part of the world, deep plowing. All through the first half of the decade the drought continued, insects invaded weakened crops that did come up, and half the farmers in the eastern part of the state lost their land and their dreams and moved to the West Coast. The full story of disaster is heart breaking. Although Montana was not, strictly speaking, part of the Dust Bowl, there were droughts in 1929-31 and 1934, 1936 and 1937. The New Deal poured more money per capita into Montana than any other state, and some farmers survived on large spreads with new machinery financed by government loans and with sounder agricultural practices (especially chisel plowing, strip cropping, which means planting in bands from 80 to 200 feet wide at right angles to the prevailing wind direction, leaving fallow the spaces between the bands, and planting shelter belts of trees). Today some of the world's finest wheat comes from Montana, most of it grown in the north central part of the state, the so-called Golden Triangle from Havre to Cut Bank to Great Falls. Much of the crop is shipped to Asia from barge ports in Lewiston, Idaho, to seaports on the North Pacific coast.

But little of this plenty is evident in the far eastern or northeastern part of the state. Jonathan Raban tried to take photographs of the landscape here, but as he showed them to his wife he realized that about all he had on film was "a hundred perfectly exposed snapshots of a badly maintained golf course."[2] The scope, the scale of the land does not lend itself to a frame, and in any conventional sense this scene is not sublime, not beautiful, not really very attractive. It is mainly empty. The Missouri remains in sight to the south of Highway 2, the Burlington Northern tracks paralleling it, the highway stretching out ahead with a few rises but nothing like a hill or a curve. Along the way are the white crosses, some decorated with artificial flowers or ceremonial herbs, marking spots where the monotony or the alcohol or the weather or the distraction of nothingness took over and someone left the road at too high a speed. Most of the accidents along here are single-car crashes, a trooper once told me. After almost succumbing to the emptiness myself, it is good to come upon the novels of Larry Watson who writes of this part of the world in ways that demonstrate that lives are lived here with concerns much like ours.

Not too far into Montana, a mere hundred miles or so, the greatest of all the man-made additions along the Missouri is encountered. The Fort Peck Dam, the largest structure of its kind in the world when it was finished in 1939, looms 250 feet above the waters of the Missouri for over two miles, with a dike for nearly two more miles. The lake backed up behind the Dam is 200 miles long and sixteen miles wide. Although generators for rural electrification were added in 1943, the fundamental purpose of the dam is flood control. In spite of the talk about irrigation, there has never been much attention to this, since there is little demand for the extra wheat that would be grown here. The Dam is best at containing the runoff of mountain snowmelt, and serves as the first line of defense against flooding in the entire Missouri Basin. It was one of the centerpieces of Franklin Roosevelt's WPA and employed over 10,000 workers in its construction over a period of several years. Towns were built for these workers with names like Wheeler (after Senator Burton K.). New Deal, and Delano Heights, but no trace of them remains today. In 1938 about a tenth of the uncompleted dam slipped into the water, taking with it railroad tracks, a trestle, a dredge, and eight lives.³ But it has lasted and remains an imposing monument to human energy. As at Gavins Point Dam near Yankton, there is a superb Corps of Engineers campground nestled in among towering cottonwoods. The dam looms overhead and you can't help but imagine what it would be like to see it give way, but apparently that is not likely. The campground is so comfortable that I have endured a hailstorm, an all-night windstorm, and a spectacular thunder-and-lightening display here and still think fondly of returning.

From this point all the way to Fort Benton is becomes impossible to follow the Missouri, since there are no roads along it past Ft. Peck Lake. Highway 2 continues on through the town of Glasgow, where in early summer there are likely to be hundreds of hopper cars on the freight sidings waiting for the winter wheat crop. The Milk River flows through Glasgow, "The River that Scolds At All Others", so named from the glacial deposits it picks up at its point of origin near Glacier National Park. More than once I have gotten turned around in Glasgow and have found myself heading north toward Canada instead of west, paralleling a railroad track and a river, but the wrong track and the wrong river. Then on to the dusty crossroads of Malta, where a decision must be made, either to continue on Route 2 to Havre and then turn south to Great Falls, or to head south once again to the Missouri where the sole bridge in a hundred miles crosses, and on to Lewistown, then west to Great Falls. I have tried both, and the latter is far more interesting. The road from Malta is empty, wheat in the flatlands, grazing where the country rolls. Once I found a pronghorn in the middle of this road and not about to move. They are curious odd-looking creatures—dwarfish with great protruding eyes and antlers that stick straight up like antennae, so that they look like comic book Martians. Their stride is different from the gracefully bounding deer I am accustomed to; it is stiff-legged, like a trotter, and more than a bit comical. There are signs to the Ft. Belknap Reservation, to an old mission, and a natural bridge, and there are other signs pointing toward settlements with names like

Zortman, which must testify to a Protestant presence at one time, as well as an Indian one.

Then with absolutely no warning everything changes. The land abruptly becomes hills with pines scattered around, many of them size-able, and the road begins to head downward toward the Missouri. The traveler once again finds himself or herself swooping into a colorful canyon formed by the river bluffs. There is a campground just across the bridge, where those fortunate enough to come downriver from Fort Benton by canoe or powerboat can put in (there are few places on this stretch of the River where there is any shore at all). This is the desolate "Missouri Breaks" country (the term referring to any sudden change in topography), and is protected as the Charles M. Russell Wildlife Refuge. The road climbs upward and in a few minutes no sign of the canyon or the River can be seen. But soon we pass the Judith Mountains on the way to the quaint town of Lewistown, and then to get back to the river we travel through butte and range country that anyone familiar with Charlie Russell's work would recognize.

―――――――――

Just north of today's Fort Benton another major river, the Marias, named by Lewis for one Maria W__d, enters the Missouri, and here one of the crucial decisions of the entire journey had to be made. Which fork was the true Missouri, the passage into the Rockies, leading to a simple (so they still thought) portage to the Columbia? Primarily because of its muddiness, so similar to the Missouri they had known so well for so long, the northern fork seemed to most of the party to be the true Missouri. Lewis and Clark were not sure. If a mistake were made by heading north, so much time would be lost that the expedition could be trapped in the mountains in winter, or be forced to turn back. If a mistake were made heading south after the crew had warned against it, confidence in the command of the leaders would be severely shaken.

The issue was heightened by the political implications of the choice; undoubtedly the caution given to Lewis by Jefferson about potential border disputes with the British had to be in his mind. Nowhere does the competence of Lewis and Clark shine forth any more clearly than at this critical moment.

From the information they had gleaned at Fort Mandan, the waters of the true Missouri had to originate in the Rockies, which must be visible from the falls the Mandans had told them about. The water at these falls was described as almost transparent. Moreover, the falls were supposed to lie "a little to South of sunset" from Ft. Mandan, near lesser ranges of mountains. These characteristics were found in the southern fork. The northern one was heading too far north. Thus from rational observation as well as information from the Indians, both Lewis and Clark were convinced. But to bring along their party, especially the respected Cruzat, acknowledged as the party's best riverman, they determined to explore the two forks separately. Lewis took six men to follow the north fork overland, while Clark headed south with four others. From a point somewhere near today's Ft. Benton, Clark saw the massive Big Belt snow peaks and the rushing torrent of the river through its canyon and didn't need to go further. Lewis' group had a longer and less conclusive journey. It was clear that the north fork drained a large plain, and it kept heading north and northwest. The hills Lewis spotted were northeast as well as northwest (on the Canadian border, as we know it today). While he was quite sure this was the wrong way, nevertheless he and Clark decided to remain tentative. He would go overland in search of the Great Falls, while Clark, being the better waterman, Lewis admitted, would proceed down the south fork with the bulk of the party. A few days later Lewis heard the sound of falling water and saw spray "like a collumn of smoke." He and Clark had been right. As John Logan Allen concludes, "This was a brilliant piece of deduction from a fuzzy set of facts and illustrates, as well as any other event during the course of the expedition, the competence and

intelligence of its commanders."[4] The Enlightenment mind was alive
and well in Montana.

At the same time, it is worthwhile to take a longer look at how Lewis
writes about his first experience of the Falls, or rather of five of them
(four still visible today, in spite of hydro dams). He first of all points out
that this experience is his alone; three of his men were sent out on the
flanks to hunt, and Goodrich is some distance behind him. He uses the
dramatic technique of narrative in time to attempt to express the
succession of experiences—"agreeable sound of a fall of water" to
"collumn of smoke" to a tremendous "roaring," all occurring at just
about high noon, after he had come some fifteen miles that morning.
He rushes to some rocks at the base of the falls for the best vantage
point, this "sublimely grand specticle, " where he still adheres to a time
sequence, an historical explanation of how rocks have fallen to create
the setting for the tumbling waters foaming and splashing there. Now
he begins a long passage of description in terms of space; he offers
estimated measurements of the width of the channel, the position of
the cliff-like sides of the channel, the height of the falls (about 80 feet,
he guesses), the placement of this scene amid the larger surroundings of
downstream channel and three-acre bottomland with its huge
cottonwoods. This goes on for over 400 words. Maybe to minds more
orderly than mine he gives a clear picture of the scene, but I get very
little except a sense of the magnitude of the Falls. At this point Lewis
mentions that a rainbow has formed in the mist above the falls, and
now we learn that his linear measuring and placement has failed him,
too. The passage is so interesting that it needs to be cited in full:

> after wrighting this imperfect discription I again viewed
> the falls and was so much disgusted with the imperfect
> idea which it conveyed of the scene that I determined to
> draw my pen across it and begin agin, but then reflected
> that I could not perhaps succeed better than pening the

first impressions of the mind; I wished for the pencil of Salvator Rosa or the pen of Thompson, that I might be enabled to give to the enlightened world some just idea of this truly magnificent and sublimely grand object, which has from the commencement of time been concealed from the view of civilized man; but this was fruitless and vain (*Journals*, IV, 285).

The world of measurement and geology and geography, in which he has been schooled, has let him down when he is confronted by such an overwhelming total experience (although he goes on to say that if he had brought along a *camera obscura*, he might have captured more of it; "even I could have hoped to have done better," he says). Aware that artists and poets have a facility for this kind of thing and that scientifically-trained gentlemen do not, Lewis feels a kind of inadequacy not heretofore revealed. The next morning as he headed further upstream, he encounters four more cascades of varying size, Crooked Falls, Colter Falls, Rainbow Falls, and Black Eagle Falls, and he begins to reflect on what he has seen in terms inherited from eighteenth-century aesthetics, which he could have picked up from the *Spectator Papers* or just about any imitator. When trying to compare yesterday's Great Falls with today's Rainbow Falls, he says, "I determined between these two great rivals for glory that this was *pleasingly beautifull*, while the other *was sublimely grand*" (*Journals*, IV, 290). One way of taming the experience was to categorize it and thereby hold at bay the intimation that something about this prodigy of nature lay beyond his ability to give it a name.

———————

Today's Great Falls is best approached from the north with a stop at Fort Benton. We find a magnificent Lewis and Clark monument beside the Missouri there, with Sakagawea at the feet of the explorers. There is also a monument to Shep, the faithful dog who met every train for five years after his master had left or died, and who lived under the platform, fed by a sympathetic stationmaster. Shep is in Ripley's *Believe It or Not*. The first time I entered the Headquarters of the Upper Missouri Visitor Center (not much larger than its name) I spoke with a young Ranger who was chafing that she had pulled Visitor Center duty in place of her regular job, patrolling the Missouri as far as the Russell Wildlife Refuge. She looked for boaters in distress, did surveying, checked the water levels and the state of the banks and the weather, and all the things the government should know about. She loved her work. It seems that, while the River is fairly tame in this stretch with regards to its current, it poses all kinds of problems to those not well prepared. She had stories of people who ran out of drinking water (the sources are few and far between), whose outboard motors fail, and who get stranded on a bar or tiny piece of shore when wicked storms come down the canyon and carry their boats away. For much of this stretch it is almost impossible to walk away from the River, and even if you could, where would you go? She offered me a list of approved river runners in case I wanted to take the trip, and implied that anyone who didn't was somehow deficient. I have picked up the same message from others.

The Fort Benton Museum, a quaint little place, does a good job of conveying what a bad scene the town had been in its heyday. Shallow-draft riverboats began to reach this far upstream, the limits of navigation on the Missouri, at just about the same time as gold was discovered to the south, so supplies and people were shipped in as gold was shipped out. This made for some interesting incidents, especially when another main cargo, whiskey, to be shipped up the Mullan Road to Western Washington and along the Whoop-Up Trail to Canada, was added to the mix. Rivermen, drovers, prospectors, Indians all fought regularly under its influence with predictable consequences: Ft. Benton was well known as a non-discriminatory killing ground. In time it became the "Chicago of the Plains," with as many as fifty steamboats a year at the local docks, with the expected resultant excitement and chaos. Eventually the Great Northern came through and put an end to the uncertain river traffic, and by then the big export was no longer gold but wheat.[5] Free with a ticket to the Ft. Benton Museum is a visit to the Museum of the Great Plains, an unpretentious place, in spite of its name, on the edge of town, dealing primarily with farming. I saw close up the evolution of farming techniques and machinery, even rigs that could scuff-plow, plant, fertilize, spread herbicide, and cover up the seeds all in one operation, fifteen rows at a time! I'm still enough a child of the machine age to find this exciting.

The highway from Ft. Benton to Great Falls is unusual, in that it clings to the ridgetop overlooking the Missouri instead of being located on the floodplain. One advantage is that we get to see some small fenced areas with government warning signs that exude mystery and menace, probably something to do with the missile defenses that dot the state. The air force base at Great Falls, Mahlstrom, used to be part of the same system to take care of us all, and it was then common to see very fast jets in close formation flying low over the farming landscape. Today the role of the Base is quite different, not involving air defense at all, we're told, so that about the only planes coming and going are transports. When I first visited Great Falls the massive stack of the Anaconda smelter still dominated the skyline, although the buildings themselves were empty, with hundreds of broken windows testifying to the popularity of that pastime. The smelter was built in 1888, not coincidentally the very year Great Falls was incorporated. Although there was very little mining in the immediate vicinity, the smelter resulted from the dispersion of ore out of Butte, first silver, then almost exclusively copper, here and to the new town of Anaconda west of Butte (the company and the town named after the admired military maneuver of Gen. Winfield Scott against the Confederate Army, but soon seen as apt for the stranglehold "The Company," the unofficial partnership of the mining company and

Montana Power, had on the entire state). While gold had proved profitable for a few decades, Virginia City being "one of the great gold camps of the American West," the development of an electric society produced an insatiable demand for copper wire. When the Guggenheim copper holdings in Chile threatened "The Company," Anaconda bought them up. When profitability seemed to point to manufacturing rather than mining, Anaconda bought the largest copper fabricator in the country as well. But in 1971 the Chilean government seized the mines and the bottom dropped out of the copper business. Even the Butte open pit, into which part of the city had slid, closed down. When Atlantic Richfield bought out Anaconda, both the big smelters were closed, and the "destruction of the old smokestack offered a traumatic and symbolic closing of a century of copper domination in the state."[6]

The days of copper furnished a lively tale of violent action and skullduggery beyond the scope of this account. Today, however, it is remarkable how relatively unscarred the city of Great Falls has become from the trauma of copper withdrawal. The flats on the north side of the Missouri have been cleared of every trace of the smelter (bricks from the stack were sold for a dollar each as souvenirs). The city lost no more than five percent of its population, Cascade County even less, and, like Pittsburgh, the town has undergone a fairly smooth transition to a service-oriented economy. I suppose Malmstrom can be called service-oriented; at any rate, with nearly 5,000 civilian workers, it is far and away the largest employer in the area. And quite a few who have served here remain in the city after they leave the Air Force. Medicine is next in employment, with two hospitals, one specializing in cancer treatment, the other in the treatment of heart disease, and there is a research institute for tissue and organ transplantation, clinics, and a rehabilitation center for the treatment of crippled children and adults as well. As befits a city that sees itself as central to its state, education also plays a prominent role, even though the major state universities are elsewhere, at Missoula and Bozeman. The University of Great Falls,

Mountain States Baptist College, the Air Force base Education Center (in cooperation with several universities), and the MSU College of Technology all grace the area, and locals are proud of their public school system which consistently produces students in the top decile of national test scores.

But it is agriculture that still dominates the city. Great Falls serves as the major grain processing and shipping center for a fourteen-county area known as the Golden Triangle. And it is also the supply center for all that farming as well, everything from seed to chemicals and fuel to specialized machine shops and retail outlets. Built as a rail hub to Minneapolis, the home of James J. Hill and Paris Gibson, the town founder, and on the original Great Northern tracks, it also was connected to the cities of the Yellowstone and eastward to Omaha and Chicago by the Milwaukee Route, and it was tied into the Union Pacific with tracks southward through Butte and Salt Lake City. Enough of those trains are still running, at least ten hefty freights per day, to make things interesting. But most of the wheat today heads to Snake River ports, such as Lewiston, for shipment to Asia. And a new venture, the manufacture of pasta, hopes to make use of some of that durum wheat right in Great Falls.

A modern airport and interstate play their part in economic activity as well. They also bring in tourists, a major component of the area's prosperity, about half of them from Canada. Many local people are ambivalent about expanding the tourist trade, since greater numbers, they fear, might destroy the very qualities that tourists come for, space and peacefulness. Tourism is a concept that has been hard to sell in Great Falls. When visitors asked where the Falls were, locals used to tell them how to get to Black Eagle Falls, just at the edge of town, and not the much more spectacular falls further downstream, because Black Eagle was easier to find. Now there is a parklike setting as far as the Rainbow Falls, with a well-designed lookout from the south side of the River. But the falls that Lewis first encountered, the true Great Falls, can

only be reached by a winding, poorly marked, broken-down asphalt
road on the north side of the River, which, the small signs tell us, leads
to the Ryan Dam, without mentioning the Falls. Once the intrepid
traveler makes it, he is rewarded with a spectacular view from a
delightful little park that looks very much like Lewis' three-acre bottomland. Not only the Falls but the gorge impresses, with sheer walls
about 200 feet dropping down to the foaming stream. With the right
kind of vehicle it is even possible to venture further to Sulphur Springs,
where the expedition camped and Sakagawea was treated for an illness
with its waters (a treatment which almost killed her), and on the south
bank to visit the site of the beginning of the portage from Belt Creek.
But these are in no danger of being despoiled by hordes of tourists,
since they can't be easily found. Once when there for a conference, we
were taken to the portage site by bus and one of the busses got hope-
lessly stuck in Montana mud. Nothing availed, until about fifty hearty
conferees finally gave the ninety-ton bus a push.

The town calls itself the "Electric City" from the several dams at the
various falls, which earlier had powered gristmills. The smelters created
a demand for power, and at one time there was enough left over to drive
an electric railway over the Rockies. Today the hydroelectric capacity is
more than needed by the immediate area, so surplus production goes
into the northwestern grid. Once when I visited the Falls, I learned that
Ken Burns and Dayton Duncan were in town to do some filming for the
Lewis and Clark television production, but I saw no trace of them.
When I viewed the program I realized why—the Falls were far more
photogenic at sunset. Later I was told that, even though the water level
was high that June, Burns had persuaded Montana Power to let more
water through the Dam for a more spectacular effect.

The town itself is a no-nonsense community, with a busy commercial area not much concerned with aesthetics, although this appears to
be changing. Recently the downtown seems spruced up, with galleries
and bookstores more prominent than I had remembered. There is

much work by Montana artists and craftspeople available, and much of it is of high quality. The two most interesting structures in town are the old Burlington and the Milwaukee passenger stations, and both have been renovated into professional and commercial offices. There are a few big old Victorian houses in the downtown area, one of them with a spectacular carriage-house built to look like a castle. Paris Gibson, an engineer from Minneapolis, who is credited with bringing the first sheep-raising operation to Montana, laid out the street pattern of the town and is still remembered in the name of a park along the Missouri and in Paris Gibson Square, which is the Center for Contemporary Arts and home to the county historical society. The displays here are sparse but the artwork is primarily highly regarded modern work. The Great Falls Public Library has been touted as "one of the finest in the northwest," but I couldn't find it on any maps and had to ask where it was. Much of the older residential area, like many other western towns, is composed of similar small houses on heavily shaded streets. Especially in Montana the towns take very good care of their trees. And the city claims to number over fifty parks, not counting the State Fairgrounds.

Across the Missouri (and the Sun) lies the newer residential section of the city, a large area beginning with flats along the River and moving up the hillsides. The higher up the slope, the more architecturally venturesome the houses become. At the top are a considerable number of homes with a sweeping view of the river and the entire plain on which the city rests, all the way to the Little Belts and the snow-capped Big Belts to the southeast. To the southwest and the west about forty miles away lies the Front Range of the Rockies, with peaks immediately looming up to 8500 or 9000 feet (Great Falls itself is at about 3300 feet). It is not unusual on weekends for the town to virtually empty out, since a major attraction of living here is the proximity to the spectacular outdoors. Much of the tourist trade must come through, rather than to Great Falls, using it as a pit stop (it is about halfway between Yellowstone and Glacier Parks). The Great Falls' "strip," 10th Ave. S., is crowded with RV supply places, as well as the usual discount stores, motels, and fast food places and is billed as the most heavily traveled bit of highway in Montana. The town, by the way, has the most confusing street nomenclature of any place I have ever visited; 10th Ave. S., for example, runs east and west, as does 8th Ave. N. Over the bridge 6th St. NW runs far to the south of 20th St. SW. Whatever.

Without question, the jewel of the city is the C. M. Russell Museum Complex in the heart of town. Gathered in the same block are the Museum, the final home of Charlie and Nancy, and the log cabin which served Russell as studio and guesthouse for entertaining his cowboy friends from his former life. Apparently he loved nothing better than cooking a dinner over an open fire in the cabin while shooting the breeze far into the night. Russell had a reputation for the largest stock of dirty jokes in the West, and Will Rogers, it is claimed, used to come to get new material. The outbuildings are interesting but the Museum is superb. From the entrance with its bronze plaques showing scenes from Russell's life sculpted by the ever-present Montana artist Bob Scriver, we are aware that something special has occurred. And other artists are shown here— one gallery has an excellent collection of Western artists of Russell's generation, and another contains a show of contemporary Western landscape artists. But this is clearly Charlie Russell's place. His personality dominates. Most of us are familiar with the oils, which at one time were thought of only as calendar art and today are celebrated for their authentic Native American and cowboy detail, as well as their display of human and animal physiology. But on display here are his achievements in many other media. One entire room is given over to his clay and beeswax sculptings, which reveal his amazing facility and dexterity, as well as his wit. Another features his watercolors, including beautifully wrought and tinted drawings on the margins of hotel stationery with a letter on the same page. Russell was constantly doing work specifically tailored to the interests of a particular friend, who would then receive it as a gift. What emerges here above all is the energy, the dynamic quality of his work, which seems always to be in motion. In this part of the world the Russell name has become a kind of icon. It is "Russell Country," the "Russell Wildlife Refuge," Highway 87 is the "Charles M. Russell Memorial Trail," there is even the Charles Russell High School, and the number of retail establishments using the name are legion. One could do much worse.

There is a modern arena in Great Falls which books all kinds of entertainment and lectures, and the town is home to a Dixieland Jazz Festival each summer, as well as a nationally known exhibit and sale of Native American Art and Western Art each spring. But most of the events focus less on aesthetics and more on the West's better known pastimes. Rodeos abound; even the State Fair gives equal billing to the State Rodeo, and the Legends of Rodeo appear in the fall, along with an antique gun show. There are horse shows and monster truck shows, and also the Country Garden Quilt Fest. But for many the high point of the year comes in late June with the Lewis and Clark Festival, which has grown from its modest beginning in 1989 to an event involving thousands of participants and spectators.

The Festival has an interesting history. The Portage Chapter of the Lewis and Clark Trail Heritage Foundation was planning for the Great Falls Centennial in 1984, as well as the hosting of the annual L&CTHF conference, when, in one of those fortuitous bursts of energy, the members present came up with the idea of tying together all the pending events into one massive package. A mural to be donated to the Great Falls Airport was nearing completion, Bob Scriver's statue of Lewis at the Missouri-Sun confluence was ready, interpretive signs were being placed at the Rainbow Falls overlook, and the first encampment, another of those historic reenactments, was to be held. So much momentum was generated that the Festival has become the biggest event of the year, with thousands of visitors coming from all over the world for an extended celebration. Great Falls has become the center for Lewis and Clark activity among many places vying for that role. The Portage Chapter is virtually the mother chapter of the Lewis and Clark Trail Heritage Foundation, with three spin-offs—the Honor Guard which runs the Encampment each year, the Fund for the Interpretive Center which has succeeded in building a six-million dollar institution near Rainbow Falls to be the national center for Lewis and Clark exhibits and research, and a commercial arm which runs the gift shop, the gallery, and some of the exhibits at the Center. The Center was officially opened during the celebration in 1998, after the local committee had raised three million dollars from private sources, which was matched by the federal government.

The Interpretive Center is a beautifully sited and designed building of stained wood, which nestles unobtrusively into the bluffs along the River upstream from Rainbow Falls. From the glass walls at the rear of the Center only the River is seen. The dominant feature of the entryway is a giant compass rose inlaid into the floor with the names of donors embedded in it. The central display area is unique in its concept; on one side of the winding corridor is the timeline of European civilization, including the progress of the Expedition across the plains, and on the other side is the parallel Native American story. The equality of the presentation places the history of the past in a new perspective, and forces us to reassess our understanding. There are "hands-on" items, such as a rope attached to a dugout, together with a gauge that shows how many pounds the dugout weighs and how much energy it takes to move it. There is also an auditorium, which runs a half-hour version of the Ken Burns-Dayton Duncan videotape almost continuously. There is a small research library, not very well equipped at present, but intended to become a center for Lewis and Clark studies in the future. And there is an ample gift shop, which brings in profits to maintain the operation. Lewis and Clark are well served here.

The two weeks of the portage from late June to early July were among the most trying physically that the expedition was to endure. With his engineering skills Clark laid out an eighteen-mile route around the Falls that cut off the southward curve in the River. It ran to a point upriver from today's city, about two miles south of the confluence with the Medicine River, today's Sun, opposite some small islands they called "White Bear Islands" because of the prevalence of grizzlies there. While the south and east side of the Missouri was more level than the opposite bank, there were still countless gullies or swales to get the canoes and stores across or around. After burying everything that could be left behind, including the white pirogue, they began the task: "Good or bad we must make the portage." Lewis had wheels cut from a large cottonwood and tackle made from the best wood he could find (including the canoe's mast), so that the men could pull the truck-like conveyance over the undulating landscape, but it was a torture to maneuver. For one brief period on a windy day a sail was rigged, so that the canoes sailed on dry land. But this was the exception. The heat, the mosquitoes, the storms (once the men complained of being bruised by hailstones and later Clark measured one as seven inches in circumference), the endless exertion—all were topped only by the agony of sharp rocks and prickly pear cactus thorns penetrating their "mockersons", so that every rest stop involved pulling the needles from their feet. When, that is, they could stay awake, since most used every chance possible to collapse in sleep. Still, both captains tell us, the men did not complain. There seemed to be a division of labor of sorts along the way; Clark was in charge of the baggage and the party's movement, as well as surveying the route, while Lewis organized the hunting, the feeding and supply details, at one point even taking a turn as camp cook. There was considerable illness during this leg of the trip.

Lewis also spent much time and much of the men's time in preparing his collapsible iron boat frame for its maiden voyage. If it worked it would provide a lightweight 30-foot canoe with a sizeable beam to make travelling in the shallows easier. It would also be possible to carry it across the mountains on what was supposed to be a day's portage to the

Columbia, although it grew more and more difficult to believe in that portage when the immensity of the mountain peaks more and more came into view. Lewis had elk skins and buffalo hides scraped and sewn, wooden seats, oars and stays carved, and, since no pines were available for pitch, he had buffalo grease mixed with tallow for sealing the seams. Almost every day he commented on the progress of the boat or, more often, his recognition that its success was growing more remote. When the portage had been completed, he held up progress for several days to insure as complete a drying as possible. Then the moment of truth arrived. The boat momentarily floated like a cork and was loaded, but because of a violent wind it had to be unloaded. By evening, when the wind abated it was discovered that the seams had not held and "she leaked in such manner that she would not answer." The frame was sunk on the spot, never to be recovered on the return journey. But the interesting point is how Lewis berated himself for the mistakes in judgement he claimed to have made in every step of the boat's preparation. If only he had not had the hides shaved so fine. If only he had used only buffalo hides. If only he had used a different kind of needle for the sewing. If only he had thought to have prepared real pitch earlier—on and on he goes, to a point beyond reason. It was the one great failure in his life so far, it seemed, and he took it hard. But in a touch of Emersonian compensation he says he is glad that he thought to bring along a grindstone, since the axes had to be sharpened often to cut trees for new canoes![7]

Ever since the Falls were sighted, strange events had been occurring. In addition to those already mentioned, a grizzly sneaked up on Lewis as he watched a buffalo he had just shot die. He had carelessly not reloaded, and the bear chased him into the River, and, when it was only twenty feet away, Lewis turned and pointed his espontoon at him, whereupon the bear unaccountably fled. Both the attack and the defense were bizarre, but this was only the beginning. After firing on what he called a "tygre cat," probably a wolverine, he was rushed by three buffalo, which then wheeled and ran away. Fields engaged three bears at the same time. The grizzlies got bigger and meaner, and soon approached mythic proportions, as did the mosquitoes. Lewis notes that "it now seemed to me that all the beasts of the neighbourhood had made a league to distroy me" (*Journals*, IV, 293–294). As well as many of the men, both Lewis and Clark were ill at different times, but neither so ill as Sakagawea, who seemed on the verge of dying from what appears today to have been a pelvic inflammation. Through almost superhuman efforts, Clark, Sakagawea, her baby, and several others barely escaped from a heretofore-unknown hazard, a flash flood, when mud, rocks, and timber descended upon them. In his rush to safety, Clark lost his gun, knapsack, tomahawk, and, significantly, the Corps' only large compass. But the way was not lost; the compass was found the next day. A mysterious booming from the distant mountains was heard not once but twice, for which no plausible explanation has ever been forthcoming. This was an enchanted landscape, more appropriate to Spenser's *Fairie Queene* than any countryside these men had ever known. Lewis speaks of this period as being like a dream, but he knows it isn't because of the prickly pear needles piercing his feet.

We have never before heard Lewis speak of dreams, nor has he ever attributed events, even in jest, to supernatural causes. He sees the animals with human motives, making "league" to destroy him. But since he escaped the conspiracy, he is able to present the events in a light-hearted tone as "amusement" or "white magic." This implies the reality of its opposite, or "black magic," as well, an idea far from Enlightenment boundaries of thought. The hero can be made invulnerable because of a spell, or he can be doomed to enthrallment or death. In either case, control is out of his hands, and he is at the mercy of a power not his own. Reason has nothing in common with magic. Lewis has tacitly admitted, whether or not he is aware of it, that the world of cause-and-effect has receded a good distance from his present surroundings.

The drive down Highway 15 from Great Falls, while not dreamlike or enchanted, is certainly one of the most exciting parts of the interstate system. After passing Ulm, the site of an ancient pishkun, or buffalo jump, where braves tricked the lumbering creatures to plunge off a cliff to their deaths, the highway enters the foothills of the Rockies, where a broad shoulder is provided to put on tire chains in appropriate weather. The River is often far below the road, which crosses and recrosses the narrow but swift moving, rock-filled stream. A tiny settlement or two lies on narrow flats between the hills and the River, and occasional single lots with isolated cabins appear to be carved out of the mountainsides. Names like "Cascade," "Wolf Creek," and "Canyon Creek" flash by. Just north of Helena a side road cuts off to the place where the two tour boats *Pirogue* and *Sacajawea* are docked for the trip into the Gates of the Mountains, a canyon named by Lewis himself.

It was here many years ago that I met Mr. Tubbs, who as a young man had come from upstate New York and had never left. He was glad to take me through the small museum at the dock, adding by his personal commentary to the exhibits on the natural history of the region and the dams in the River. It was inconceivable to him that I claimed the need to move on, for he never did, and the sight of herds of elk coming down to the River to drink was more precious to him than the delights of Missoula. He had a point. When I finally took the boat tour many years later (the weather had been too cold or stormy on two previous attempts), it was a revelation. In addition to the guide's literate and informative commentary, there was the place itself, a hushed slice into the limestone walls rising above us (Lewis estimated them at 1200 feet, a height picked up by tour guide, but my guess is about half that high).

Lewis thought he was travelling through a gorge of granite; at least he wanted it to be granite for the sinister effect thereby produced. It was growing dark when he entered the canyon, so that the search for a camping place was difficult. The overall effect on him suggested again that aesthetic category he referred to at the Falls, the sublime. Today it is a special place for viewing wildlife. Mountain goats pose on inaccessible points, big-horned sheep feed in isolation, ospreys nest in their haystack-like dwellings on the cliffs, and bald eagles circle overhead. The boat lands and pauses for awhile at a trailhead into the surrounding mountains, near the site of the Mann Gulch forest fire, which took the lives of thirteen young firefighters many years ago, a melancholy note that fits the shadowy surroundings. There are dams both upstream and downstream from the canyon, but since they are for hydropower alone they don't affect the River all that much. This is one of the very few places along the Trail that has remained much as it was when the Corps of Discovery passed through, and in the hushed silence that thought is awesome.

The city of Helena a few miles south is the first settlement along the way that has almost nothing whatsoever directly to do with the Missouri, which flows some ten miles east of it. The River provided power for the huge smelter east of town, and a large lake for recreation has been formed behind the Dam, but that is about all. It is only accident that it is even that close, since Helena grew from the vein of gold discovered at Last Chance Gulch, today a sloping downtown street, filled with coffeehouses and upscale shops. A central feature of the city is its neighborhood of nineteenth-century mansions, homes for the famous fifty millionaires of Helena. Almost no one whose fortune came from Butte or Anaconda wanted to live there in those days. There is also a magnificent and spacious Catholic church and a Catholic college in this area, and a large, modest residential area on the Valley's flats. A bit further out is the stately Capitol, several outlying governmental buildings, and the Montana Historical Society, with its fifteen-foot stylized sculpture of a buffalo skull and its room of Charlie Russell paintings. The Valley gives way to hillside in two directions, and here is found street after curving street of West-Coast-type dwellings. I have heard from several sources that, unlike most Western cities, Helena tends to look inward, so that its civic life is limited, and these discrete neighborhoods may be one of the reasons. Or it may be due to the fact that many of its more affluent residents are government employees or lobbyists, who tend not to become as much involved in local affairs. There is another side to this: anyone who does want to become involved in committee work or public leadership merely needs to show up at the meetings. There are not many posters downtown advertising local events, and few public places downtown remain open after dark (one of them, a good restaurant, is in a building once occupied by a notorious house of ill repute). Helena reminds me more of an Eastern city—with a view.

At this point the River bears east and south another 60 miles to its source at Three Forks, where the Jefferson, the Madison, and the Gallatin Rivers merge to form the Missouri. I had envisioned a clean meeting place, something like a three-way electric socket, but it isn't quite that tidy—it takes a few hundred yards for all three to come together within the confines of a modern state park. But all three of the rivers are still good-sized, powerful streams, and I have seen each in flood obliterating ranch houses and campgrounds along the banks. Clearly, none of them behave like a beginning, more like middle. Again, Lewis and Clark faced a fundamental problem: which of the three provided the route to the mountains? The Gallatin was soon rejected as coming from an area too far to the east. Time was growing short to cross the mountains, some of which even in August showed extensive snow on their crests. Clark took a small party and in a speedy fifty-mile journey up the Madison, determined the Jefferson to be the true mountain route. Once again it was clear that this expedition was not a straight-line progress from one point to the next, but a series of crises leading to even more complex problems. How much of their cultural baggage had to be left behind, cached, perhaps, on the plains behind them?

1   Cited in Jonathan Raban, *Bad Land: An American Romance* (New York, Pantheon Books, 1996), pp.181–182. Three other books helpful in understanding the agricultural settlement of Montana are Clark C. Spence, *Montana: A Bicentennial History* (New York, W.W.Norton, 1978), Joseph Kinsey Howard, *Montana: High, Wide, and Handsome* (New Haven, Yale University Press, 1943), and Michael Malone, Richard Roeder, and William Lang, *Montana: A History of Two Centuries* (Seattle, University of Washington Press, 1976).

2   Raban, p.64.

3   Spence, p.152.

4   John Logan Allen, *Lewis and Clark and the Image of the American Northwest* (New York, Dover Publications, 1991), p.277. This work was originally published as *Passage Through the Garden: Lewis and Clark and the Image of the American Northwest* (Urbana, University of Illinois Press, 1975).

5   Much of this information is derived from Malone, et. al., pp.72–77.

6   Malone, p.327.

7   *Journals*, IV, 369–370. The degree to which Lewis is preoccupied with the folding boat and his responsibility for mistakes made in preparing it is truly revealing. Clark barely mentions the boat, as if he had never invested much its success, but Lewis writes about it virtually every day during this period.

CHAPTER 9

The Dark Side of the Shining Mountains

We begin to feel considerable anxiety with rispect to the Snake Indians. If We do not find them or some other nation who have horses I fear the successful issue of our voyage will be very doubtfull or at all events much more difficult in it's accomplishment. We are now several hundred miles within the bosom of this wild and mountanous country, where game may Rationally be expected shortly to become scarce and subsistence precarious without any information with rispect to the country not knowing how far these mountains continue, or wher to direct our course to pass them to advantage or intersept a navifable branch of the Columbia, or even were we on such an one the probability is that we should not find any timber within these mountains large enough for canoes if we judge from the portion of them through which we have passed. However I still hope for the best, and intend taking a tramp myself in a few days to find these yellow gentlemen if possible.

Lewis, July 27, 1805 (*Journals*, IV, 436)

After the month getting around the Falls and ever since leaving the lower portage camp on July 15, apprehension about finding the Shoshonis, or the Snakes, as Lewis and Clark called them, had been growing. Not a single Indian had been spotted since leaving Fort Mandan the previous April. The sites of camps had been seen, most old but some recent, smoke signals had been sighted, and prairies had been set afire, perhaps as a danger signal or maybe as a hunting technique to move game. Plains Indians often used fire to renew the prairie grasses for the following season, but in the middle of the rich and seemingly endless Montana grasslands this would probably be unnecessary at this time. It is easy to envision braves hidden by some rise in the ground or on a rocky height impassively watching the Corps of Discovery pass by, as in all those Western movies and at least one great Charlie Russell painting. What is less intelligible is why they did not make contact. Close observation must have shown that this was no war party (there was that woman with her baby), and every tribe in the West was always eager for trade. Still, they had never seen such a large, well-equipped party come upstream, and fear of the unknown must have been a powerful inhibitor.

The River was becoming more and more difficult, with steep cliffs coming to the water's edge, and the canoes often had to be poled or towed, usually in rocky, cold water, so that feet once again became cut and swollen. When the party arrived at the Three Forks, false starts were made and time wasted, as Clark took a small party and reconnoitered up the Jefferson, overland to the Madison, and back to the Forks, a journey of over fifty miles in three days. On the day of Lewis's journal entry above, Clark had returned feverish and totally exhausted, and his condition must have only added to Lewis's apprehension.

But much worse suffering lay ahead. Although Sakagawea began to recognize landmarks, even the camp where she had been captured by the Minitaris five years earlier, the River was becoming almost impossibly shallow, game was growing scarce, Shannon disappeared and was lost again for several days (this happened frequently to Shannon), accidents began to pile up. A beaver gnawed down a willow that had held Lewis's note for the party; a canoe upset in rapids and badly injured Whitehouse, as well as damaging some supplies; the exhaustion of the men added to the misery of bloody feet, boils, and hunger. The physical hardships were multiplying the further upstream they proceeded, and were greater than those of the portage, greater than anything they had thus far experienced on the expedition, partly because they came from so many different sources.

Under these conditions, Lewis begins to behave somewhat erratically, or at the very least, with questionable judgement. What can only be termed his racism when it comes to Native Americans emerges more clearly. He (together with Clark and Jefferson, too, for that matter) had always addressed tribal gatherings in the familial language as children, with Jefferson as the Great Father in Washington. This may simply have been a means of dealing with intelligible concepts for the sake of communication. But Lewis apparently believed the categorization, or at least was careful to place a distance between the capabilities of the Indians and himself. In the July 27 passage above he takes consolation in his superiority: "…if any Indians can subsist in the form of a nation in these mountains with the means they have of acquiring food we can also subsist." This may be read merely as a touching faith in their guns, although it downplays any value in the fact that the Shoshonis had lived here for years and knew the territory. But his comment on Sakagawea a few days later, when she is able to identify the place where she had been taken prisoner, is totally unambiguous. Because she appeared to reveal no sorrow in recollecting those bloody and tragic events, he says that "if she has enough to eat and a few trinkets to wear I believe she would be perfectly content anywhere" (V, 9). This is of a piece with his passing comments about "those yellow gentlemen" and remarks to come about being thoroughly sick of the Shoshonis' "national hug." In his eagerness to be identified by the Shoshonis (he may have had the sense of being watched), he had American flags broken out and raised on the canoes, and when his four-man party set out on foot into the mountains, he had McNeal carry a flag on a staff to be posted at each stop, as if the Indians would have any idea what *that* was all about. And ever since the fiasco with the collapsible boat, he had been testy with the men and berated them, first with their wasting of meat when they found game, later when they failed to intuit his wishes when they approached the first-sighted Shoshoni. Much of this may have resulted from anxiety over Clark's debility, not only with fever and fatigue, but also with his inability to walk because of a painful boil on his ankle. All the responsibility—for the mission and for the lives of the party—was now his, and things weren't looking very good.

———————————

Midway between today's town of Twin Bridges, where the Beaverhead and the Ruby Rivers form the Jefferson, and the town of Dillon, there is a rock formation known as Point of Rocks, which rises over 350 feet from the River. Sakagawea caused some excitement when she saw it and recognized it as near the summer retreat of her people, who should have been nearby (it is unclear whether she called it Beaverhead Rock, from its resemblance to that animal's profile—to me it looks like nothing whatsoever—or whether this is Lewis's misreading of its being on the Beaverhead River). Today Dillon, the commercial center for the Beaverhead Valley, is a bustling town of about 4,000. This doesn't sound like much until you put it in perspective: there are only about nine places in the State with a population over 10,000 and four more over 5,000. Moreover, Dillon is the largest town in an area greater than Massachusetts, Connecticut, and Rhode Island combined. Interstate 15 skirts the edge of town and is the highway that ties Butte, Helena, and Great Falls to the south, meaning Salt Lake City, and from there to California. The valley in which it is located is beautiful, with snow peaks visible on each side and lush fields well watered from the streams and snowmelt. The highway also brings fishermen, hikers, snowmobilers, hunters, and just plain tourists to the thirteen motels and lodges and twenty restaurants in Dillon itself, to say nothing of the outlying places with names like Wisdom and Wise River. But Dillon does not give the impression of being primarily a tourist town. Rather, it seems to be a self-contained community supplying everything needed for civic life: excellent shopping, a historical museum, to be distinguished from a visitor center next door, many parks, a community concert season, a local band and orchestra, a community theatre, a weekly newspaper and a radio station, complete medical facilities with a 31-bed hospital and a roster of thirteen MD's, as well as ancillary care, state social service agencies, fifteen places of worship including a Quaker Meeting and a Bahai'i group, and even six veterinarians. And although the local people don't make much of a fuss about it, there is a local college, Western Montana State, at one time a normal school, which has been brought into the State system as a branch of the University of Montana, and has Divisions of Arts and Humanities, Math-Science, Business & Tech, in addition to Education. To a flatlander there is a quality of energy and expectation in the town's very air, which is beginning to thin since the elevation is over 5400 feet.

Near today's Dillon the dramatic climax of the expedition's entire outward bound journey was shaping up. By this time the canoes had to be dragged over the streambed, and Lewis was getting too impatient to wait for them. He selected three of the crew to accompany him on an advance party. Each man was to carry a blanket, weapons, and trinkets for trading—nothing else—and the group was to travel rapidly up the Beaverhead to its fork with today's Horse Prairie Creek, about twenty miles southwest of Dillon, where a dam has created a sizeable lake called Clark Canyon Reservoir, a popular camping and fishing spot. Lewis left a note for Clark asking him to wait here, since it was clear that the canoes could never make it up the creek. About ten miles farther on (in the vicinity of a contemporary settlement called Grant, where a sign over the general store advertises it as the "Horse Prairie Hilton," and the small school building has a calculation posted to show that it is located exactly halfway between the North Pole and the Equator), Lewis finally saw what he was waiting for, a lone horseman, "mounted on an eligant horse," armed and curious, carefully watching Lewis's party from a distance of a mile or so. This man, the first seen since Ft. Mandan the previous April, had to be a Shoshoni, Lewis believed, and the lives of the entire party depended on making contact with that tribe of horse collectors. In his eagerness he did everything he could think of to reassure the brave: he lay down his gun, he flapped his blanket in the air three times, a universal gesture, he confidently reports, of friendship among all western Indians (except, apparently, the Shoshonis, for Lewis has to report "this signal had not the desired effect"), he moved forward with some trinkets displayed, calling out *tab-ba-bone,* which he asserts means "white man" in their language, and he pushed up his shirt sleeve to show the color of his skin. Where Lewis had gotten his information on the Shoshoni language is unclear, but he was probably wrong. Linguists today call it a nonsense phrase or one meaning "stranger," "one originating from the sun," or from the east, or maybe "look at the sun," which might explain why the horseman turned to peer over his shoulder (V, 72). Lewis's display of his arm would reveal little, since he has lived in the outdoors all spring and summer, and the dangling of trinkets must have appeared bizarre, to say the least. Drouillard was also trying to signal the horseman, while McNeal and Shields advanced, the latter missing Lewis's signal to halt. After the horseman, in apparent anxiety and confusion, wheeled and rode off, Lewis bitterly berated Shields (who said he had not seen the signal) and believed he had been responsible for losing contact ("I now felt quite as much mortification and disappointment as I had pleasure and expectation at the first sight of this indian. I felt soarly chargrined at the conduct of the men particularloy Shields to who I had principally attributed this failure.... I now called the men to me and could not forbare abraiding them a little for their want of attention and imprudence on this occasion" (V, 70). Even his spelling deteriorates.). But looked at from the Shoshoni's point of view, the brave did the prudent thing in avoiding these apparently crazy and possibly dangerous people coming at him from three directions simultaneously.

The little group proceeded on, headed for a break in the Beaverhead Mountains, today's Lemhi Pass, at about 7400 feet, Lewis recording their every action in meticulous detail, some of them rather strange. For example, he prepared a bundle of gewgaws, attached it to the end of a pole, to be fixed next to the remains of their breakfast fire, so that the Shoshonis "might from this token discover that we were friendly and *white persons*" (italics added: V, 70). And there is that American flag carried everywhere and planted whenever they stop. When they finally encountered a group of Shoshonis who quickly fled, Lewis contemplated tying bundles of trinkets around the necks of their dogs, but the dogs didn't cooperate, either, and ran away. The next day, amid fresh indications that the Shoshonis were nearby, they took time from their pursuit to enjoy their situation. McNeal stood with a foot on each side of the now-disappearing creek and "thanked god that he had lived to bestride the mighty & heretofore deemed endless Missouri" (V, 74). A few miles further on, after crossing the Continental Divide, Lewis stopped to drink from a west-running brook, where he "first tasted the water of the great Columbia river." At the same time. Lewis confirmed what he had expected—visible in the west were range after range of "immence high mountains;" the portage to the Columbia will not be Jefferson's journey of a day, if it is ever possible at all. The death of the dream of a Northwest Passage occurred at this moment.

The rest of the intensely dramatic story has been retold so often that I hesitate to repeat it again, but certain features, I think, deserve special emphasis. Soon Lewis and his men came upon three female Shoshonis, an old woman, a young girl, and a young woman who fled. The other two, seeing escape was not possible, sat on the ground and held down their heads as if expecting to die. None of Lewis's trinkets altered their despair, but when he painted their faces with vermilion, they revived and led the party to the sixty or so warriors in camp not far away. Lewis believed it was the paint, which he took as a symbol of peace, as the factor that made the difference, again following his doctrinaire notions of what Indians do and do not believe, but it is far more likely that the *direct touch* produced the desired effect, touch that troubled Lewis in a few moments when he was embraced by the warriors, so that he was "all carresed and besmeared with their grease and paint till I was heartily tired of the national hug" (V, 79). Was the civilized Lewis bothered more by the grease or the hug? Moreover, Lewis lit a pipe to smoke, but before partaking, the Shoshonis sat in a circle and took off their moccasins, urging Lewis to do the same, taking their leisure in barefootedness. But Lewis had to rationalize this: "This is a custom among them as I afterwards learned indicative of a sacred obligation of sincerity in their profession of friendship...or which is as much as to say that they wish they may always go bearfoot if they are not sincere; a pretty heavy penalty if they are to march through the plains of their country" (V,79). There is no record elsewhere in Indian ethnography of such an interpretation. Sense had to be made of these unusual happenings in terms of the categories of thought that Lewis brought along with him. For the Shoshonis it was all simpler and more spontaneous than that; they were at home, in their valley, no longer apprehensive about the strangers, and at ease amid their meager surroundings.[1]

During an evening of celebration Lewis received his first taste of salmon. Because of the salmon, he understood that he was on the edge of the Columbia watershed. His men danced nearly all night (one highly speculative scholar believes Lewis, too, celebrated, to the extent that he contracted syphilis that very evening or the next, which eventually led to his suicide). Lewis began the task of gaining the Shoshonis' confidence and their horses (he estimated the size of their herd first at 400, later at 700), which were indispensable for the descent to the Columbia (he was to learn shortly that no water passage was possible). He first listened to their story and shrewdly assessed the Shoshonis' desperate need for trade; every time they went to the plains to hunt buffalo, they were driven back into the mountains by the better-armed Blackfeet and Minitaris. Here they had almost no sources of food and only three guns among the entire tribe to hunt with. Lewis witnessed their strenuous and futile efforts to hunt antelope. Lewis as usual believed the way to gain their cooperation was by displaying power, which could not become fully apparent until the rest of the party arrived, and so the ground shifted to his effort to persuade them to accompany him back to the Beaverhead. They were extremely reluctant to leave their sanctuary, having only recently been pursued and defeated by Plains tribes when they crossed the Divide probably much like the time when Sakagawea was captured. And while their spokesman claimed to trust Lewis, some among his men did not, fearing that they were about to be decoyed into an ambush. Lewis responded with a four-fold attack: 1.) white men don't behave treacherously but act upon their word, he self-righteously proclaimed; 2).if you don't cooperate, white men will not come to trade with you and bring the guns you need; 3.) there must be men of courage among the tribe who would test the white man's word for the sake of future benefits; 4) those benefits would be immediately realized when the party is encountered, since there are supplies and goods, including food, with them. Lewis was sure that questioning their courage was the lever to action, for he says of Cameahwait's reaction (more on his name in a moment) that "I had touched him on the right string; to doubt the bravery of a savage is at once to put him on his metal" (V, 96). But it is equally likely, given the gaunt appearance of the tribe, that the prospect of immediate food was the persuader, especially given their reaction the next day when Lewis's party kills some game, which is fallen upon and devoured raw: "some were eating the kidnies the melt and liver and the blood running from the corners of their mouths, others were in a similar situation with the paunch and guts but the exuding substance in this case from their lips was of a different description" (V, 103).

More and more slowly they proceeded, with still no sign of Clark, who, although now able to walk himself, had a crew with many sick and injured who were trying to move the heavy canoes where no canoe should be expected to go. Now the most remarkable moment of the entire journey took place. Cameahwait "with much ceremony" placed the most distinctive item of Shoshone clothing, the fur tippets, on Lewis and his men, in order to confound any ambush plans, as Lewis immediately perceived. The visitors would be attacked first because of their garb. In return, Lewis placed his cocked hat with its feather on Cameahwait's head, and notes that *"we were soon completely metamorphosed"* (italics added; V, 104). Yet when they arrived at the fork there was still no sign of Clark and the party, so once again the Shoshonis became nervous. Fully aware of the gravity of the situation, Lewis writes: "I knew that if these people left me that they would immediately disperse and secrete themselves in the mountains where it would be impossible to find them...& of course we should be disappointed in obtaining horses...and I feared might so discourage the men as to defeat the expedition altogether" (V, 105–106). He had arrived at the most crucial moment of the entire journey. He is required to give up his identity, a very serious matter for an officer and a gentleman, especially from Virginia.

At this point two things occurred. Lewis gave his gun to Cameahwait and had his men also give their guns to other braves. This went beyond Cameahwait's strategy to deceive a potential enemy, for its placed absolute power in the hands of the Shoshonis to use as they wished. Given Lewis's usual disdain for the "savage" mentality, this act seemed to be out of character, and displayed either trust in his companions or, more likely, desperation to keep the contact alive. But he did it immediately and without lengthy forethought. Equally out of character was his next act, "recource to a stratagem in which I thought myself justifyed by the occasion, but which I must confess set a little awkward" (V, 105–106). He lied. Coming upon the note he had left for Clark, this one not a victim to a beaver, he pretended it was *from* Clark saying that the party was nearby. Still treating the Shoshonis as children, he offered a knife and some beads to a brave who had volunteered to accompany Drouillard to take an "answer" to Clark as a reward "for his confidence in us" (the brave did not request or need such a reward), but most of the party dispersed into bushes to hide. Sure enough, the gamble paid off. Soon Clark, Charbonneau, and Sacagawea came into view, and somewhat later the canoes with York, who Lewis was sure had played a big part in the braves' remaining, since their curiosity had been aroused by the report of a black man. Next, almost miraculously, Sakagawea recognized a woman of the party as one who had been captured with her and later escaped, and then recognized Cameahwait as her brother (or maybe her cousin)! The closing of the linguistic gap completed the relationship of the Corps of Discovery with the Shoshonis as well. Drouillard, thought by Lewis to be a master of all Indian sign language (Lewis had earlier expressed his full confidence in his ability to communicate, but, as we have seen, he was less than perfect in understanding and being understood), gave way to Sakagawea, who translated from Shoshone to Minitari, which Charbonneau then translated into French, so that Labiche could translate into English. Lewis now gave his set speech promising trade and defense, since their mission was to extend the jurisdiction of the United States government to bring goods to the Shoshone and protect them from their enemies if they only cooperated with the Great Father in Washington. Lewis, as usual, passed out medals with the countenances of Washington and Jefferson on them, and distributed other gifts, showed off York, the "Segassity" of Seaman, and the wonder of the air gun, and in return got the horses and a guide, and a profession of lasting friendship. The earlier "metamorphosis" of the races had been reversed. The Shoshonis were once again in their place as passive receivers of civilized American supremacy, or so it seemed to Lewis.

The fluidity of the situation that had created such anxiety for Lewis is over. No longer must he cope with a "savage" mind, which operates so differently from his own, but he can once again revert to careful, scientific description of the Shoshonis and their customs. It is Lewis, after all, who first informs us that the Shoshonis had no organized leadership structure, and each had the opportunity to be a chief, depending on circumstances. And he learned that they had no fixed names, either, but instead took on names relevant to acts in their lives. Thus Cameahwait literally means "he does not walk," paralleling his reluctance to advance with Lewis, but Lewis is also aware of another name, Tooitecoon, "fires a black gun," which certainly celebrates Lewis's handing over his rifle. On another day and under other circumstances, his name could be almost anything else. Albert Furtwangler cites a linguist on this behavior:

> The spirit which actuated the event that selected his name was propitious; To a Shoshoni, the particular desig-nation, together with his physical body—the recipient of that name—were most secret things. To tell that name, or have the body photographed, was to lose part of his nature, which he would miss in the hereafter. When asked to give his name, he is unwilling to do so, but an Indian with him may give it; yet if there is a way of evading the matter, the Indian with him will not give the true name, but will make up a name from something that may occur to him at that particular moment. (Shoshoni place names are invented similarly on the spur of the moment.)[2]

Lewis had momentarily participated in the metamorphosis more fully than in mere appearance only. When he gives up the last appurte-nances of the white man, his hat and his gun, he ceases to be Lewis and goes forward as a brave in his tippet (which he kept and highly prized, to the extent that he had his portrait painted in it when he returned). Lewis "does not walk" because he is no longer Lewis. And although he does not yet know about Cameahwait's other name, he participates in it by giving him his gun. This transformation of identity, the violation of order, must have been very difficult for Lewis to accept, but he does, I think, intuit what is happening even as he rationally resists it. On the return route, Lewis and Clark found their caches untouched, but no sign of the Shoshonis, who had vanished from their ken forever. The transformation was temporary. But the undercutting of Enlightenment standards had a permanent effect on Lewis. He experienced a doubt about his own solidity, his identity, a shock for anyone, but especially so for a man of Lewis's background and temperament.

But what about Clark? Since he had no part in the anxious wait but was instead concerned with the effort of moving the party onward, what was his response to the meeting? It is instructive to compare the Captains' entries at this point for they differ considerably in tone and to some extent in content. Lewis, strangely enough, describes the events of this August 17 meeting with a curious flatness: the Shoshonis are excited and the chief repeats his "fraturnal hug," the meeting of Cameahwait and Sakagawea, his sister, proves to be "really affecting," but more so the reunion with the woman who had been taken prisoner with her by the Minitaris. When the canoes arrived, "we had the satisfaction once more to find ourselves all together," says Lewis (V, 109). From this point on he is all business, caught up in the details of earning the good will of the Shoshonis in order to gain the necessary horses and of transporting their goods to the Shoshonis' camp. But all this must be done with care, Lewis points out, for "to keep indians in a good humour you must not fatigue them with too much business at one time." He tells us that "it was mutually agreed" that Clark should set out the next day with eleven men to determine if water travel to the Columbia would be possible. And he ends the day saying that "the sperits of the men were now much elated

at the prospect of getting horses." It is the reunion of the force that
dominates his account of the day (V, 112–113).

Clark's version of this day, however, is quite different in emphasis.
When the party first spotted the braves, he tells us, Charbonneau and
Sakagawea "danced for the joyful sight." As he approaches the party he
recognizes Lewis and his men dressed "in their Dress" and they are met
with great signs of joy. And the Indians "Sung all the way to their Camp."
This festive occasion, as Clark presents it, was an emotional one, far
more so than Lewis's buttoned-down account presents, and Clark
underscores this by emphasizing the singing and dancing, which almost
takes the form of liturgy. What occurs next is even more noteworthy: the
Shoshonis tie in Clark's hair some pieces of shell resembling pearls,
which, he says, have come from the seacoast. Lewis never mentions this
remarkable detail. Afterwards, Clark says, "we then Smoked in their
fassion without Shoes and without much cerimoney and form." What is
happening here? Why is Clark treated so differently? We have heard
before of other tribes' interest in his red hair, just as they were awed by a
black man. This act, however, seems to go beyond anything we have
experienced thus far, and beyond the emotion we should expect from
the Shoshonis under the circumstances. Could it be the case that Lewis's
condescending treatment of them as children is accurate, that the
ornamentation of Clark is a form of childish exuberance or perhaps a
simplistic form of mistakenly worshipping this god-like creature? This
doesn't fit well with what we know of them. Perhaps the following
statement, Clark's description of the smoking ceremony, clarifies the
situation. He sees the shoelessness for what it probably is, a celebration
of relaxation by the group after tension, "without much cerimoney and
form," without the need to turn it into an emblem or allegory of some
other meaning, as Lewis had felt compelled to do (V, 114). Later in the
day's account Clark describes the Shoshoni custom of changing names
and he seems completely comfortable accepting what he thinks is
Cameahwait's name as his own for the remainder of their stay. Could it

be that the Shoshonis sense in Clark someone who is genuinely interested in them and their responses, less manipulative and more direct, seeing them less through the filter of their usefulness to the Corps (although certainly aware of this) and more directly as persons? Lewis can say condescendingly that "like most other Indians they are great egotists and frequently boast of heroic acts which they never performed" (V, 119). But we never hear this tone of voice from Clark.

The very next day was Lewis's birthday, which occasions the most remarkable journal entry of the entire trip. I include it in full (it is tacked on to the end of an entry describing how they have traded for horses):

> This day I have completed my thirty first year, and conceived that I had in all human probability now existed about half the period which I am to remain in the Sublunary world. I reflected that I had as yet done but little, very little indeed, to further the hapiness of the human race, or to advance the information of the succeeding generation. I viewed with regret the many hours I have spent in indolence, and now soarly feel the want of that information which those hours would have given me had they been judiciously expended. But since they are past and cannot be recalled, I dash from me the gloomy thought and resolved in future, to redouble my exertions and at least indeavor to promote those two primary objects of human existence, by giving them the aid of that portion of talents which nature and fortune have bestoed on me; or in future, to live for *mankind*, as I have heretofore lived *for myself*.—(V, 118)

How are we to take this, especially in its context? On one level, it makes no sense at all. Lewis has substantial achievements to his credit— a successful army career, management of an estate and head of a family, including mother and siblings, secretary to the President of the United

States, at one point even delivering the President's State of the Union address to Congress, not to mention the achievement of safely leading the Corps of Discovery 3.096 miles (according to Clark's calculation), managing the lives and fortunes of up to 44 people and collecting knowledge, which will be of considerable assistance to the future of his country. True, Jefferson had written the Declaration of Independence before this age, but that is competing in rarified territory. Surely, Lewis must hold impossibly high expectations for himself. For a long time I tended to view this passage as another literary exercise, a form of secularized spiritual inventory borrowed from the Puritans. Then, too, eighteenth-century literature, especially devotional literature, is full of this kind of passage; even Dr. Johnson was fond of such gloomy self-assessments.[3] According to this approach, this passage would be parallel with his description of the Great Falls, which also follows a rhetorical framework common to the time.

But what if we see this passage as a sincere expression of his state of mind and soul at this moment? In other words, is there a way in which we, too, can understand Lewis as a failure to "make a difference," as people today are fond of saying? In his own eyes he has not provided a solid financial basis for his family, always a primary concern for an Albemarle gentleman. He has been unable to find a young woman who will marry him, a problem that will dog him the rest of his life. He has no plan for a permanent career after the expedition is over, although he undoubtedly trusted a grateful country to reward him suitably. But these shortcomings are not the same as failing to "further the hapiness of the human race," and, moreover, all can be rectified in the future. None are out of reach for a man his age.

Could it be that the experience of "metamorphosis" has so shaken this 31-year-old that all his certainties, his own identity included, have been called into question? The concept of separate identity, and with it, of order and reason, may have been shaken by the special intimacy of his relationship with Cameahwait. Although Lewis seems to revert quickly to his former self and his assumption that the savage mind is a lesser thing, it is still true that only when he sheds his identity as Captain Lewis do events turn out right for him. To call into question the values one has lived by and given allegiance to can profoundly affect a person and different people are affected in different ways. For some such an experience can lead to exalted revelation and joy and for others darkness and doubt. Lewis was touched and seen in a totally unexpected way, and he may well have been unable to deal with this experience in ways that made sense to him. If he couldn't understand this encounter with a Shoshoni, what could he understand? Maybe not what the "hapiness of the human race" entailed. At any rate, it is the case, as we shall see, that Lewis's young life begins a downward arc at this point, leading to theft, murder, a painful gunshot wound, depressing political infighting, great and unexpected debts, and, only four years later, death. Lewis has now arrived, literally and figuratively, at the dark side of the Shining Mountains.

In the State Capitol in Helena, down a narrow, twisting stone-floored corridor reminiscent of a middle school, lies the House of Representatives' Chamber, home to a massive 12'x26' mural by Charlie Russell, perhaps the best thing (and the biggest) he ever did. It startles the viewer by having in the foreground a group of mounted Shoshonis wheeling their horses in evident wonder and excitement, and beckoning others over to the painting's right, where the middle ground has Sakagawea conversing with a brave, and Lewis, Clark, and two other unmounted, rifle-toting figures standing by and watching. Surrounding the figures is the detritus of an Indian camp—buffalo skull or two, some curious dogs, lodges, and burnt-out cooking fires. Out of the humdrum of the encampment emerges the turmoil these visitors have brought, and the focus of the entire painting is on the emotions of the Shoshonis.

Russell has included it all, the charged moment of encounter with the world of white men, which is the defining moment in the history of Native Americans, the seed of the end in the beginning.

I wanted to view that Shoshone camp, but as of this writing, I haven't made it yet. The first attempt, up a two-lane but adequate road for about 20 miles to a gravel cut-off, was made after a 10-inch snowfall in June in my van, not known for its traction but high enough off the ground to make the attempt feasible. The snow didn't trouble me that much, but in June snow melts, and the road to Bannack, I saw, was completely under water. The track to the Lemhi Pass (or what I took to be the right way—there were no signs) had no shoulders above water. There are some small ranches up here, so there was little danger of being stranded, but since I wasn't even sure this was the right road, and since it didn't look like turning around would be possible on such a narrow path, I chickened out. On the second attempt a year or so later, I learned that I had made the right decision, because the gravel ends about three miles further on, becoming one of those tracks the maps call "unsurfaced—local inquiry may save time." This time, a week or so later in June, the snows were gone but the rains had come. Still, in my rented Camry I was able to dodge some massive muddy potholes until I passed a sign that promised "Lemhi Pass—1 mile." The track headed upward, now deeply rutted and extremely muddy, but so long as I steered free of the ruts, I could move forward at about 5 M.P.H—until I missed the high ground and ended in the ruts. The result was about forty-five minutes of maneuvering in order to back down the hill for a mile or so, covered in mud from spinning the wheels (inside as well as outside, since I had to stick my head out the open window to see when the front wheels were straight). So I, too, had an adventure here, but Lewis and Clark at least made it. My last venture was the least dramatic, again in June, between thunderstorms. I didn't even try the journey through the mud this time. I look forward to another attempt, since I, too, am determined to straddle the beginnings of the Missouri and drink from the source of the Columbia.

———————————

The Expedition now underwent a month of hell. Game had disappeared, and rations were meager, to say the least. Clark's exploration of the Salmon River proved that the Shoshone were right— there was no way to make use of river travel on that rapids-filled, bankless chasm. Clark laid out three plans: proceed by land with as many horses as possible and a Shoshone guide to a navigable branch of the Columbia; divide the party with one group as above and the other attempting the "River of No Return"; or send one party back to the Great Falls to bring back dried meat and cross the Divide from the Medicine, while the other group attempted the land route down the mountains. They had learned that in one sense their two-month loop to the Missouri's source and back to the Lolo Trail had been unnecessary, that they could just as well gotten horses from the Flatheads whom they met in that area. But after having survived so much together, separating the Corps and virtually sentencing one party to death, while not unheard of in military organizations, must have seemed unthinkable. By August 21st the first frost had frozen the captains' ink, the Shoshone were preparing to leave for the Missouri hunting grounds, and a whiff of famine was already in the air. A good part of the problem resulted from the need to head northward to the one known way across the treacherous mountains, the Lolo Trail, used by tribes for generations, and that trip was itself steep and dangerous.

By the 27th Clark has reached the Trail, where there was nothing to hunt. He points out that the Indians gladly shared what few salmon they had and appeared contented, while "my party hourly Complaining of their retched Situation and [contemplating?] Doubts of Starveing in a Countrey where no game of any kind except a fiew fish can be found"

(V, 175). Whereas Lewis has repeatedly spoken of how the party has retained cheerful spirits in the face of every hardship, this comment strikes me as the more believable. Already Clark finds that "my flesh…is declining." But the worst was just beginning. Horses wandered off at night in search of some forage, only to fall and be crippled, even rolling down steep inclines, the snow began, and little can be more exhausting than slogging through snow, especially when it was also falling from the trees so that the men were constantly wet. They ate one colt, then, another, finished off the canned soup that Lewis had providentially brought from Philadelphia, and were down to eating bear oil and twenty pounds of candles. Even Clark's mild elation at the Bitterroot River ("I was the first white man who ever wer on the waters of this river") was short-lived as starvation loomed. On September 18 the captains employed a frequent strategy and sent Clark with six hunters ahead in a desperate search for food. The very next day the men spotted a prairie down on the flats, about 60 miles away, and began to take heart that their mountain ordeal was nearing an end. But the main party was just about finished; as Lewis notes: "I find myself growing weak for the want of food and most of the men complain of a similar deficiency and have fallen off very much" (V, 226).

On the day after that, Clark's party met the Nez Perce, a handsome people, he says (wouldn't anyone look good at this point?) among piles of camas roots lying about everywhere. They had hit upon Weippe Prairie, one of the most important root-collecting points in the Northwest, where tribes from as far away as the Pacific came to gather this staple of their diet. The Nez Perce were friendly, fed them, gave them knowledge of the country to the Columbia, furnished them with two guides, and agreed to tend their horses until they returned. Another happy ending. As Lewis puts it in his last journal entry for a long, long time: "the pleasure I now felt in having tryumphed over the rocky Mountains and decending once more to a level and fertile country where there was every rational hope of finding a comfortable subsistence for myself and party can be more readily conceived than expressed, nor was the flattering prospect of the final success of the expedition less pleasing" (V, 229). Note how the expression of personal joy is paired with a glimpse of fame, a view to be taken by others. This is not a simple man!

But there was to be much more suffering in their lives. They were entering a new and strangely barren, windswept country, where the environment had totally changed again. Everyone, including the captains, fell victim to serious intestinal disorders brought on by the change in diet (or again having a diet), or perhaps the new, hot climate as well. The building of new canoes was limited by the number able to work (Lewis was immobilized for days). Their axes were so worn down that cutting was difficult. With uncharacteristic testiness Clark complains, "I continu verry unwell but obliged to attend every thing" (V, 249). There was no game to be found. When they set off from Nez Perce territory they were watched everywhere by crowds of new tribes of Indians, whose language and customs were different and less friendly.

The country they passed through from Lemhi Pass is today paralleled by some of the most spectacular highway in the country, even though the "rough places have been made smooth," more or less. U.S. 93 from Salmon, over the Divide at the Lost Trail Pass and north to Hamilton and Lolo, runs along the wild Salmon for a ways and then follows the Bitterroot to a junction with U.S. 12. Now the route is mainly down, with roaring rivers foaming along beside the road, sometimes dotted with rafters running the rapids, snow peaks all around, pointed firs everywhere, and at least through much of June, plenty of snow at the crest of the Pass. My last trip down was early in the morning before logging trucks inhibit one's speed, and my tape deck was blaring out the Kyrie from the Verdi *Requiem*. What a rush! It takes all morning to make Lewiston, past little settlements of retirement or vacation cabins, past the paper mill town of Orofino, Idaho, past the headquarters of the remaining Nez Perce Nation.

Lewiston (not to be confused with Lewistown, a much smaller place in the center of Montana), at the confluence of the Clearwater and the Snake, is approached by the Lewiston Hill Grade into the rimrock canyon of the Snake where truckers frequently are known to blow out their brakes. It, too, is a paper mill town, as the gagging odor quickly indicates. It has a bleak past as a supply center for the gold and silver mines of the Idaho Territory, whose first capital it was for a year about the time of the Battle of Gettysburg, when congressmen had other things on their minds. There is a wild story of how the locals refused to allow the territorial seal to leave when Boise was named the new capital, and U.S. troops, pushing through the town's sheriffs, had to retrieve it at gunpoint by blowing a safe in the now-empty governor's office.[4] When I first visited the town almost twenty years ago, it was a rundown, sad place. But Lewiston has undergone something of a renaissance since the Snake has been tamed by a series of dams and locks, and today is a major seaport of the West, 465 miles from the Pacific. Fully one-quarter of the nation's feed grain and 35 percent of its wheat moves down the Snake-Columbia system in barges twice the size of those on the Mississippi because of channel dredging and lock-building, to be loaded onto ocean-going freighters in the Portland vicinity. Other barges carry computer products from the burgeoning high-tech industry of Idaho and Utah, as well as manufactures such as coated milk cartons.[5] While prosperity has perked up the town to some extent, the battle with environmentalists and government agencies over the approaching extinction of the salmon seems to have embittered many. The changing of water flows and temperatures makes it impossible for the young salmon to survive the journey to the ocean, even when some adults seem to be able to make it upstream to spawn. A plan to build a flexible Kevlar tube eight feet in diameter and 350 miles long avoiding dams, predators, and slow-moving water that would transport baby salmon by means of a temperature and speed-controlled flow matching that of the undammed rivers, a kind of fish waterslide, got no farther than public derision. Any attempt to manage the water flow for the benefit of fish, as opposed to the barges, has been blocked and blamed on those prosperous dilettantes west of the Cascades who are seen as not having a clue as to what real work is and who have an increasingly remote government on their side. How this conflict will be resolved is still unsure, but meanwhile there are fewer and fewer salmon. And the barge traffic continues to grow and will therefore become harder and harder to control. As the Expedition ran out of game crossing the Shining Mountains, so today the disappearance of the salmon impoverishes the area.

1   I owe much to Albert Furtwangler, *Acts of Discovery: Visions of America in the Lewis and Clark Journals* (Urbana, University of Illinois Press, 1993), Chapter 6, "Signals of Friendship," pp.110–134. I hope I have been able to carry his ideas a step further.

2   Furtwangler, p. 125.

3   See, for example, Johnson's *Meditations*, in R. W. Chapman, ed., *Boswell's Life of Johnson* (London, Oxford University Press, 1960), p.341.

4   The story is told in Blaine Harden, *A River Lost: The Life and Death of the Columbia* (New York, W.W.Norton, 1993), p. 146.

5   Harden, p. 25.

Chapter 10

The End of the Trail

While Setting on a rock wateing for Capt Lewis I Shot a Crain which was flying over of the common kind. I observed…Several Indians on the opposit bank,…others I Saw on a knob nearly opposit me at which place they delayed but a Short time before they returned to their Lodges as fast as they could run…as I approached near the Shore, I landed in front of five Lodges which was at no great distance from each other, Saw no person…I approached one with a pipe in my hand entered a lodge…found 32 persons men, women, and a few children,…some crying and ringing there hands, others hanging their heads. I gave my hand to them all and made Signs of my friendly dispoition…. They said we came from the clouds &c &c…and were not men &c. &c.

Clark, October 19, 1805 (V, 305)

Except for a minor road running for twenty miles, of a type the map calls "other," no highway borders the Snake River past Lewiston all the way to the Columbia, some 120 miles distant. There is no reason for a road. The River has carved a canyon through basaltic rock, and four major dams control the flow of a stream dropping over 500 feet in that distance (the Mississippi, for example, drops about 100 feet in 700 miles). The landscape along the way is "gritty," a wind-swept rocky treeless moonscape of undulating hills scoured clean of vegetation, where even sagebrush has a hard time of it. The appropriate word to describe the country is "scabland." The map shows only one town on the River between Lewiston and the confluence with the Columbia, a dot of a place called Ayer, virtually unreachable by road. And at the confluence (called Hades by the first railroad builders) there is the town of Burbank, population 710, which consists mainly of a tank farm, grain elevators, and one bar, but almost no visible people. Yet only minutes away is the Palouse region with topsoil 150 feet deep in places, some of the richest farmland in the world. In 1889 a Nebraska farmer bought a hundred acres of land in the area, and with the harvest of one season he paid for his land, seed, and fencing, and had $98 left over to put in the bank.[1] Once when driving through the area I thought the map showed me a shortcut south to the town of Dayton, on my way to Walla Walla. But within a few minutes I found myself trying to navigate a twisting one-lane rut through fields of wheat and grasses, meant, I later discovered, only for farm machinery. The gas station attendant in Dayton remarked, "They should take that road off the map," and I heartily concurred. To the north, within ten miles of the Snake, is a comfortable town, Pullman, where Washington State University is located. Further directly north lies Spokane, the center of what once came to be known as the "Inland Empire," because it had rail connections to the east and west and was the supply and transportation center for a vast agricultural area. Only thirty miles or so south the Blue Mountains emerge, heavily wooded peaks approaching 8,000 feet. The geological and geographical variety in such a short space is truly stunning.

———————

As they entered the Snake-Columbia river system, Lewis and Clark yet again emerged into another totally different world. Clark tried to express the newness of the region: "The face of the Countrey, on both Side of the river" he says, "is Steep ruged and rockey open and contain but a Small preportion of erbage, no timber a fiew bushes excepted" (V, 339). While rushing streams and dangerous rapids presented them with moments of great danger (canoes were overturned and goods flooded with regularity), at least this was *action* rather than passive endurance of suffering and illness just experienced. Clark's entries reflect this relief at once again being engaged. More importantly, they were surrounded with signs of human habitation and, much of the time, unlike the days crossing Montana, crowds of Native Americans came to stare and meet with them. From their mat lodges with flat roofs, which indicated to Clark the lack of rainfall, to the fenced burial grounds, to the mounds of drying (and stinking) fish everywhere, and further down river, the first houses made of wood they had seen since Illinois—Clark scrupulously noted it all. At the confluence they discovered a major trading market of the area, where they were welcomed, apparently warmly, by Wallulas, who asked them to stay awhile so that all their people would have the chance to see them. More likely, the tribes had their eye on the guns and trade goods brought by the expedition, for if they could control access to these they would, like the Teton Sioux along the Missouri, dominate their neighbors. Lewis and Clark, however, refused the invitation, perhaps understanding more of the situation than they had in the past.

As they moved past the Big Bend of the Columbia, they encountered an entirely different reaction from the people known as the Umatillas, as

Clark describes in the passage at the head of this chapter. These words require further clarification, and it is found in Biddle's version of the encounter, where he cites a conversation with Clark. The Umatillas had observed the fall of the crane but not the shooting or the shooter, until after the crane had landed. At the time a few clouds were passing overhead. These impressions were connected as follows: the sound of the rifle (which they had never before heard) announced what was to follow; the appearance of men and bird simultaneously with the passage of clouds indicated that all had dropped from the clouds; while birds come from the clouds men do not, and therefore these are not men but some kind of gods; and since the bird is dead, the gods are dangerous, and thus we must prepare for our own deaths. This belief in divinity was confirmed when Clark uses his burning glass to "bring down fire." It took some persuasion to convince the Umatillas that they were mere mortals, Clark reports, but they soon put the episode behind them.[2] When we think of how often explorers have lost their bearings and have come to believe themselves to be gods, Clark's attitude is instructive. The sixteenth-century explorer Cabeza de Vaca became overwhelmed with his apparent ability to heal native peoples and saw himself as Christ-like. Columbus was so taken with his name as meaning "Christ-bearing" and "dove" that he constructed an entire theology wherein he was to be seen as the descent of the Holy Spirit to save mankind. Countless voyagers in the Northwest went mad with religious inspiration, as the missionary Asahel Munger, who claimed to have revelations that the Whitmans had to be driven out from their Walla Walla mission, and who later drove nails through his hands and set himself on fire.[3] Unlike these people, Clark appeared only amused by being mistaken for a god. Remember how he was honored by the Shoshonis, who braided seashells in his hair. He has enough confidence in his own identity not to lose his aplomb when others see him as more than he is. This is why he is such a trustworthy reporter.

Although no matter what specific tribes they encountered on their voyage down the Columbia, certain characteristics were shared—the natives smiled a lot but when one's back was turned they would steal anything they could lay their hands on, and this habit became extremely irritating to the entire party. Ronda tries to explain this thievery as a cultural distinction; the river tribes saw the things they took from the expedition as payment for services rendered, and they were seeking acknowledgement of their own importance.[4] The same can be said to explain petty larceny in any culture, but it hardly justifies it. The river tribes lived amid billions of pesky fleas, and they traded shrewdly for the dogs the party needed to supplement the diet of roots and salmon that they began to hate (Clark alone did not like dog meat). Their perceived villainy affected the captains, who now violated a heretofore unshakable rule, not to take anything belonging to Indians, when they "confiscated" some rare boards for firewood. Another difficulty came with the river itself: they encountered several bad rapids along the way to the Columbia, but these paled in comparison with the rapids at Celilo Falls (today completely gone because of the dams), the Narrows at The Dalles (a tautology, since "Dalles" means "narrows"), and the mighty Great Gorge, where the Columbia cuts into the Cascades. They took great risks in running some of these rapids almost casually, even when they knew they should make portages, but it was now mid-October and time was precious. At least in the Gorge they were back in the world of trees and game and the animal rations they were accustomed to.

By the time they reached the Narrows Lewis and Clark were encountering more and more frequent items of European trade—brass kettles, scarlet blankets, sailors' hats and jackets. Just as Ft. Mandan had introduced them to a vast trade center for the Missouri and Great Plains tribes, so now they were in the midst of the Pacific-Plateau system, where coastal tribes met with those east of the Cascades, who in turn traded with the Nez Perce, who themselves were linked to the Shoshone and

Middle Missouri trade system.[5] Fish, roots, robes, and European goods passed back and forth, as well as stories and songs. This time Clark recognized more fully this "great mart of trade," and understood the something of the political issues among the tribes and also why bargains were no longer possible. These tribes had extensive experience negotiating with others, even with Western sailors, and were very shrewd customers, so that the expedition's trade goods bought less and less in the way of foodstuffs. The party marveled at the great salmon runs and the hundreds of Indians hanging on to scaffoldings built over the Falls to bring in the catch. They in turn amazed the Native Americans with their daring (or foolhardiness) in running their canoes through some of the worst rapids. Because of rumors of attack by unfamiliar coastal Chinookans, the party had to be watchfully armed as they moved through this inhospitable country. Even when the River plunged into the Columbia Gorge, and forests provided game once again, the party still was preoccupied with threats of violence, inadequate diet, and those ever-present fleas.

The Columbia has not always been a kind place to the very people who make their home along it. Already by the time of Lewis and Clark, western diseases introduced by the trading ships were spreading upstream, so that in a generation the native population had been cut in half. One writer states that "the history of Indian-white relations in the Columbia Plateau is first and foremost a history of the ravages of disease."[6] In the Willamette Valley the estimate ranges as high as 90% mortality, which, in turn, made it possible for settlers to enter this pastoral paradise. In addition, a fervor for converting the Indians to Christianity, fueled by a religious revival in the East added to the tragedy, especially in the case of the Protestant missions established by earnest but naïve believers (when they weren't unbalanced), who were totally unacquainted with Indian languages and cultures. Prominent among them were Marcus and Narcissa Whitman, whose story has been retold many times but who still reverberate in our memories.

The mission they founded near present-day Walla Walla was practically on the Oregon Trail. They intended to convert the Cayuse and other nearby tribes, who never could understand mission's emphasis on settling down to farming in order to overcome sin, when the rivers flowed with fish and the land had roots free for the taking. Like tribes closer to the Coast, they, too, were beginning to feel the effects of disease, and they observed settlers coming along the Trail, 500 in 1845, 2000 in 1846, 5000 in 1847. Moreover, apocalyptic messages from a native prophet were spreading and gaining credence. When a measles epidemic hit the area (fatal to the Cayuse but not to the whites), the tribe believed that the medicine Whitman was administering was a poison (he had been poisoning their dogs and injecting an emetic into his melons to deter theft), and so they planted a hatchet in his head to release evil spirits. Before they finished they had killed a total of fourteen at the mission, including Narcissa.[7] One "New Western" historian wants to question who the victims really were, the Whitmans or the Cayuse, who, after all, were surely misunderstood by the whites.[8] This reminds me of the sophistry proposed in T.S. Eliot's *Murder in the Cathedral,* when the King's thugs propose that we accept Thomas a Becket's murder as "suicide while of unsound mind." To excuse the slaughter on the grounds that the Cayuse were also victims ends up belittling them by assuming they are incapable of moral discrimination as finely tuned as the white man's.

Today the Interstate from the confluence westward is so broken down that the ruts toss a car about like a boat on the waves. It reminds me of how the early settlers traced parts of the Oregon Trail from the grooves worn by wagon wheels in the rock. But when nearing The Dalles one only needs to look up and see the perfect snow-capped cone of Mt. Hood, looking like a child's drawing of a mountain peak, to

know we are no longer on the Great Plains. The Columbia flows on
mightily beside the highway even though no longer as it once did. It has
been described as "not a cozy river, not the kind a man can feel belongs
to him," and "an anomaly in a dry country, an ill-tempered ribbon of
deep, dangerous water, a resource that is at once fundamental to and
distant from the lives that depend on it."[9] As much as it intoxicates
engineers, it intimidates those who happen to be born near it." The
fifteen major dams along its length and the 100 more on its tributaries
have reduced its current to one mile per hour. A nerve center in
Vancouver, across the River from Portland, controls the dams' gates, so
that every six seconds the flow is altered, depending on power needs of
Seattle and Tucson and Las Vegas. Pools between dams fill during the
night when demand is reduced. If the River feeds the grid more power
than it can handle, the system is kept from shorting out by a massive
electrical resistor consisting of three towers wrapped with wire coils
(called the Toaster), which glows red hot for half a second to bleed out
excess power.[10]

When the dam was completed at The Dalles in the mid-fifties, Celilo
Falls, the economic center of the Columbia tribes for thousands of
years, disappeared in six hours.[11] Even prior to this, giant ferris wheel
contraptions were in place to scoop up fifty thousand salmon a day for
the canning industry, thereby depleting the salmon culture.[12] Today the
rapids have all been tamed for the benefit of the barge trade. And one
of the Grand Coulee Dam's great contributions has been hydropower
for the massive nuclear weapons production facility at Hanford. This
has led to an unexpected economically valuable resource, the radioac-
tive waste cleanup from the leakage, estimated to bring from 50 to 250
billion dollars to the area (New York's Love Canal cleanup cost $250
million).[13] And much of the territory along the River has been irrigated
to transform deserts into highly productive fields and orchards,
including the apple and french-fry capitals of the world. Imagine if you

can barges twice the size of those on the Mississippi full of frozen french fries headed downriver.

Such economic progress has come at a cost. First, to the Native Americans, whose most productive bottomlands were flooded, a story we have heard before. They have received none of the irrigation water for their remaining fields, but they do get free residential electricity, if they can afford to make use of it. But the greatest cost has been paid by the salmon, which are disappearing faster than anyone expected, the rate accelerating in the 1990's. The Pacific Northwest has been defined simply and emblematically as "wherever the salmon can get to." If so, then the region is shrinking. The Pacific salmon is one of nature's more complex creatures, with at least 400 distinct stocks known, differentiated by where they spawn. From hatching in the gravel of a mountain stream, they must travel through the slackwater of the pools and past the dams, sometimes over a thousand miles, to spend up to four years travelling a 4000-mile circle in the ocean, hunted by modern trawlers and ancient seals and sea lions, and then return to the location of their birth to mate and die. But a salmon run, like a chain breaking at its weakest link, can collapse anywhere. Logging and farming muddy the streams and destroy the shade and hiding places that young fish need. The turbines at the dams kill about half of the fingerlings, not, as might be expected, by chewing them up, but by exploding their bladders through changes in the water pressure. For those who survive, water temperatures have been elevated and the current slowed, so that where in the natural state it takes a month for the fish to reach the Pacific, it now takes two or three, so that they often lose their imprinted drive to return to the ocean. One solution is to remove the fish from the river by pumping them into barges or tank trucks and then dumping them into the river below the last dam, Bonneville, but this doesn't work very well. Breeding fingerlings in hatcheries doesn't work well, either, for genetic differences among species are ignored, and success is counted by how many fish are put into the river, not how many return. Furthermore,

hatcheries create special problems: about 99% of hatchery smolts carry
a kidney disease that prevents their return from the sea. A hatchery fish
is ten times less likely than a wild salmon to come home. 80,000,000
hatchery-bred fingerlings are dumped into the river while the number
of returning adults has plummeted alarmingly—the Chinook, the most
important commercial species, declining by 80% in the 1988-92 time
period, the coho declining by 95%. The Idaho salmon is close to extinction, and in 1994 not a single Chinook was seen on the upper Grande
Ronde River in Oregon.[14]

There is, of course, grave concern expressed on all sides. Blame is
placed on the river's fishermen, primarily the Native American tribes,
for taking too many fish (the sport fisherman is carefully regulated), but
the tiny proportion of fish disappearing in this way doesn't answer the
problem. Sea lions love to feed on and even play with salmon in the
open ocean. I have visited the observation room at the Bonneville Dam,
where all fish heading upstream pass by a window and are counted, and
where just about every one of the four-foot-long salmon has scars on its
flanks from sea lion swipes. But, again, the number destroyed in this
fashion is miniscule in comparison with the once-fecund salmon runs.
For over fifty years the primary action in commercial salmon fishing
has moved further north, to Alaska and British Columbia. The major
role played by the dams is inescapable. Recognizing this, in 1994 the
Northwest Power Planning Council called for a plan whereby barge
traffic would be suspended for two months of the year to permit a
drawdown of the Columbia, in order to speed up the current, and
thereby get more salmon to the sea. The plan, it was claimed, would add
$2 per month to electric bills in the region, at present the cheapest
power in the nation. But there is apparently a slim chance of putting it
into effect. One United States senator has said that it is better for some
salmon to become extinct than for electricity rates to go up. And the
barges must continue to move, for 25% of the nation's feed grain and
35% of its wheat, not to mention much of its computer hardware and

software, come downstream, with 40% of the grain surplus to domestic needs shipped overseas to help our balance-of-payments problem.[15] Ours is probably the last generation to know the Pacific salmon, which for Lewis and Clark ran as a solid silver stream, so that it looked like it was possible to walk on their backs across the Columbia.

Nowhere in my travels have I been to a spot where climate so abruptly changes. At The Dalles I recall the blazing sun, strong westerly wind, and, above all, the parching aridity of the Great Basin country. I once camped there on a fine May day but got no sleep at all that night, because I was worried about my tent blowing away. Then, in a matter of a few miles, the traveler is in the Columbia Gorge, that magnificent cut in the Cascade Mountains, and everything changes to the misty green of evergreen forests, leaping waterfalls, and wild flowers everywhere. From a ten-inch annual rainfall at The Dalles, Cascade Locks, thirty miles further west, will have 100 to 120 inches a year. At a campground there where I frequently stay, when I asked why, with so much annual rainfall, the sprinklers were running in July, they admitted that the rain didn't always come when it was needed. The summers provide moderate, sparkling days for windsurfing at Hood River, to the disgust of the bargemen, who must avoid hitting them, even when they seem heedless of the danger. The winters transform the coastal rains to snow on Mt. Hood, just twenty or so miles south, for spectacular skiing near the famous old Timberline Lodge. And then, at the confluence of the Willamette with the Columbia, is Portland.

The Willamette Valley was the promised Eden at the end of the Oregon Trail, which terminated at the river's falls thirty miles upstream from the Columbia. On the journey outward Lewis and Clark completely missed the Willamette, since they were hugging the north shore, and an island blocked their view of its mouth. They were also preoccupied with the fact that they were encountering tidewater, meaning that their quest for the Pacific was nearing an end. But the trappers to come found out about the Valley and by the 30's word began to spread back east, when one of those strange junctions in history occurred. In the midst of that religious revival sweeping through the East appeared a delegation of Nez Perce at St. Louis, asking that their people be taught about Christianity, and this call received an immediate and fervent response. Jason Lee established a mission at Salem, the Whitmans at Walla Walla and Lewiston, and a group of Methodists at The Dalles, the Clatsop Plains, and Oregon City. Again, the site of Portland was at first bypassed. The attempt to save Indians' souls did not go well (one Cayuse complained, "God is stingy"), but settlement prospered, since rumors of a pastoral paradise coincided with a severe economic depression in the disease-ridden Ohio Valley. Thus the Oregon Trail was born, and it funneled 53,000 settlers into the valleys of Oregon between 1840 and 1860.[16] An agreement was reached with the British that American territory would extend to its present boundary and statehood soon followed.

American and British relations in this part of the world had been difficult, ever since the original discovery of the Columbia River. In 1792 an American merchant captain, Robert Gray in his ship *Columbia Redviva*, had been the first to cross the Columbia bar, at the time one of the most treacherous on earth, and he gave the River its name. But he traded with the Indians in the estuary alone. It remained for an Englishman, Lieutenant William Broughton, Captain Vancouver's second-in-command, to sail as far as the Columbia Gorge, and thereby explore the full extent of the Columbia's tidewater. Because of his voyage, the British claimed the territory. But the Americans made their presence felt when John Jacob Astor set up his fur trading post at the town which bears his name, only to see it fail after a short time and be sold to the British North West Fur Company, whence Astoria became Fort George, and the territorial question became further muddled. At this point the British began to exploit their advantage, and by 1825 had established a flourishing outpost of Empire at Fort Vancouver, across from the mouth of the Willamette. Yet in one of history's ironies, the man sent to manage the enterprise with responsibilities to control the Indians, trap out the entire Northwest, and prevent American settlement, proved to be the settlers' best friend. Dr. John McLoughlin, a humane man as well as efficient administrator, assisted them with supplies, counsel, and even money after witnessing their sufferings; when his government objected to his support of the "enemy," he resigned to retire to the town he had founded, Oregon City, the first incorporated town in the West.[17]

From this point on American dominance was unquestioned, and the British, finding that the fashion for fur hats was passing anyway, more or less gracefully bowed out after years of negotiation. They agreed to a border north of Puget Sound, which has remained to this day. In little more than a decade came territorial status followed by statehood as the Willamette Valley and its tributary valleys filled up along its 100-mile extent, past Salem and Corvallis, to Eugene. Farmers were amazed at the fertility of the valleys and the mild, healthful climate. Portland, however, did not at first dominate over other towns until the California Gold Rush brought about an insatiable appetite for the produce of the Valley, which was shipped from Portland's natural harbor. Given the New England origin of many of the settlers and their commercial know-how, it was inevitable that Portland (its very name determined by a flip of a coin known today as the "Portland penny," between two Yankee merchants—it could have become Boston) prospered under such conditions.[18] When the railroads arrived, first the transcontinental lines, then a link with San Francisco, Portland's steady, if unspectacular progress was assured.

By the time the Lewis and Clark Centennial had rolled around, local businesses thought it would be beneficial to the city to get on the exposition bandwagon, which was then sweeping the nation. Beginning with Philadelphia's celebration of the nation's centennial in 1876, there followed the Cotton Exposition in New Orleans, the Piedmont Exposition, the great Chicago Columbian Exposition, the Nashville,

Omaha, and Buffalo Expositions (not to mention the Corn and Coal Palaces described earlier). But the most directly watched celebration was the massive Louisiana Purchase Exposition in St. Louis in 1904, where Lewis and Clark were also properly celebrated. It was decided that a 1905 festivity would benefit the city by making Portland better known, and, if it was smoothly carried off, Portland could gain a reputation for civility and efficiency, instead of carrying the derisive name of "Stumptown" into the new century. Even though the federal government had no interest in Lewis and Clark, there was concern for developing the Pacific Northwest, and so Congress approved funds for the Exposition, which was to put Portland and the entire area on the map. That it did. The Exposition was quickly and handsomely built on unused land northwest of downtown along the Willamette River. It ran smoothly to good crowds, totaling about two and a half million, and impressed the world; Portland was described as "well-built and metropolitan in appearance...in every respect an Eastern city" (meaning that no visitor needed to fear the crudity associated with the pioneer West). In a decade its population more than doubled, new buildings went up all over town, new bridges were built, the flats east of the Willamette became the primary residential area, and an era of confidence in the future was ushered in, a confidence, it should be added, which has existed to the present day.[19]

As was true of Sioux City when it developed its Corn Palaces by cooperative effort, Portland has celebrated itself as a city with great community spirit. Some have attributed this to the ethnic and racial homogeneity (while there are minorities here, it is a relatively "whitebread" town). Others point to the attention devoted to public spaces and artworks: the handsomely sculpted public drinking fountains, called Benson Bubblers, the full-sized sculptured animals in the downtown area, the cascading fountains in the many parks, the magnificent and easily accessible Washington Park with its Rose Gardens, the wholly open fun of Pioneer Courthouse Square, the multi-story *tromp d'oeil* mural on the walls of the Oregon Historical Society Building portraying the Lewis and Clark Expedition members, as well as fur traders and Oregon Trail pioneers, above all, the massive statue of "Portlandia," affixed to the Portland Building. Still others credit the far-sighted public officials who in the past, well in advance of most of the nation, looked to preserve the best of the city by stringent zoning requirements, serious attention to rapid transit, and an openness to citizen input. The city has gained considerable attention for the way it has governed itself, and several of its leaders have gone on to Washington to try to apply what has worked here to the national scene.

The city was built a long way from the confluence with the Columbia, over ten miles away, at a bend in the Willamette, which narrows at that point, and which then flows northwest almost paralleling the Columbia. The Port of Portland with its ship, rail, and truck facilities, stretches along this part of the River. The downtown sits on a modest height on the West Bank of the Willamette, at the foot of hills that roughly parallel the River. To the southwest those hills contain some of the most expensive residential neighborhoods and a large medical center with the State University's medical schools and the University and Veterans Hospitals, among others. The northwest also is a highly desirable residential area, where Victorian homes, some of them edging up the flanks of the hills, have been integrated into a gentrified shopping and entertainment district of upscale attractions. Driving along 23rd Street in the middle of a weekday afternoon, I have been caught in gridlock worthy of Manhattan, consisting mainly of BMWs, Mercedes, and Jaguars. The area also contains the magnificent Washington Park, where winding roads lead to many attractions, such as the Zoo, an arboretum, a forestry museum, some Japanese gardens, and the International Rose Test Garden, where thousands upon thousands of roses are grown as the focus of the annual Rose Festival. On an even partially clear day, all you need to do is raise your eyes from the roses to see Mt. Hood looming to the west. Running further northwest is Forest Park, the largest park within a U.S. city, some 4,600 acres of greenery disturbed only by the occasional trail. Beyond the hills lie the burgeoning suburbs, where much recent development has occurred.

East of the River are much larger flats, where most of the city's expansion in the first half of this century occurred. The flats are broken most noticeably by the presence of Mt. Tabor, an actual volcano within the city limits. But Rocky Butte in the northeast and Kelly and Powell Buttes in the southeast also provide some elevations. Close to the Willamette and the downtown is a busy commercial district around the Lloyd Center, one of the first enclosed malls in the country, which differs from most in being near the heart of the city. Close by is the striking new Convention Center and the Oregon Arena, home to the beloved professional basketball team, the Trailblazers. Portland appears to be a city of mainly single family homes, and the northeast area is striking in its profusion of well-kept homes and yards, many quite small in the western bungalow style, but most displaying lavishly blooming flowers much of the year. There is an area almost due east of downtown, called the Hawthorne District, which is reminiscent of Berkeley, Boulder, or Ithaca in its "hipness," and its comfortably seedy (but not low-rent) residences. Further to the south lies much greenery and the New England-like campus of Reed College, the city's (and the West's) most distinguished liberal arts college.

The least interesting part of the city is its northern section. The area along the Columbia, mostly bottom lands and not heavily populated, contains the airport, the county fairgrounds and exposition center, a raceway, and several golf courses. In the triangle between the Columbia and the Willamette, however, is a residential area, which, while not exactly comparable to ghettoes in other cities, is the home of many of the less affluent. At the same time, it is also home to the University of Portland, an expensive college founded by the same Roman Catholic order that built Holy Cross and the University of Notre Dame. It sits on well-manicured grounds on a bluff overlooking the Willamette. Not too far away is the gothic St. John's Bridge, designed by the same man who later built San Francisco's Golden Gate Bridge (but he is reported to have considered this one his masterpiece). I once parked on the heights near the Bridge and watched Toyotas being unloaded from a Japanese ship into the Southern Pacific rail yard, to be sent all over the country.

As a residential city Portland has charm and comfort. But what the traveler notices most is its downtown, which seems in scale and detail very different from anyplace else. This results in part from strict regulation as to what can be built there; height, consideration of views, and general architectural harmony are all regulated. It also results from the always-enforced limit to the size of blocks. Early in Portland's life streets were placed 200 feet apart to increase the number of desirable corner lots. This creates or adds to the sense of openness lacking in the metropolitan canyons of San Francisco or even Denver. But regulations of this sort are often subverted. Philadelphia long ago got around the hard and fast law that no building was to be taller than the hat on William Penn's statue on top of City Hall. It is the will and the energy of the people in Portland that has not only preserved but also developed the special quality of the downtown. There was, for example, a perfectly usable freeway running along the riverfront which was torn up to become parkland. This is now Waterfront Park, which is treasured for exercising, concerts, picnicking, and just plain river watching. For much of the year it also houses a craft market of heroic proportions, well patronized by locals and tourists alike. From Portland's founding land had been set aside for what has become the Park Blocks, six to the north of downtown, and twelve to the south, which are lined with elms (yes, elms, virtually extinct in the East), well landscaped, dotted with fountains and benches, and bordered by a unique mix of public and private buildings, including the Art Museum, the Center for Performing Arts, the "Schnitz"(another concert hall), the Oregon Historical Society, many churches and older apartment buildings, and at the south end, the campus of Portland State University. There are other blocks where private traffic is banned, so that busses may load and unload for all destinations, and the rapid transit train, the MAX, has its terminal. The greater downtown area of over 200 blocks is a "fareless" area, so that public transportation here is free.

A good example of how the city has remained "people-friendly" is the story of Pioneer Courthouse Square, blocks away from any courthouse. Its site, virtually in the center of the commercial district, was where the first school had been built, a big, New England-style building complete with cupola. After a thirty-year lifetime, the school was razed, and the Portland Hotel, a steeply roofed Queen Anne-style chateau of seven stories, was erected, to be the pride of the city. But its useful life also passed, and finally in 1951 it, too, was torn down, the location serving for the next thirty years as a parking lot. But in the renaissance years of the 80's, the city awakened to the need for something more meaningful at its heart, and created the Square, which has a sunken center where all kinds of activity takes place—concerts, exhibitions of all sorts (once when I visited there was a collection of antique cars), sometimes just idle conversation.[20] There is a Powell's Bookstore, a travelers' version of the huge warehouse store a few blocks away. On each of the 50,000 bricks constituting the Square is the name of a donor who contributed $15 to $30 to complete it. Around the edges are a very busy Starbuck's, food carts, and all sorts of public art. There is the famous life-size silhouette of the businessman with an umbrella hailing a cab, entitled *Allow Me.* There is the 25-foot column, the *Weather Machine,* which every day at noon emits a puff of steam and a trumpet fanfare, and then symbols emerge—a golden sun goddess, a copper dragon, or a blue heron for sunshine, storms, or unsettled drizzle respectively, one of which ultimately returns to forecast the day's weather. There is the whimsical signpost pointing to destinations as varied as Mt. Washington (2 mi.), Walden Pond (3278 mi.), and Tipperary (a long way). And the Square is not monumentally aloof. It gets heavy use from morning coffee drinkers to brown bag lunchers to concertgoers, as well as those who just want to loaf in whatever sun the Weather Machine has been able to predict.

One more story of public enthusiasm for the character of the downtown may help convey the city's special flavor. A local architect, Michael Graves, was commissioned to create the Portland Building, and a man named Raymond Kaskey designed and executed a 36-foot copper sculpture of a lady called *Portlandia* to kneel over the building's entrance. She was inspired by Lady Commerce on the City seal, and she is depicted with loose hair, one arm holding a trident, the other reaching down over the doorway (the hand, by the way, has been known on some occasions to have a yo-yo suspended from it). As one writer describes her, "With her nine-foot-long thighs and plunging décolletage, some have even called her X-rated." Sentimental or not, the lady is impressive. In 1985, she arrived in Portland by barge and then had to be trucked through the city streets to be installed. With no advance planning, over 50,000 people turned out in the rain to parade alongside her from the warehouse to her ultimate destination, and to cheer mightily when she was put into place. The point of the story is to underscore the sense of public enthusiasm about this piece of public art, which has become a kind of icon for the city. Pride in the public spaces and monuments is widespread, and the sense that these are *ours* reverberates everywhere.[21]

Indeed, Portland's satisfaction with itself can sometimes border on smugness. Not only are its location, its organization, its community spirit to be taken as incomparable, but also its restaurants, its music, its coffee. I have never heard a single snide remark about the annual Rose Festival, with its series of parades and its high school queen who gets to sign her name in concrete at one end of the Rose Garden (but only her first name, so that stalkers are discouraged). In spite of Old Town with its fair number of lounging derelicts who are sometimes assumed to be lurking felons, Portland gives the impression of being healthily normal, as advertisers for years assumed when they used it as a test town. Its profile includes a white population of 85%, with 7% African American, 5% Asiatic, and 3% Hispanic, with a few Native Americans, far less diverse than most American cities its size. As one wag claims, you could pick up the metropolitan area and drop it into the Midwest and no one would notice, although the view would be different.[22]

And the climate. Without much ice and snow, Portland could seem a paradise, but only if lack of sun is deemed desirable. Residents are testy on this subject, constantly defending their community against charges that it always rains—sometimes they become downright hostile, pointing to the fact that the annual precipitation is about the same or less than most eastern cities. They neglect to mention that most of it comes in the winter and spring, and when it doesn't rain it is still likely to be cloudy. Even if the rainfall is less than at the Pacific Coast, the "grayfall" is equally oppressive, as cloud masses from the Pacific pile up against the Cascade Range, just to the east. Sometimes a realistic Portlandian will acknowledge the problem, but will be quick to point out that it's not as gray as Seattle.

And there are problems that aren't going away because of civic spirit. Portland has become attractive to outsiders because of the influx of high-tech jobs (in the seventies and eighties Tektronix, Electro Scientific Industries, and Floating Point Systems, followed in the nineties by Intel, Hewlett Packard, Epson, Fujitsu, and a host of smaller, cutting-edge companies), and this has drawn large numbers of Californians to the area, especially from Silicon Valley.[23] Californians have sometimes made a nuisance of themselves, or worse, because their equity in higher-priced housing has made local prices seem so reasonable they have tended to drive up local real estate beyond the reach of locals. Everything looks cheap when compared with what they have left behind in the Bay Area. And they have brought with them a certain aggressiveness or brashness, which rubs the more staid Portlandian the wrong way. In addition, many of them have been accustomed to sterile bedroom communities miles from their employment, and they have begun to transform towns like Beaverton and Hillsboro into suburban enclaves resembling Pleasanton and San Ramon. This is often viewed here as a waste of precious open space, and a threat to the integrity of the city. Much of the civic struggle in Portland these days has to do with keeping the suburbs under control.

At the same time, more and more low-income people have been drawn to the city, only to find adequate housing out of reach. I was told repeatedly that there are no ghettoes in Portland, and I have seen nothing comparable to the burnt-out, trashed neighborhoods of places like Pittsburgh or St. Louis. But there are certainly areas where residences are sub-standard. The city and county are working at improving housing, but have fallen far behind the need. The network of public agencies and private charities is very active but cannot move fast enough in most areas, although they have done what appears to be an excellent job in dealing with youth crime and gang activity. But one measure of a city in trouble is a rise in domestic abuse cases, as the frustrations of living get turned inward, towards one's own family members. And Portland has reported a dramatic increase in recent years.

I have been led to believe, however, that one underlying problem, perhaps the most serious of all, has to do with the prevalent attitude of "Westernness." Portland's civic-mindedness has come into direct conflict with the classic belief system of the cowboy, the self-fulfilling myths of independence and self-reliance. Behind every social issue is the response of the "he-man" Westerner—leave me alone in the middle of my own space. Too often, people here are determined to provide for services to others only if they are not inconvenienced by such actions. A case in point is Oregon's tax revolt, the enactment a few years ago of Measure 5, a state law limiting property taxes, reminiscent of California's Proposition 13. While it has significantly reduced local taxes, it has come close to crippling many aspects of society, from medical assistance for the underemployed to State colleges and universities, libraries, and parks. But it is the public schools that have suffered the most, losing up to half their local funding. This was supposed to be counterbalanced by an increase in state funds, which, however, have been hard to come by. At the same time, the growing numbers of suburbanites do not see these problems as theirs, and they resist attempts to develop regional solutions. The ingenuity of some administrators has postponed the collapse of the schools, but, according to some I have spoken with, just beneath the surface of Portland's apparent success and sophistication lurks an uglier reality waiting to erupt.[24]

Of course, no discussion this brief can penetrate to the core of a city as large and varied as Portland. Large cities defy superficial analysis, and this is one reason I have had little to say about places like St. Louis and Kansas City along the Lewis and Clark route. But Portland, I believe, is a special case. It has developed into a possibility for a fully functioning community of major scale, unlike any other in the nation, but so many questions remain that its future is unclear. Whether it fulfils its promise as a "landscape of hope" or degenerates into merely another urban tangle is still open.

As the party proceeded on toward the coast, October was turning into November, and they were buffeted by wave after wave of Pacific storms. The River was so frightening that it was necessary for them to creep along one bank, since they could not manage their canoes in the current. For today's outdoor sojourners, travelling under power or along trails guarded from the elements by Gore-Tex, and capable of making fires by a variety of means, constant rain can still sap one's morale. For these travelers in clothes which were rotting and falling off, things were considerably worse. There were few suitably protected places to make camp. Food was scarce and often eaten raw, since fires were difficult to build. In those moments without rain, the fog descended so thickly that often the other shore of the River was not visible, and the world was one giant whiteout. In addition, there was the further irritation of coping with the inveterate theft of the Indians they met; at one point while they were searching every native for Clark's missing tomahawk-pipe, a coat was stolen! But on November 7 the fog lifted and Clark saw open water. He writes in his undersized notebook (DeVoto says he kept it strapped to his knee), "Ocian in view! O! the joy!", one of the most genuine outbursts of emotion in the annals of exploration.[25] The first version of the Journal is somewhat more subdued and commander-like: "we are in view of the opening of the Ocian, which Creates great joy." Not a single exclamation mark. He embroiders on this later, (we know it is later because the day's entry includes a highly unusual phrase describing the visibility of the Wahkiakum women's private parts: "when she stoops or places herself in any other attitudes this battery of Venus is not altogether impervious to the penetrating eye of the amorite," which is taken word for word from an entry of Lewis's not written until January), as follows: "Great joy in camp we are in View of the Ocian, this great Pacific Octean which we been So long anxious to See, and the roreing or noise made by the waves braking on the rockey Shores (as I Suppose) may be heard distinctly" (VI, 31, 32). Here is a case where meaning has not been improved by revision.

But he was wrong. All this turbulence was merely the broad estuary of the Columbia, the prelude to the full fury of the ocean crashing against the headlands and the forbidding bar. The Pacific itself was not viewed until over a week later, when their misery had increased to the point that the object of their eighteen-month journey appeared almost parenthetically: "The tide meeting of me and the emence Swells from the main Ocean (imedeately in front of us) raised to Such a hite that I concluded to form a Camp on the highest Spot I could find in the marshey bottom, and proceed no further by water as the Coaste becomes verry [dangerous] for Crafts of the Size of our Canoes—and as the Ocian is imedeately in front and gives us an extensive view of it from Cape disapointment to Point addams…"(VI, 48). The high drama of the moment was overshadowed by difficulties of surviving. For several days the only place to camp was on a collection of floating logs where rain-loosened stones kept showering down on them from the sodden cliffs overhead. Nevertheless, the men, perhaps in spite of their situation, seemed to delight in carving their names on trees all over the area. Clark, who is never characterized as a complainer, every day includes in his journal such statements as this: "It would be distressing to a feeling person to See our Situation." His entry for November 22 sums up his frequent response: "O! how horriable is the day."

The expedition had been stopped as never before, and something drastic had to be done if they were to survive. At this point came the famous "vote," about which much has been made, as the first election in the west, all the more remarkable because a black slave and an Indian woman were allowed to participate. For such a momentous occasion, the details are remarkably obscure. It is necessary to go to the journals of the enlisted men to learn that the captains called them together for their "input," as we might say today.[26] Clark never mentions a vote, although there is a tally, which is difficult to decipher. Instead, he argues for a particular position at considerable length and with great cogency: we need game, which is supposed to be more plentiful on the south side of the river; we need salt, which we can produce from boiling the ocean's water; we may be able to meet with a ship if we are near the ocean; the climate at the coast must be milder than that of the mountainous area upriver. Everyone except Joseph Fields agrees that the south shore should be explored to see if it satisfies the requirements for survival. Fields wants to head back inland immediately. The real vote is then on what should be done if the south side of the estuary proves unable to support them. 29 crewmembers are listed by name, including York, but Charbonneau is not recorded as voting. Clark puts the results in three categories, "falls," (presumably meaning a return all the way to Celilo Falls on the other side of the mountains), "Sandy River," (west of the Cascades but far enough inland to be protected), and "lookout up," (which must mean returning upstream to the best possible location to be found). The latter category receives a slightly higher number of votes than the Sandy River location, but six members want to head all the way back to the Falls. Interestingly, Sakagawea, or "Janey," as Clark sometimes calls her, is off the chart, with an independent and sensible comment— "in favor of a place where there is plenty of Potas" (VI, 83-85). But the case for the south shore had been so overwhelmingly made that their immediate course of action was clear. The tally of alternative sites for their winter quarters was in the nature of a false vote, since it was contingent on the unsuitability of their first choice, and it could be reversed by another vote later. The journals of the enlisted men make this clear; while all three claim that the officers conferred with the crew, none makes any mention of a contingency plan beyond crossing the River. This, then, was no more an exercise in democracy than the consultation at the Marias, where the officers heard out the men but followed their own opposing judgement. Nevertheless, it must have helped their morale under such desperate conditions to think that they had some part in determining their own fate.

The story of that miserable winter is well known. The Oregon Coast did itself proud, with only twelve of the 106 days without rain. Not only was their clothing made of hides rotting away, but the meat of the elk and deer they were able to shoot often spoiled before they could get it back to the Fort. And their old adversaries, the fleas, were as bad as ever. A party was set up at the ocean at a healthy distance away to evaporate sea water for salt, and the rest of the men set to work building shelter, called Fort Clatsop, consisting of seven rooms in two rows with a stockade around them. By Christmas Eve of 1805, in spite of the thieving depredations of the Clatsops, which proved to be a constant irritation, everyone was under cover, so that a celebration was in order. Clark noted that he was awakened by the discharge of firearms, shouting, and song under his window, after which presents were exchanged, the captains giving tobacco to the smokers and handkerchiefs to the non-smokers, while Clark notes a fleece shirt, drawers, and socks given to him by Lewis, "mockersons" from Whitehouse, an Indian basket from

Goodrich, some black roots from Clatsops who had visited the day before, and, of special interest, "two Dozen white weasils tails of the Indian woman" or, in the notes, the "squar of Shabono" (VI, 137). This seemed an extravagant act by Sakagawea. Where did they come from? Have they been among her personal possessions throughout the journey, and, if so, why had she not used them to warm her son? Had she been trapping on the sly while others were constructing the fort? We will never know.

But the fact of this gift, plus the fact that Clark mentions it in such a sidelong manner (elsewhere he gives her a name, often "Janey"; why not here?), has helped to fuel speculations of a romance between these two. Fictional accounts since then have included everything from special glances to hints of much, much more. Earlier, when Sacagawea was deathly sick with an infection, Clark had kept us carefully posted on her condition, and when he, in turn, was in bad shape, she baked bread for him with flour she had been saving for her baby. It was from Clark that we first learned how Sacagawea saved the items that had gone over-board when the white pirogue was swamped. And there is the fact that Clark subsidized the education of "Pomp," as he liked to call her son, and looked after her daughter as well. Clark's notation of her death in 1812 at Ft. Manuel is taken by most scholars as definitive, in spite of the tradition that she lived to a ripe old age elsewhere as a fabled storyteller. The consensus is that "Clark would know."

Is this enough evidence to support a romantic entanglement? To some, perhaps, but to me, no. There was clearly respect for this intelligent, self-possessed, and plucky young woman. The way in which she approached the captains to go on the expedition to see the reported whale tells us a good deal about her. Clark and twelve of the men were to journey beyond today's Tillamook Head to Cannon Beach, where, according to the Indians' report, a whale had been washed ashore. They wanted to bargain for some of the meat and oil to supplement their diet, as well as get a look at this scientific curiosity. Just before leaving,

Lewis tells us (Clark is almost certainly copying Lewis's entries at this point), that "the Indian woman" asks for permission to accompany them. It sounds like she may have been nursing a grievance, for she tells him that she had traveled a long way with them "to see the great waters" (she had not yet been to the ocean), and "now that monstrous fish was also to be seen, she thought it very hard she could not be permitted to see either." Lewis says she was "very impotunate to be permitted to go," apparently surprised by the vehemence of her request and her assertiveness (VI, 168). With Clark's agreement, she and Charbonneau joined the party. By the time they reached the 105-foot whale, the Indians had completely stripped it, leaving only the skeleton, but Sacagawea at least saw the ocean and the whale's remains. Once she spoke out, the males treated her with respect, but it was up to her to remind them that she was a person with her own interests. Lewis did not appear to be susceptible to her qualities, but Clark, as he usually did with Indians, saw her as an individual. This, however, in spite of the implications of many of those who have written about her, does not inevitably spell "romance."

I have been along the coast in the winter and can readily verify that it does indeed rain there. When I spent some time in Florence, the locals seemed quite proud of the fact that 120 inches of rain had been recorded that year. Some of the time, though, it was a fine rain, what we Easterners would be likely to call a mist or a shower. But mist doesn't add up to 120 inches, so obviously there was plenty of real rain, too.

On the way west from Portland, Highway 30 follows the Willamette along its oblique course toward the juncture with the Columbia, past mile after mile of docks and ship-loading facilities, where most of those barges from the Snake River end up. Further along the Columbia, the country is wild, apart from a few struggling lumber towns and the remains of a decommissioned nuke, with the rampant growth of rain forest to the south side of the road, and marshy floodplain on the riverside. There is another road from Portland to the north coast, the Sunset Highway, which is more scenic, and which offers, in the appropriate season, strawberries and asparagus for sale around every bend, before it heads into the dramatic Coastal Range and on to the ocean at Seaside. But to follow the Corps of Discovery's route it is necessary to shadow the River, even though their progress was along the north shore, the Washington side. As the highway approaches Astoria, one's breath is literally taken away by the cleansing winds blowing in—they always seem to be blowing in—from the open Pacific.

Like Clark, we can easily be fooled into thinking the Ocean is in view long before it really is, because the Columbia's estuary is so huge. A bridge from Astoria to Washington built at the narrowest point is over four miles long, believed to be the longest continuous three-span through truss series bridge in the world, another in the long series of superlatives we have encountered. While the river traffic goes under this bridge, and the shipping channel follows close to Astoria's business district, the Port of Astoria, capable of handling any cargo ship afloat today, is seaward of the bridge, facing the twin headlands of Point Adams and Cape Disappointment, on the Oregon and Washington shores respectively. There are likely to be up to a dozen ships in port or riding at anchor waiting to load or unload at any given time. In addition, there may be a seemingly helter-skelter collection of ships on the River, easily observed from viewing platforms located at strategic points throughout the town.

The founding of Astoria occurred not many years after Lewis and Clark returned, but it was not directly related to the explorers' efforts. The British had already established a traffic in furs at isolated outposts in the northwest by 1800 and promised to make this lucrative trade totally their own. But John Jacob Astor, already an eastern millionaire, saw an opportunity to compete with the British. He planned a two-pronged approach: sending a well-equipped ship to establish a permanent trading post at the mouth of the Columbia, and then following up with a cross-country expedition (following the route of Lewis and Clark) to make trading contacts along the way. Washington Irving's book *Astoria* provides a detailed account of the entire adventure. The ship *Tonquin* arrived in March, 1811, and immediately a fort was built, at about the site of present-day 15th St. This means that Astoria is the oldest permanent American settlement west of the Rockies. The tenuous claim of Captain Gray to American possession of the territory was thus solidified, at least for a time. But the town was plagued by troubles from the beginning, for a variety of reasons, prominent among them the difficult relations with the local tribes, who were already experienced in trading with white men and knew the market value of their otters and other pelts.

The story of the end of the *Tonquin* well underlines the developing conflicts. Sailing north to extend trading with other tribes, the ship encountered hostility because of the captain's somewhat surly refusal to meet the prices asked or even to bargain. He was a stiff-necked Scotsman and by all accounts a difficult man, who was a competent seaman but sorely deficient in diplomatic skills. After a day in which he had insulted the Indians by rejecting their offers and had threatened to set sail (his native interpreters had warned him not to trade with these people in the first place), canoe after canoe full of apparently friendly Indians came out to the ship and boarded it, accepting trades which the day before they had rejected. One observer, however, noted they seemed to want mainly knives. Sure enough, at a signal, they pounced upon the crew and killed most of them, as observed by the sailors in the rigging who were setting the sails. The surviving crewmembers reached the deck cannon and were able to drive off the Indians, whereupon that night they escaped in one of the ship's boats. The next day the ship drifted apparently abandoned, and so scores of Indians boarded it, intent on plunder. Suddenly, there was a tremendous explosion, which killed a hundred or so of the attackers and blew the native interpreter into the water, where he was rescued to tell the tale. A wounded ship's clerk still on board, named Lewis, an apparently suicidal fellow, had set fire to the ship's powder magazine as an act of vengeance. Needless to say, the news of the loss had a chilling effect on the young settlement, whose few remaining inhabitants felt they would be overwhelmed at any moment.[27]

But part of the overland party arrived in the winter of 1812 and helped to create a degree of hopefulness for the post's survival. It was not only restive Indians that were to be feared but Englishmen as well, for war was imminent and the North West Company across the River was much stronger than Astor's tiny outpost. In fact, Astor had persuaded the federal government of the importance of Astoria, so that a warship was to be sent to defend it. Astor outfitted a second vessel to accompany the *U.S.S. Adams* at his own expense. But it was not to be; the crew of the warship was needed in the Great Lakes, and Astor's ship was blockaded in New York Harbor.[28] He then tried to cut his losses by negotiating a separate peace through his agent (who shortly thereafter became a partner in the British North West Company). When a British man-of-war appeared in the harbor to take possession of the settlement, all of it had already been purchased by private parties, leaving no spoils for the crew. On December 12, 1813, the American flag came down from Astoria and the Union Jack was raised over what was now called Fort George.[29]

But the story does not end here. The Treaty of Ghent ending the War of 1812 called for a return of all territory captured by the British to American hands. Astor, never one to lose graciously, maintained that this meant Astoria was to revert to American control, even though he had sold it quite legally before the British warship arrived. He got the ear of President Madison and Secretary of State John Quincy Adams, who were in the process of developing a continental strategy for American identity, which required a presence on the Pacific shore. They promulgated the fiction that Astoria was conquered territory. Moreover, the British were losing interest in extending the empire in this direction themselves, and they knew they could still do business here even under American auspices, and so their admittedly weak claims to the territory were abandoned. By 1818 Astoria was once more in American hands, but not much changed. Astor said, "If I was a young man, I would again resume that trade—as it is I am too old and I am withdrawing from all business as fast as I can."[30] The strange asymmetry of Astoria had taken another turn.

The next 180 years of the town's history are certainly less exciting. The bracing, not to say harsh, climate has had something to do with its relatively slow growth, as has that highly dangerous bar across the mouth of the harbor, only tamed by extensive dredging in the twentieth century. Many Scandinavian immigrants, however, arrived to sail these waters. By the late nineteenth century fishing and logging offered a measure of prosperity, so that the many Victorian homes gracing the slope up from the estuary could be built. Some overly exuberant publicist has called Astoria the "Little San Francisco of the Northwest," because of those houses. But they played a part, literally, in the town's recent prosperity. Because of them several Hollywood films have been made here, since they can pass for New England dwellings if you don't look too closely (the trees are very different), at considerably less cost than filming across the country. When I first visited Astoria in the early 80's the lull in fishing and logging had taken their toll and the place seemed dispirited. But today prosperity has brought a new shine to this town of over 10,000 residents.

The annual Astoria Regatta has been celebrated for over 100 years, and the Scandinavian Festival has a long history as well. But in recent years new community celebrations have appeared, such as the Broadway-style melodrama, *Shanghaied in Astoria,* which is repeated each summer and a reconstructed encampment across Young's Bay at Ft. Stevens celebrating its Civil War history. There is a new fairground, where a celebration called "OckoberFisht" takes place. In December comes the Umbrella Parade. Galleries and little theatre productions are found all over town. Restaurants and lodgings have been spruced up. But most revealing of all is the Astoria Column. Originally, in the 1920's, the Great Northern Railway had proposed a flagpole at Astoria to celebrate the route of the railroad, but instead a monument patterned on Trajan's Column in Rome was built atop the 600-foot Coxcomb Hill, extending 125 feet high with an observation platform on top reached by a 164-step interior staircase. The view of the entire estuary (on a clear day) is incredibly spectacular. But this was not all. A frieze executed in the Italian technique of "sgraffito" was created, whereby a bas-relief was carved in the top coat of plaster, allowing the chocolate-colored background to show through. Then the entire frieze was painted, with the history of the area spiraling around the column from bottom to top. It was a remarkable achievement, but by the 1980's the coastal climate had almost completely obscured the frieze. So its restoration was undertaken, paid for mainly by the community, and today the frieze is beautifully visible in shades of brown, from the native wilderness depicted at the base, through Gray's discovery of the Columbia, Lewis and Clark's winter here, the Astor venture, the British occupation, to the coming of settlers and the railroad at the top. Individuals, businesses, and clubs contributed $1,000, "stepping up" for each step in the staircase. Schoolchildren built and filled Column piggybanks. Foundations made major contributions. In all, $750,000 was raised. This Column alone would bring visitors to the area, to say nothing of the town's other attractions.[31]

A few miles south of Astoria, across Young's River the road to Ft. Clatsop National Memorial is clearly marked. Along a backwater that drains into Young's Bay, called the Lewis and Clark River today, the captains chose the site for their winter quarters. Nothing remains of the original Fort Clatsop, and archeologists have been unable to verify with certainty the exact location of the original fort, but in 1955 area citizens using Clark's sketches constructed a replica on what was believed to be the site. In 1958 it was given to the National Park Service, and it remains under this jurisdiction.[32] It is a remarkably well preserved spot, with over a hundred acres of untouched wilderness surrounding the reconstructed fort and the visitors' center. Surrounded by the tall firs of the rain forest, it echoes to birdcalls in the early morning, much as when it was first built. Even the parking lot is screened by trees, so that many visitors can be absorbed into the surroundings. The trail to the canoe landing is much as it must have been originally, and on the way a 30-foot-long dugout under construction illustrates how canoes were built. It is one of those magical places along the trail where it is easy to feel the presence of the Corps of Discovery.

A few miles away at Seaside the original site of the salt-making operation, verified by word-of-mouth through several generations of Native Americans, can be viewed, but under very different circumstances. Seaside is a busy resort town, full of gift shops, lodges and motels, rental properties, a massive boardwalk which projects outward into the ocean, and plenty of tourists. The stone fireplace with pails to be filled with seawater for evaporation lies jammed in between houses and must be surrounded by an iron fence to keep it from being vandalized. A historical marker provides appropriate information and warns that violators of the space will be prosecuted. On the boardwalk there is a monument marking the "end of the trail," and this is true in more than one sense. The party's identity has truly evaporated, like seawater into the very clouds that the Umatillas had thought was their home.

1 Norman G. Clark, *Washington: A Bicentennial History* (New York, W.W.Norton, 1976), p.69.

2 Biddle's *History,* II, 648.

3 N. Clark, p. 26.

4 Ronda, *Indians,* p.172.

5 This highly intricate international system is thoroughly described by Ronda, pp.169–171.

6 The anthropologist Eugene S. Humm, as cited by Harden, pp.61–62.

7 N. Clark, pp.24–26; esp. Robert Clark, *River of the West: Stories from the Columbia* (New York, HarperCollins, 1995), pp.96–125.

8 Patricia Nelson Limerick, *The Legacy of Conquest: The Unbroken Past of the American West* (New York, W.W.Norton, 1987), p.41.

9 Harden, p.55.

10 Harden, p.70.

11 R.Clark, p.329.

12 R. Clark, p.310.

13 Harden, p.154.

14 Harden, pp.218–227.

15 Harden, p.237.

16 Terence O"Donnell, "Oregon History," in *Oregon Blue Book* (Portland, Secretary of State, 1997), pp.400–401; p.403.

17 O"Donnell, p.403.

18 Elaine S. Friedman, *The Facts of Life in Portland, Oregon* (Portland, Portland Possibilities, Inc., 1993), p.1.

19 Carl Abbot, *The Great Extravaganza: Portland and the Lewis and Clark Exposition* (Portland, Oregon Historical Society, 1996), esp. pp.15,54,39.

20 Terence O"Donnell and Thomas Vaughn, *Portland: An Informal History and Guide,* cited in Friedman, p.262.

21 Friedman, p.262.

22 Friedman, p.97.

23 Gordon B. Dodds and Craig E. Wollner, *The Silicon Forest: High Tech in the Portland Area, 1945–1986* (Portland, Oregon Historical Society, 1990).

24 Friedman, pp.129–130.

25 Bernard DeVoto, ed., *The Journals of Lewis and Clark* (Boston, Houghton Mifflin, 1953), p.279.

26 Gass (X, 177): "the party were consulted by the Commanding Officers...." Ordway (IX, 256): "our officers conclude with the opinion of the party...." Whitehouse (XI, 398): "Our Officers had concluded on crossing the River..."

27 Washington Irving, *Astoria, or Anecdotes of an Enterprize Beyond the Rocky Mountains,* ed. Richard Dilworth Rust (Boston, Twayne, 1976), pp.72–79.

28 Ronda, *Astoria and Empire* (Lincoln, University of Nebraska Press, 1990), pp.272–273.

29 O"Donnell, *Oregon Blue Book,* p.398.

30 Ronda, *Astoria,* pp.302–315.

31 *Astoria Column[s]* (Astoria, Friends of Astoria Column, n.d.).

32 Appleman, pp.348–349.

CHAPTER 11

Trees Like Fireworks

while we were encamped last fall at the entrance of the Chopunnish river Capt. C. gave an Indian man some volitile linniment to rub his kee and thye for a pain of which he complained, the fellow soon after recovered and has never ceased to extol the virtues of our medecines and the skill of my friend Capt. C. as a phisician. This occurrence added to the benefit which many of them experienced from the eyewater we gave them about the same time has given them an exalted opinion of our medicine. My friend Capt. C. is their favorite phisician and has already received many applications.... We take care to give them no article which can possibly oinjure them.

Lewis, May 5, 1806 (*Journals*, VII, 209–210)

The party hunkered down for the winter, and engaged in looking for food or trading for it with the shrewd Clatsops (Clark calls them "tite Deelers," later changing it to "Close dealers"). They also passed the time by mending their clothing and building up a supply of moccasins for the return trip. For the captains, there was writing and more writing, as well as questioning the Indians, whenever they could. They learned that chances of a ship were nonexistent at this season, since the English and American traders had to get away from that coast in winter in order to keep their ships from being dashed to pieces on the rocky shore. Clark at one point talks about "the Great Western Ocian, I can't say Pasific as Since I have seen it, it has been the reverse" (VI, 103). Lewis had learned that the ships headed away to the southwest and shrewdly posited another more southern port as yet unknown. In fact, the ships headed for Hawaii (VI, 187, 191n.). But the captains made several copies of a record of their achievements, together with a map of their route, and left them at the Fort (which they turned over to the Clatsops), in order that any trader who showed up would learn about them (VI, 429). Although Jefferson had hinted to Lewis in his original letter of instruction that a ship might be available to pick them up, the U.S. Navy was virtually non-existent by this time, and, moreover, there were no indications that the party had survived. From the expedition's point of view, the prospect of a return by sea was not appealing, because they knew it would take longer. They were right. One of the captains' notices fell into the hands of Samuel Hill of Boston, whose ship *Lydia* arrived at the mouth of the Columbia just after they had left. The *Lydia* spent the trading season loading up with furs, and it arrived in Canton in November. There the notice was obtained by an American, who sent it to a friend in Philadelphia with the further information that the Corps of Discovery had been in good health and spirits and had left on March 23 for the States. This information arrived in Boston on the same ship on May 12, 1807, almost eight months after the expedition had returned to St. Louis![1]

As noted, the captains wrote a good deal during the rainy winter. They obviously caught up on their Journals. Clark worked on maps and put together an estimate of distances between watercourses, over 400 of them, from Ft. Mandan to Ft. Clatsop, arriving at a total of 4134 miles. He and Lewis co-authored an estimate of the numbers of western Indians, tribe by tribe. But all of this work seemed like doodling; none of it has the cogency or descriptive authority of the writing done at Ft. Mandan, which was to be sent back immediately with the keelboat for Jefferson's eyes. It was a distraction from the constant wetness, the rotting meat, the irritating local residents, and the utter boredom of that winter. They had learned to cope with suffocating humidity, bugs, and danger of a Missouri summer, the numbing cold of a North Dakota winter, the physical pain of the Great Falls portage, even the great deprivation and hardship of the Bitterroots, but this slow, grinding, gray monotony was almost too much. Lewis's verbal outburst against the Clatsops on February 20 and the fact that he and Clark rationalized the barefaced theft of a canoe both indicate a loss of control, unthinkable for Enlightenment gentlemen. As Ronda points out, the experience at Ft. Mandan had been one of cooperation with the Indian tribes, but here a "we" against "them" mentality had developed, from their sense of isolation in an alien world (VI, 330–331; VI, 426).[2]

Does this help to explain the curious writing behavior of Lewis and Clark? We have no answer to the question why Lewis stopped journal writing again for over three months at the end of 1805. The earlier lapses could be explained by possible lost sections, as Donald Jackson has theorized, but now his entries began on January 1, 1806, in a fresh notebook, a fact too obvious to be coincidental. And by not writing, he was disobeying a direct order from his Commander-in-Chief, an act not to be taken lightly by a military man. Can there be some justification? Clearly, Clark shows there was plenty worth recording during this period. While Lewis had periodic bouts of illness, there was little so serious as to prevent writing. No discussion exists that they had agreed to divide up the journal-keeping chores, although this could have been a possibility. Did something happen to Lewis, some depression or loss of purpose, brought on, perhaps, by the almost unbroken sense of failure ever since the episode with Camaweahat? We recall that on at least two occasions, with the Shoshonis and with the Nez Perce, the party would, in all likelihood, have perished if not for the aid of the "savages," and this could be a bitter realization for a man of "reason." The far side of the Shining Mountains had proved to be not empty but crowded with unmanageable people, so that diplomacy was less possible, and it was full of weather that made maneuvering incredibly difficult—to say nothing of the fact that the dream of the Northwest Passage had died.

Another fact needs to be dealt with. Immediately as of January 1, Clark began to copy Lewis's entries almost word for word, as he rarely had prior to this time. The only significant differences between the captains' entries occurred when they were separated. What does this mean? Clark still followed the letter of Jefferson's instructions, but it has become clear that journal-keeping now receives a lower priority than heretofore. A common experience of writing journals, reported by most who do so, is that the act of writing becomes increasingly important over time, so that it not only becomes a habit but a need. This is not true for Clark, or, apparently, for Lewis, either.

Although few scholars actually say so, there is sometimes the implication that Lewis's failure to write for long periods foreshadowed the depression that led to his suicide. For a time I harbored that suspicion myself. We all went for justification to Jefferson's memorial to Lewis, which appeared in the Biddle edition of the expedition's history published in 1814. Jefferson claimed that Lewis had exhibited "from early life" the symptoms of "hypochondriac affections," which had been "a constitutional disposition in all the nearer branches of the family of his name." He went on to claim that he had observed "sensible depressions of mind" when they had lived together in Washington. He also noted that "constant exertion" of body and mind "suspended these distressing affections." But, he speculated, the "sedentary occupations" of his life as Governor in St. Louis brought on once again this depression, which "began seriously to alarm his friends." This was especially true of the days preceding his decision to return to Washington, Jefferson continued, when he was in a "paroxysm" and betrayed a "derangement of mind" on the journey, according to Jefferson's informant, an Indian agent named Neely, who accompanied Lewis.

Setting aside for the moment this diagnosis (no one else has been able to confirm a family history of mental instability of any sort, and certainly not in Lewis's father, who had the misfortune to contract pneumonia and die from it after participating in the battle of Saratoga), depression can have little to do with the question of writing in the Journals. Lewis takes up writing again when "constant exertion of body and mind" was at low ebb, just the opposite of what would have been predicted from Jefferson's description, and he apparently stopped writing when he was most active, as if he was running out of time. Jefferson had alluded almost in passing that Lewis's troubles resulted from alcoholism, and Steven Ambrose frequently refers to him as an alcoholic. But there had been no alcohol around for a long time, so that whether or not this was true (and many seriously doubt it, since, again, evidence is lacking), it can have no bearing on when Lewis did and did not write his journals.

More so than Clark, Lewis seems to be writing for an audience, Jefferson especially, accepting his responsibility to describe flora and fauna, Indian customs and reactions to their mission of pacification, and the geographical formations which encouraged or inhibited the movement of trade We have noticed that even his presentation of personal observation, as in the passage at the Great Falls, tends to be rhetorical and formalized, certainly when compared with Clark's spontaneity. Even Lewis's revealing birthday passage of 1805 has a rhetorical ring to it, as does this account of emerging from the terrible deprivation and suffering of the Bitterroot descent:

> the pleasure I now felt in having tryumphed over the
> rocky Mountains and decending once more to a level and
> fertile country where there was every rational hope of

finding a comfortable subsistence for myself and party can be more readily conceived than expressed, nor was the flattering prospect of the final success of the expedition less pleasing (V, 229).

Could it be that, when his sense of the audience has strengthened, he feels compelled to write? And what would strengthen that sense?

The January 1 entry, short though it is, does not suggest any apology or change in tone from earlier entries, with one exception. He begins by describing the company's attempt at a New Year's celebration, by waking up the officers with a discharge of a volley of small arms, the only mark of respect within their power, he says, "to pay this celebrated day." But watch closely what follows:

> our repast of this day tho' better than that of Christmass, consisted principally in the anticipation of the 1st day of January 1807, when in the bosom of our friends we hope to participate in the mirth and hilarity of the day, and when with the zest given by the recollection of the present, we shall completely, both mentally and corporally, enjoy the repast which the hand of civilization has prepared for us (VI, 151–152).

Although the expedition will not be able to leave for home for almost another four months, the turn of the year brings with it a turn of perspective. The future does not hold mystery or the unknown; it is to be a return, a homecoming. After having to cope with a messy, uncomfortable, mean present here among strange, constantly dripping trees and equally baffling people, it comes as an overwhelming relief to think of going home. On March 23 Lewis says tersely, "at 1 P.M. we bid a final adieu to Fort Clatsop." It is Clark, in a strikingly different entry from Lewis, who reflects on the Clatsop experience:

at this place we had wintered and remained from the 7th of Decr. 1805 to this day and have lived as well as we had any right to expect, and we can Say that we were never one day without 3 meals of Some kind a day either pore Elk meat or roots, not withstanding the repeeted fall of rain which has fallen almost Constantly. (VII, 8).

One explorer has had enough of exploration; he yearns for the familiar. The other speaks almost nostalgically about the Clatsop days. In spite of his rhetorical parallelisms, antitheses, and balances, Lewis's genuine sense of relief in the earlier passage comes through. This alone could provide motivation enough for once again taking up his pen. He is looking forward to seeing friends and family in Virginia. He is going home. His audience is changing to his family and friends.

Lewis's journal entries remain businesslike, even though his exasperation with the crowds of Indians continuously surrounding them becomes evident and seems to grow. At one point he reports pummeling a man who attempts to steal an iron socket for a canoe pole (?), and he threatens to shoot the next man who tries to steal anything. He accuses some chiefs of stealing horses, which, it turns out, have wandered off on their own, but he reveals no remorse for the false accusation. Members of one tribe even steal Seaman, and in fury he orders a pursuing party to fire upon them, if necessary, to get the dog back (they do, and this is the last time Seaman is ever mentioned—what does happen to him?). There are many entries that coolly report on the usual business of the expedition as well, but, curiously enough, no real expressions of joy or anticipation beyond that New Year's Day passage.

The Columbia on the trip home was no less dangerous, in spite of the fact that they were headed upstream, because the water was higher and the current stronger than in the fall. As if tired of fighting it, the party proceeded along the southern bank by land, whenever possible. It was with genuine relief that they got clear of the Columbia and once again returned to the Nez Perce, whose behavior differed so radically from the river tribes. Not only were they friendly and generous, but they were scrupulously honest as well, qualities more appreciated by the party than ever. The horses they had left behind in the fall were awaiting them, having been cared for by the tribe (although the care became a source of friction between two chiefs), and one brave even brought them two canisters of powder his dog had dug up from the cache.

The good feeling was reciprocal. The memory of Clark's ministrations to the sick on the trip west remained alive, and crowds of people greeted him each morning. Remember, it was Lewis who had the rudimentary medical instruction and maintained the supply of medications; it was Lewis's mother who raised the garden of medicinal herbs and passed on her lore to her son. But Clark assumed this role, modest about his accomplishments, but effective nevertheless in the treatment of "schrofla, ulsers, rhumitism, Sore eyes, and the loss of the use of their Limbs". His most spectacular case involved a paralyzed chief whose appetite and pulse remained constant, and who was restored to movement primarily by the use of medications and sweat baths. He also had successes with a serious illness of Bratton and a growth on the neck of Sakagawea's baby. Each morning of their stay among the Nez Perce he held office hours: "a great number of men women & Children were wateing and requesting medical assistance maney of them with the most Simple Complaints which could be easily releived, independent of maney with disorders intirely out of the power of Medison…" (VII, 243, 245-250). The captains sensibly speculated that many of these ailments resulted from the diet of the Nez Perce, especially their lack of meat. Clark tells us in considerable detail what he prescribes for various people and that "all of those pore people thought themselves much benefited by what had been done for them" (VII, 273).

Again, however, Clark did not lose his sense of balance when he was treated as a miracle worker. He had taken obvious satisfaction in his ability to help, and even an evident pleasure at the exercise of rational, diagnostic skills. Not incidentally, he had been able to provide a service that has brought the party badly needed food now that trade goods were just about depleted. But there was never an indication that he allowed his successes to go to his head, to see himself a magician or divine being, as the Nez Perce were doing. Instead, he appeared to be mildly amused by his status while living in this relative paradise, where the party remained longer than at any place other than the winter forts. In an uncharacteristic passage, Lewis notices that the "quawmash" is in bloom and "it resembles lakes of fine clear water, so complete is this deseption that on first sight I could have sworn it was water" (VIII, 22). Such is the transforming power of peacefulness. The tranquility made the thought of leaving and once again crossing "those Snowey tremendious mountains" all the more daunting. Clark says, "even now I Shudder with the expectation with great difficuelties in passing those Mountains"; compare this with Lewis's milder "I am still apprehensive that the snow and the want of food for our horses will prove a serious imbarrassment to us" (VIII, 24). Even while they had been regaining their health and enjoying athletic contests with their friendly hosts, the memory of the ordeal of the previous fall hung over them; Lewis had recorded in May the following: "I am pleased at finding the river rise so rapidly, it now doubt is attributeable to the melting snows of the mountains; that icy barrier which *seperates me from my friends and country*, from all which makes life esteemable.—patience, patience—" (italics added; VII, 267). Clark's entry varies to some extent; he borrows Lewis's "icy barrier," but adds a passage on his consultations with the Indians as to when they may be able to cross.

When they left in early June, against the advice of the Nez Perce, they found that they had to return because the snow was still too deep. This was the only time in the two and a half years of the expedition that they had to backtrack. A couple of weeks later they set off again, this time with a Nez Perce celebration on their behalf, when trees were lit afire, so that the scene looked like a display of fireworks, beautiful against the backdrop of the night. The object, they were told, was to insure fair weather for their journey, and there was no word of doubt or belittlement of this superstition from the captains (VIII, 50); are the men less susceptible to magic?—none of the other journals mention the burning trees).

The area of their camp is today on the small reservation granted to the Nez Perce after their surrender to the Army, the heroic and tragic story of Chief Joseph's outwitting and outfighting the white men, who had to humble his people in order to assert their control. The region is occupied with many small sawmill towns. The occasional clear-cut is visible, not so ugly as in Oregon, where the steepness of the hillsides has created erosion, which prevents anything else from growing, but ugly enough. For some reason driving up the Lolo Trail on Highway 12 is less satisfying than driving down. Logging trucks clog the highway, and by mid-morning the strobe-like effect of sunlight flashing through the trees tires the eyes. There are fewer rafts visible running the river, and driving against the current doesn't seem as exciting as following it. Probably it all has to do with the time of day, since I always seem to hit this stretch of highway later in the day going up than coming down. At any rate, it is easy to sympathize with Clark's epic-like recital of the descent (not found in Lewis):

> Descended the mountain to Travelers rest leaveing those tremendious mountaines behind us—in passing of which we have experienced Cold and hunger of which I shall ever remember. <as we> in passing over this part of the Rocky mountains from Clarks river, to the quawmash flats from the 14th to the 19th of Septr. 1805 we marched through Snow...in addition to the [c]old rendered the air cool and

the way difficuelt. Our food was horses of which we eate three.—(VIII, 68).

Even if I have seen snow at the summit, I have at least been able to travel a dry and clear highway and picnic from my cooler chest on the way down.

About ten miles from the hot springs, the city of Missoula has grown up on the banks of the west-flowing Clark's Fork River. The town has become notorious or desirable in Montana, depending on one's point of view. East of the Divide people tend to speak of it as home for crazies of all sorts, especially ones drugged by alcohol or controlled substances, and to be avoided at all costs. Undoubtedly, the University of Montana, hardly known as a radical bastion but different in habits from much of the state, has contributed to the reputation. A group of fine writers has clustered around the University, which developed one of the first and most successful writing programs in the nation, and these people, being communicators, have helped create an aura of doom, which in turn can lead to a dangerous freedom.[3] To an outsider, the reputation seems highly exaggerated. Although there are the requisite number of seedy bars around town, and the incidence of long hair is higher than in Montana's general population, class-change time at the University exhibits a remarkable number of straight-appearing students crossing the campus. And one of its nationally known programs, forestry, is hardly famous for producing or even tolerating, far-out crazies. Still, the reputation persists and appears to be proudly nurtured by some in the community.

After reaching the summit and indulging in the Lolo warm springs (and learning of the "barbaric" custom of leaping from the baths into the cold stream), the captains revealed their plans for further exploration.

They may have been going home, but plenty remained to be done. It is possible that, since their main mission, to find a commercially practicable route to the Pacific, had been a failure, they felt driven to bring back as much other news as they could. At any rate, they were to engage in several missions by dividing the total party into three roughly equal groups. First, they wanted to find a shorter practical route from the Lolo Pass to the Missouri, and Lewis did so. The route his party of ten took to the Great Falls, based on information from the Indians, cut about 400 miles from the return journey. The rest went with Clark to recover the cache at Camp Fortunate, at which point Clark's group again divided, with half going to the Great Falls to the caches there, while the remainder, including Clark and ten others, followed the course of the Yellowstone to the Missouri. At this point, the plan was to reunite the entire party, with the exception of three of Clark's group, who were to return immediately to the Mandan villages with the horses and a letter to a British trader trusted by the captains, who they hoped could convince some Sioux chiefs to return to Washington. Why explore the Yellowstone? Because Lewis had told Jefferson from Fort Mandan that they would, since they had heard stories of the abundance of furs in that area.

But the last mission, the exploration of the Marias River, was the most problematic of all. Jefferson had claimed that the captains should pay special attention to rivers entering the Missouri from the south. And there is some attention given to the Kansas, the Platte, and the Yellowstone. But far more often, there is keen interest in rivers from the north—the James, the Vermillion, the Milk, and especially the Marias, which had appeared to be the course of the Missouri when they first encountered it. Could Jefferson have intentionally tried to confuse readers of the semi-public document containing the expedition's charge? Some have thought so. The Louisiana Purchase included all land drained by the Missouri River and its tributaries, and so it was necessary to discover precisely where those tributaries came from to determine what land was in fact United States territory. The British in the north were already poised to move further into the interior in pursuit of furs. Borders needed to be established by exploration and, hopefully, by settlement, as soon as possible. The Marias exploration, then, was to serve a useful political purpose, even though it was dangerous.

But was Lewis prudent in the manner he chose to accomplish it? Because the number of horses had been reduced to ten (seven had disappeared before the portage around the Falls), he decided to take only three men with him into the depths of the Blackfeet hunting grounds. The Blackfeet were to known to be hostile to just about everybody. (The story that later Blackfeet hatred of the white man stemmed from the incident with Lewis is questionable, since they were widely known to be the grumpiest tribe in the northwest long before this.) Lewis and his men were able to determine that the Marias did not drain an area much beyond the latitude of 48 °, 40'N., not as far as hoped to provide a buffer against the British trading posts in Saskatchewan, but it was apparent from their earlier travels upstream to find the course of the Missouri that the Marias had its source to the west, not the north. Further verification was not essential.Maybe Lewis was counting on the fact that Indians had been so scarce in the entire Montana region on the way west. Maybe he thought that speed and firepower would suffice. Maybe he wanted to make up for the failure as an officer in the U.S. Army in giving up his identity in order to persuade the Shoshonis. Maybe he was simply trusting to luck once again. But this time it ran out. Lewis intimates as much, when he tells us on the day before the encounter why he couldn't take a proper reading: "as if the fates were against me my chronometer from some unknown cause stoped today, when I set her to going she went as usual" (VII, 127). The events to come, then, are preceded by an omen of almost supernatural proportions.

The story of that edgy encounter with the Blackfeet band, their attempts to steal weapons and horses, the ensuing violence when two of the Indians were killed, one knifed by Reuben Fields, the other shot by Lewis, and the headlong flight from a larger band of Blackfeet just over the horizon is a classic tale in the best traditions of the western. And the adventure itself certainly broke the monotony of their lives on the Great Plains. But we have to wonder if it was worth the risk. Like the plan to explore the trail to Santa Fe during the winter of 1804, which courted even greater intervention by the Spanish (we know there were Spanish troops combing the territory later hunting for the expedition), like that occasion when Lewis was a courier in the Ohio Territory and had to flee for his life through hostile Indian lands, even like some of those dangerous cliff-climbing episodes where he fell or almost fell, Lewis from time to time seemed to enjoy the thrill of danger for its own sake.

After riding about 120 miles in a 24-hour period, they neared the Missouri and heard the rifles of their hunters. The boat party Clark had sent downriver had arrived, so that the total contingent now numbered twenty, probably enough to repel any attack from the Blackfeet, especially since the canoes were available for a fast getaway. Lewis even had meat from the vast buffalo and elk herds they passed through cooked for the following day, when they stopped for the evening, making an extra 15 miles a day possible. They made no further forays away from the River and arrived at the mouth of the Yellowstone in just over a week. But the "chapter of accidents" has not closed. Clark was ahead of him, having moved downstream from the Yellowstone because of a shortage of game and a surplus of mosquitoes. The party was still separated.

Monday, August 11, was one of the lowest points of the entire expedition for Lewis. There was little game visible until Lewis shot a swimming buffalo, which turned out to be unfit for food. He next spotted a grizzly and landed the canoe to kill it, but it ran away. He was unable to get a successful reading of the sun with his instruments. Finally, the party encountered a herd of elk on a thick willow bar. Lewis shot one, and as he tracked it down, he was wounded by a ball, which hit him in the left thigh and right buttocks, causing a painful wound. He was sure that Cruzatte, one-eyed and nearsighted, had mistaken him for an elk and called out "damn you, you have shot me." But there was no answer, so there was the possibility that Indians had ambushed him. He made his way painfully back to the canoe, informed the men, armed himself with his rifle, his pistol, and the air gun and "determined...to sell my life as deerly as possible" (VIII, 155). After about twenty minutes of suspense the hunters returned with Cruzatte and reported that there were no signs of Indians. Lewis in anger demanded to know why Cruzatte had not heard his cries and even entertained the suspicion that the shooting was intentional, that in modern parlance, he had been "fragged." In considerable pain, he tried to stretch out in the canoe, but there was no comfortable position possible, and he felt a fever coming on, which would make it impossible for him to sleep. To top off the day, another note from Clark indicated that Pryor had been robbed of the horses and escaped downriver in a bullboat he had made. But without horses he was unable to go on ahead to the Mandan villages, and so the plan to enlist the British trader's assistance in persuading Sioux chiefs to visit Washington had to be abandoned—another failure. But the next day Lewis's party overtook Clark's and "found them all well." The concern he felt at "parting from my worthy friend and companion" had ended (VIII, 158). But writing had become painful for him, and he announced that he was giving up to Clark the task of keeping the journal.

Meanwhile, Clark's trip to the Yellowstone and downstream was comparatively routine. In five days they moved from Travelers' Rest to Camp Fortunate, the site of their successful meeting with the Shoshonis almost a year earlier, a distance, Clark estimated, of 164 miles. They recovered from the cache there several canoes and some tobacco, which cheered the men, who had been without it for about three months. They moved quickly to the Three Forks, where the party divided, with half headed down the Missouri to the Great Falls, while Clark proceeded overland through some of the most fruitful and spectacular country yet encountered to the Bozeman Pass, joining the Yellowstone near the site of present-day Livingston. Sacagawea was familiar with this territory and was of considerable help. They had encountered frost, and some of the horses disappeared one night, but they were found a few days later with no sign of Indian activity, as Clark had feared. They were in the heart of Crow country, and the Crows were noted even more than the Blackfeet as horse thieves. They traversed much rocky terrain, so that some horses' hooves were worn down so badly that Clark instructed the men to make elkskin booties for the worst afflicted. But the problem was soon overwhelmed by another: one morning they arose to find half the horses gone, this time not to be recovered and presumed stolen by the Crows. Unlike the previous summer, signs of Indians had been all around them. After sending a four-man party overland with the remaining horses, Clark completed the building of canoes and sped downstream to the proposed rendezvous with Lewis at the mouth of the Yellowstone. After a few days' confusion (because Clark had pushed past the confluence in search of game and fewer mosquitoes), Clark laconically notes on August 12, "at meridian Capt. Lewis hove in Sight with the party..." (VIII, 290).

It is interesting to note how the character of Clark's journal writing changed during this period. He seemed to feel liberated to be himself once again instead of copying Lewis. On the first day out of Travelers' Rest he once again was sizing up the fruitfulness of the territory and noted how fond the horses were of a particular species of clover. He was full of wonder at the "tremendious chain of Rocky Mountains white with snow" and the "butifull extensive vallies" rich with a variety of plants and flowers. When he encountered an abrupt rock formation along the River he named it after Sacajawea's baby, "Pompey's Pillar," and carved his name and the date, which remain to this day the only one of the many signatures of the party still visible, although it has been necessary to protect it from defacement by a screen and plastic plate installed by the railroad, whose tracks pass by (VIII, 225). In fact, it is the only undeniable trace of the expedition still in existence. Unlike Lewis, who never mentions it, Clark tells us what the downstream traders have related of the warfare between the Mandans, Arikaras, and

Minitaris, whom, the captains believed, they had persuaded to live together in peace. The grand alliance against the Teton Sioux, one of the most important objectives of the entire trip, had unraveled almost immediately after the party left. Clark could handle bad news as well as good without panic or undue emotionalism. He tended Lewis's wound and they made it to the site of Fort Mandan in two more days.

The Yellowstone Basin today is the center of economic growth in Montana. Billings, an energy town, is the center for oil development, pumping, and refining from several huge fields in the Montana-North Dakota area. At the same time, hundred-car strings of loaded coal-cars leave regularly from the extensive freight yards, the result of the region's surface mining. Billings has passed Great Falls and Butte as the state's largest city, and there seems no slowdown in sight. It has in common with other boomtowns the energy and rawness of a new place. Further upriver lies Bozeman, which has become something of an upscale community, with small agribusiness and information technology firms fueling its revival, as well as the growth of Montana State University as a major factor in the area's economy. Not to be ignored, either, are the wealthy persons, movie stars, retirees, and others, who have bought up much of the surrounding area, especially near the ski centers, and shop in the boutiques of the city. I think I have seen more BMW's here than anywhere else in Montana. Bozeman is well in the running for the most spectacular city setting in the nation, between the Big Belts to the north and the looming Absarokas to the south, together with range after range of Rockies to the west. It is an appropriate setting for the excellent Museum of the Rockies, at the edge of the University campus. For some, however, the valley is getting too crowded. Livingston, about twenty miles further east and on the highway to Yellowstone Park's northwest entrance, is rapidly graduating from tourist ticky-tack to a fashionable address.

Apart from a few settlements along the rivers (the Musselshell and Powder and Rosebud, as well as the Yellowstone) and the sites of mines and oil fields, eastern Montana is virtually empty grazing country. While driving along these back roads I have had a pronghorn, apparently bored by so much space, race my car for a ways. Passing through crossroads places like Ingomar or Grass Range, I have noticed every head turn to watch my car go by. When travelling east, it seems like a major center has been reached when arriving at Miles City, with its historic downtown, it community college, its Range Riders Museum, and its government livestock research facilities. I have met people in a campground here from California who have come for the hunting and people from Illinois looking for a homestead. Further downriver, near the Dakota border, are the towns of Glendive and Sidney, both dominated by agriculture services—the area around Sidney is heavily planted in sugar beets, while the yellow blossoms of canola or maybe mustard (it's hard for a novice to tell the difference) brightened my last trip along the River. Jonathan Raban's fine book, *Bad Land*, is set in country not far from here and conveys well the special quality of life, or perhaps the lack of life. It nevertheless can become hypnotic.

After reuniting all its members, the expedition sped downriver on the current, making the Mandan villages in two days. Here they encountered some old friends among the Indians, but they found that peace among the tribes had barely lasted until they were out of sight. Their fort had burned down. The party began to break up, as Colter asked and received permission to return upriver to make his fortune (and his niche in history, as survivor of the famous chase by Indians while he was naked and as the "discoverer" of what was to become

Yellowstone Park). Charbonneau and Sakagawea prepared to return to their home among the Mandans. Arrangements were discussed for Pomp to come to St. Louis in a year, to live with Clark, who would supervise his education. As the party continued downstream (with one Mandan chief and his retinue), they had an ugly if minor encounter with the Teton Sioux, whom Clark found it necessary to threaten ("keep away from the river or we Should kill every one of them &c. &c."). The Sioux, Clark tells us, "blackguarded" them (i.e. "reviled them in scurrilous language", according to one dictionary), but were apparently not numerous enough this time to cause any real trouble (VIII, 349). When they arrived at Sergeant Floyd's grave, they found it opened and left only partly covered. Clark dismissed the possibility that animals had done this, believing instead that a Sioux chief had opened the grave to bury his dead son with Floyd, thereby hoping to share in the white man's future life, which he supposed to be happier than the Sioux'. Trader after trader was encountered heading up the Missouri, which was fast becoming a busy highway. Meanwhile, the party received the news of a nation considerably altered since they had left: General Wilkinson, Wayne's second-in-command during Clark's tenure in Ohio (Clark knew him and at one time admired him), had become Governor of the Louisiana Territory and had engaged in a standoff with Spanish troops in Texas (he was also a spy in the pay of the Spanish); the British warship *Leander* had fired on an American merchantman off New York Harbor, bringing the real possibility of war; Aaron Burr had killed Alexander Hamilton in a duel (VIII, 346). All these events would influence the captains' futures.

And then, suddenly, it was over. On September 20, the party saw some cows on the bank, "which Caused a Shout to be raised for joy," and then the village of La Charette came into view (VIII, 367). Amid the feasting and dancing the villagers sponsored that evening, Lewis and Clark learned that they had been given up as lost by the entire world. The next day they arrived at St. Charles, where the Expedition had

officially started from two years, four months, and five days earlier.
They were greeted joyously by the entire town and more partying
ensued. They moved on to Fort Bellfontaine the following day, a fort
which had been established just the previous year as the first army post
west of the Mississippi, by Wilkinson as a base for Indian trade and
military deployment. Here they were able to requisition some
appropriate clothing for the Indian chief and his party and for
themselves as well. Then on September 23, a Thursday, they paid a brief
visit to Camp Wood, where they had spent the first winter of 1803-04,
before sailing back across the Mississippi to St. Louis. The entire
population lined the banks to cheer for them. Their first response was
to plunge into socializing and then letter writing. Clark's final words in
his Journal were these: "a fine morning we commenced wrighting &c."
(VIII, 372). There was still much ahead: the trip to Washington for a
first-hand report to Jefferson, visits to homes and loved ones. But more
immediately, the details of wrapping up the expedition occupied them.
They had to pay off the men and discharge them. All the equipment and
supplies remaining were auctioned off. News had to be exchanged with
the traders who were heading up the Missouri. But the winding down
from their way of life for two and a half years, we can speculate, must
have made all this practical business seem like a dream. It is not difficult
to understand their state. Whenever I have returned from my forays
along the trail, I can barely comprehend the rolling green hills of
Western New York, even while I rejoice in reaching them. I always feel
disoriented for a few days, too, at the lack of a genuine horizon and a
westering breeze.

Did the Nez Perce's burning of the trees bring luck to Lewis and
Clark? Since they returned safely, the answer appears to be obvious. In
later life Clark moved from one success to another, overcoming his bitter
disappointment at not receiving the rank he was promised; we learn of
the depth of his sense of betrayal from a letter written years later and
cited in Biddle's edition of the Expedition's history.[4] He became a trusted

and successful public servant and leader, and a friend to all western Indians, whose lives he tried to improve. In addition, he married the girl of his dreams and raised a fine family. Even so, he experienced more than his share of family sorrows with the death of two wives and several of his children. For Lewis it was a different story. His wounding by Crusatte took on almost mythic proportions. After the celebrations ended, he was left with the governorship of the Louisiana Territory, a job he was not well suited for and not happy with, almost besieged by ambitious subordinates and greedy profit seekers and apparently abandoned by Jefferson, who seemed to have lost interest in him. He was not able to ready the journals for publication, whether from procrastination or misfortune, a subject that deserves further exploration. He could not find the right woman interested in marriage, although he tried very hard. And three years after returning from the Pacific, he was dead. For him, the appropriate analogy is not the burning trees of the Nez Perce but the charred remains of Fort Mandan.

1   John Bakeless, *Lewis and Clark: Partners in Discovery* (Mineola, Dover Publications, 1996 [1947]), p.302. See also Letters, I, 300, and Appleman, p.202.

2   Cf. Ordway's account, IX, 278. Ronda, pp.211–212.

3   An interesting survey of Montana writing is found in William W. Bevis, *Ten Tough Trips: Montana Writers and the West* (Seattle, University of Washington Press, 1990). On "doom" see esp. pp.8–9.

4   "Memoir of William Clark by Dr. Coues," *History*, I, lxxii.

CHAPTER 12

"The Only True America"

…You have navigated bold & unknown rivers, traversed Mountains, which had never before been impressed with the footsteps of civilized man, and surmounted every obstacle, which climate, Nature, or ferocious Savages could throw in your way. You have the further satisfaction to Reflect that, you have extended the knowledge of the Geography of your Country; in other respects enriched Science; and opened to the United States a source of inexhaustible wealth….You have uniformly respected the rights of humanity, actuated by principles of genuine philanthropy, you have not sprinkled your path with the blood of unoffending savages.

Address to Lewis and Clark by Pat Lockhart, Chairman,
By order & on behalf of the Citizens of Fincastle, Virginia
8th of January 1807[1]

And so they were back. But what did it all add up to? What did they accomplish? Nobody seemed quite sure. Two days after their landing at

St. Louis, a banquet was given in honor of the party, followed by a splendid ball. The newspaper account of this event (in the Frankfort, Kentucky paper, since there was none in St. Louis yet) didn't quite know what to say, except "what [respect] is not due to those who penetrate the gloom of unexplored regions, to expel the mists of ignorance which envelope science, and overshadow their country?" From the reported eighteen toasts, it is clear that those present didn't have a clue. There is repeated a vague hope that the expedition will be good for business. Celebrations of Christopher Columbus, the Capital of the United States, Agriculture and Industry, and the fair daughters of Louisiana (the latter at the end of a good deal of drinking) all follow.[2] Beyond the captains' personal bravery and endurance, their achievement seemed shrouded in uncertainty.

By December 2 President Jefferson included testimony to the explorers in his message to Congress, but here, too, there is some interesting ambiguity. In his initial instructions to Lewis, Jefferson had focussed on one goal above all others: "The object of your mission is to explore the Missouri river…as, by it's course and communication with the waters of the Pacific ocean…may offer the most direct & practicable water communication across this continent for the purposes of commerce." Virtually everything else is an amplification or a refinement of this aim. And it is here that the expedition failed most completely. There was no direct and practicable water route, and even Lewis, in his official report to the President, had to concede that, except for articles "not bulky brittle nor of a very perishable nature," the sea route around the Cape of Good Hope was still to be preferred. Deprived of this accomplishment, Jefferson could only say that the expedition "has had all the success which could have been expected," and so he shifts to the undisputed geographical knowledge, the "character" of the country, and the knowledge of the inhabitants found there. Later, in other communications, Jefferson will celebrate the knowledge of plants and animals gained, but there is no mention of "scientific" advances here. It is also interesting to note that he cut from a draft of this message the specifics of the adventure, together with a more detailed description of their activities, preferring a short, generalized statement.[3] By the very flatness of his remarks he seems to second Henry Adams's judgement on the expedition almost a hundred years later: "they added little to the stock of science or wealth.... The crossing of the continent was a great feat, but was nothing more."[4] Adams goes on to find the development of the steamboat by Robert Fulton that summer far more important for the opening of the west.

There is evidence for Adams's judgement. Not only was the hope for commerce thwarted by the discovery that there was no viable Northwest Passage, but the necessary concomitant for commerce, the cementing of alliances with Indian tribes, was only partially successful and therefore not really successful at all. In addition to the enmity earned when Lewis killed the Blackfoot brave, the argument with the Teton Sioux was never resolved, so that on the return trip, each shook fists at the other as the expedition kept to the water in passing. The promised truce between the Mandans and the Arikaras was broken almost as soon as the party left Fort Mandan, and the Columbia River tribes, while not particularly hostile to the Americans, saw no advantage in exclusively dealing with them. The friendly Shoshonis and Flatheads had vanished. Only with the Nez Perce and perhaps the Yankton Sioux were the kinds of relationship the captains sought truly formed. The British still traded extensively with the Plains Indians, especially in inferior guns, and they continued to dominate the commerce around the mouth of the Columbia. When the Astoria settlement was formed by the American fur trade a few years later, it lasted only briefly before the British took over. Only the fact that they weren't interested in settlement at this time but in trade alone prevented the territory from permanently coming under the Union Jack. No matter how good Clark's maps were, they were not needed by the mountain men and trappers first traversing the west, who followed Indian trails and compared notes with each other to learn their way. And the promise of contributions to science by the discovery of new plant species and animals, except for a few that made it back from Fort Mandan, was thwarted for almost a century by the failure of the publication of this information.

But success and failure need to be measured on a sliding scale. In fact, the nation that the explorers returned to in 1806 was considerably different from the one they left in 1803. Jefferson was first occupied in reshaping the direction of the government, which involved immediately eliminating all taint of "English" or monarchical-appearing ways, the antithesis of republicanism. This meant removing as many opportunities for corruption as possible, and the way to accomplish this was to shrink governmental expenditures to new lows. At the same time, the republican ideal was best served by the expansion of the population into new lands, not only to advance the idea of independent yeomen subsisting by their own efforts, but also to create agricultural surpluses. These, in turn, were to be at the heart of foreign trade, which was to bring prosperity to all. In Jefferson's vision, New England was the past, the West the future. The Louisiana Purchase was the key to it all, so far as the distant future of the republic was concerned. Jefferson believed that settlement west of the Mississippi would not begin for a hundred years, until land up to the River was developed, but he also saw that control of the Mississippi meant that the Old Northwest could prosper by means of the river trade.

But by 1806, the emphasis had changed from foreign trade. The first news of the larger world Lewis and Clark received as they neared the end of their journey was of General Wilkinson's marching against the Spanish and the British firing upon an American merchantman, practically in New York Harbor, killing an American seaman. Moreover, Napoleon, in spite of his lack of interest in the United States, was causing all kinds of problems by arbitrary definitions of what cargoes could be confiscated by the French. It was touch-and-go to see whether war would come first with the British or the French. At the same time, Aaron

Burr, no longer Vice President, was creating mischief in the west by recruiting a private army to attack Spanish holdings, maybe even conquer Mexico, and perhaps break off the western states to form a new nation. The issues to be confronted were quite different and considerably more complicated, less capable of quick action than those of 1803.

The accomplishments of Lewis and Clark in opening up the West, then, proved to be no longer so relevant to the questions at hand. Political leaders must always cope with the immediate; the long-range vision waits in the wings. This, I think, accounts for what appears to be a coolness in Jefferson's description of the expedition and his apparent lack of further interest in its results. Once it was clear there was to be no immediate quantum leap in commerce by means of a northwestern passage, Jefferson undoubtedly did focus his attention elsewhere. The West was primarily for another day. When the rounds of celebratory banquets were completed and Lewis and Clark suitably rewarded (it was assumed) by government posts in St. Louis, any action on their findings could be deferred (although there was still the entertainment of Indian chiefs in Washington to be attended to). The posts—Lewis as Governor of the Louisiana Territory and Clark as Indian agent for the Territory and brigadier general of the Louisiana militia—were important in themselves but, as we shall see, frustrating and lacking in support from Washington. We do have Jefferson's protestations that he had not heard frequently enough from Lewis, and it is true that there are very few surviving letters. But it is highly probable that Lewis felt ignored, perhaps even betrayed, by Jefferson, in the matter of the government's failure to honor some expenses for the expedition. If he had cared to exert himself, Jefferson could have easily settled these matters. Later Clark expressed his wounded pride that Jefferson never delivered on the promised commission as Captain (and much of his life was to be dedicated to coping with the failure of Virginia and the federal government to reimburse his brother George Rogers Clark's debts on behalf of the public good). Jefferson's decrease in interest is understandable, but so is Lewis' coolness to his patron. There is some suggestion that Jefferson sent Lewis to Burr's treason trial in order to receive trustworthy reports of the proceedings, but this is the only significant relationship between the two after the expedition's return that we have heard about.[5]

As so often has been the case in our past, the people were not waiting for governmental policy to become formalized. We have seen that on their return Lewis and Clark had already encountered numerous travelers heading up the Missouri, and some of their own number never came back to St. Louis, preferring instead to test their fortune in the west. The Missouri was becoming a busy highway. Pike and his company had returned in April from exploring the sources of the Mississippi just a few months earlier, whereupon General Wilkinson sent them out again in July to the headwaters of the Arkansas and Red Rivers. Settlers were crossing the Mississippi in growing numbers for places such as the Cape Girardeau, St. Louis and St. Charles areas, and the Indiana and Illinois Territories were not to remain wilderness much longer. Already this country was becoming bewilderingly untidy.

If the world around them was rapidly changing, what about the explorers themselves? Had they changed? It would take an insensitive clod not to be affected by the vision of those vast buffalo herds stretching to the horizon, and the exhilaration and awe resulting from the experience of the Rockies' snow peaks cannot help but alter one's inner landscape as well. But can we find evidence of changes beyond this inevitable enlargement of one's soul? In one case, Clark's, I think we can, but with Lewis I am not so sure.

Remember that these men are from the same background of Virginia republicanism, where character was determined by one's dedication to a careful blend of individual initiative with public responsibility. A man looked after his family, often his extended family, by stewardship of the land, which often meant acquiring more and more of it. He acted so as to secure freedom of expression and freedom from particular religious constraints, but public good always meant civic good; there was rarely any confusion about private interests inevitably fulfilling the public betterment, as was soon to become the case in the burgeoning market economy. Manners were important as a measure of respect for others, and education was valued for what it could contribute to self-awareness, as well as to the furthering of enlightenment ideals. But such a view of the world was virtually an anachronism by 1806. Even before this, the Founding Fathers like Adams and Jefferson had realized that the revolutionary values they had subscribed to were mostly of the past. The "empire of liberty" coming into being was not what Jefferson foresaw at all. Instead, it was emerging as the freedom to make a buck in a hurry by speculation, trade, and even sharp dealing. This frenzy of moneymaking, unparalleled in the past (although a frequent theme of American life ever since), must have been baffling to those still attempting to cling to classical republican ideals of civic virtue.

There was another world view available to Lewis and Clark, that of the Native Americans, who in their notions of the special relation between people and the natural world and the animism of that world, provided an alternative to both republicanism and the modern market economy. As we have seen, Lewis was rarely very receptive to Native American ways of viewing the world or even very interested in them, except as curiosities. His extended discussions of their habits, dress, customs, and language almost never get beyond the level of scientific description, that is, treatment of them as *objects*. Not only did he persist in addressing them in the paternalistic mode of the father speaking to children, but also he was personally offended by their presence, their smell and greasiness, as his repugnance of the "national hug" indicates. Indians were distanced by being called "those yellow gentlemen," and Sacagawea is almost never considered a person. I have discussed the shock to his beliefs when he finds it necessary to change garments, even identities, with Cameahwait, and how he may well have intuited this act as the turning point in his life. Nothing goes as he hoped from this moment on, including his death, be it suicide or murder, on the forlorn Natchez Trace.

But it has been demonstrated that Clark responds differently to the Native Americans. True, when it was his turn to play the anthropologist, he, too, could treat them as objects. He shared in the formal language (scripted by Jefferson) of addressing assembled tribes as children of the Great Father in Washington. But time after time he revealed openness to the very different outlook of the Indian. He understood without losing his equilibrium the Nez Perce treatment of him as a god in providing medical care. He was interested in the connection made between his shooting of the bird and the Columbia tribe's association with a divine omen. He alone told us of the Arikaras' belief in the talking rock. Over and over again, tribes intuitively recognized in Clark a special friend, climaxing in his treatment by the Shoshonis, who braided seashells in his hair. Although Clark was so angered by the Teton Sioux that he was ready to fire on them, it was a justified anger, which had resulted from man-to-man provocation, not the imposition of a domineering will. It is Clark who immediately credited the heroic acts of Sacagawea and who developed a special relation with her and her son, to the point where he will eventually assume charge of "Pomp's" education. On returning he will become superintendent of Indian Affairs in the Louisiana Territory for the rest of his life, even when he did not hold the title. There was little indication in his earlier life, whether in Virginia, at Fallen Timbers or Greenville, down the Ohio to Memphis, or in the Kentucky-Indiana region of his family's holdings, that Clark was to know and respect Indian ways to this extent. In all likelihood, he gained this respect on the trail, and this was one significant result of the journey west.

In the new Lewis and Clark Interpretive Center at Great Falls, the display is unusual in that on one side of the aisle the history of the American Indian is depicted, and on the other the Europeans, including Lewis and Clark. The equal importance thereby posed seemed to me at the time I first saw it to be an exercise in political correctness. But I was wrong. Time after time in our respective histories these two cultures have not only influenced each other, but also depended on each other. And if my view of Lewis and Clark has any merit, here is a case in point. I have tried to show that the life of each man after the return from the west was in large measure *determined* by his response to encounters with Native Americans. Clark's entire future career was shaped by his attempt to implement a policy toward Indians that would encourage their integration into American life and deter their association with the British and Spanish, and to do so in a manner as thoughtful of their well-being as that of the nation. While there were failures to halt the depredations of both whites and Indians, and while future history did not follow the Jeffersonian vision for Native Americans, Clark could rest easy as his life ended that he had been a sometimes-effective voice on their behalf. As for Lewis, when his expectation of national recognition and financial security faded after his return (as well as hopes for domestic tranquility; Lewis was always looking for a wife and deeply disturbed that no woman he deemed worthy would have him), he found himself enmeshed in a detail-ridden job governing the Territory while surrounded by fault-finders and scoundrels, and hounded by financial affairs he would rather have ignored. The journal of the expedition remained unpublished, not, I think, the result of procrastination, as is usually charged, but because the part of it of genuine value to Lewis, the *scientific observations*, were rough and needed the revision of experts, who were not available to help. Lewis apparently bought into Jefferson's words on the importance of these observations, which, after all, had furnished the public justification of the expedition. Maybe he genuinely believed this was his purpose. Surely, he appreciated the company and the praise of the scientific establishment in Philadelphia. When Gass's journal (as well as Private Frazier's) was rumored to be on the verge of publication, Lewis (probably with the assistance of Jefferson) immediately advertised how incomplete and partial any such account would be, because Gass knew nothing of scientific matters. His mean-spirited utterance has usually been viewed as a response to the loss of any profits, especially since he had already collected money by means of subscriptions. But it can also be seen as a more substantial comment on what he believed the expedition to be about.[6] To Lewis, his journal was not the adventure story it has since become, but a record of the people, animals, plants, and geography of this new western world (with occasional memorable reflections on the responsibilities of command). The tribes encountered along the way are to be viewed in this light, not as participants or adversaries or friends, but as objects of study, along with the prairie dog and the salmon.

The Journals of the two men have from time to time been viewed as an American *Odyssey*. If we are thinking of a superficial metaphor for a tale of adventure, the designation makes some sense, at least for Clark. Homer's work is about *justice*; as the opening page reveals this is to be the year, the gods tell us, when justice will prevail. Justice demands a *homecoming*, a return, not merely from the past but to a reconciliation with the present. Upon his return Clark's first letter was to his brother and his first visit was to his family. Then he travels to Virginia to woo and win his bride. The story of this romance is affecting. Years earlier, when Julia was only twelve, Clark had come upon her and her cousin stalled in the road by their balky horse, which they were futilely trying to move by swatting him with a stick. Clerk was wiser in the way of horses and got him moving, but he was smitten and immediately knew that some day he would marry this girl. In fact, he ultimately marries both of them;[7] when Julia died after twelve years of marriage, Clark wed the other girl, Harriet, who by this time had been widowed. Clark leads a fulfilling life as a public figure in Missouri and as head of a large and close family, even though he seems to have had more than his share of family tragedies. Clark does roughly compare with Odysseus.

But not Lewis. A more appropriate model for him would be Aeneas. Like Aeneas, he is the dutiful son of his father figure, Jefferson, and he dutifully follows his wishes to found a new nation, to find a new homeland, but only at great personal cost and disappointment. Like Aeneas, too, the great adventure of the quest ends ambiguously, without the satisfaction Lewis thought it would provide. Perhaps there was even a measure of despair, since fulfilling his public obligations had led to the frustration of his private hopes and dreams. Attempts to read the end of Lewis's life in terms of malaria or alcoholism or last minute insanity simply don't satisfy our sense of the man's complexity. If he committed suicide, then it was a fitting continuation of the pattern of self-doubt that had been developing since his thirty-first birthday. If it was murder, then it coincided with a dark fate hounding the once-promising bright young man to deprive him of his future.

At the risk of badly simplifying complex issues, let me suggest that these two polar attitudes towards the west are still very much with us. The older, Jeffersonian notion that the west is a place of pastoral plenty and original innocence, where the corruption and intrigues of the east can be shed and the desert can be made to bloom, still exists in a variety of forms. The endless expanses, the snow-capped peaks, and, more recently, the red-rock canyons are staples of advertising, and this suggests that such images stir consumers. After all, the Marlboro man sold a lot of cigarettes. The physical west has become associated with individual liberation. A belt buckle with a carving of an elk, proclaims "Montana is what America was."[8] What was once expressed in national terms as "manifest destiny" is now translated into terms of personal fulfillment. But more than this, the societies of the new west are presented as models of economic viability. Unburdened by antiquated superstructure and aging construction, and possessing few visible ethnic and class problems, places like Boise or Bozeman are held up as viable models for urban growth. The "New West" profits by the experience of older urban areas and avoids their problems by being born into a different age.

Or, to follow the thinking of Robert Kaplan, the "newest" new West is leading to a future dominated by "suburban pods," vast and shapeless areas of prosperity where development is fueled by direct commercial and intellectual ties with international markets, bypassing traditional forms of cities, free from dominance by state or even national governments. Such places will be concentrations of wealth, where inner cities have no place and commercial areas will be even more dispersed than at present, almost completely detached from their neighboring cities. He finds such pods already in formation in the locales around Omaha and Kansas City, but especially in Orange County and Vancouver. With some modifications, such as a heavy Pacific Rim component on the West Coast, these areas will be remarkably alike. For some of us this vision of homogenized centers of wealth centered in sprawling non-communities, where residential areas must be gated, and the adjacent cities become wastelands of poverty, decay, and dependence, is stupefying and more than a little obscene. St. Louis and Los Angeles are to grow more and more like Teheran and Singapore. Nevertheless, Kaplan may be as right as he is persuasive.[9]

Even as we talk about it, the optimistic view of the west begins to shade into darker hues, and the notion that the west can be any kind of ameliorated paradise begins to disappear. Of course, the West Coast was given up as lost a long time ago, as "Californication" spread, defined mainly by the growth of urban space and characterized by a particular set of dollar-based values leading to self-indulgence and perhaps narcissism. Seattle's "yuppiedom" is a virulent strain of the original. Hopes for the Sierra Nevada and the Great Basin were slower to die, but it has become increasingly apparent to many that the western world has just about vanished. In the most remote Sierra valleys can be found heaps of human garbage, and secluded mountain fastnesses yield gated hideaways of the rich and powerful. In the great forests of Washington and Idaho, helicopters harvest virgin timber. In deep Utah canyons the residue of uranium mining leaves its traces as drilling rigs sink new holes next to national parks and monuments. The gray-brown pall over the Grand Canyon is the result, not of blowing sand, as I once innocently speculated, but of the coal mines nearby and the power plants miles away. Species are disappearing because the habitat needed for survival becomes commercialized in one form or another. Environmentalists constantly have to fight to stave off encroachment after encroachment by those who would build roads, dig mines, and construct power plants, and they sometimes succeed. But all the sensible ones are mindful of David Brower's resonating words, that "In this line of work, all victories are temporary, all defeats permanent."

It is no accident that a group of writers living in the west, some of them among the finest writing today, some of them even natives, express a dark, sometimes even tragic view in their work. Their characters exhibit a measure of self-destructiveness, which reflects despair about themselves and their world, or at the very least, a profound nostalgia for something which has been lost. We could all construct our own list of such writers, but mine would include James Lee Burke and James Crumley, Tom McGuane, Larry Watson, James Welch, Leslie Marmon Silko, maybe Larry McMurtry. Quite often the land itself—in its ruin or its timeless contrast with the human—plays a central role, as in Norman MacLean's *A River Runs Through It* or *Young Men and Fire,* his book about the death of the smoke jumpers at Lewis's very Gates of the Mountains. It sometimes seems today as if a pall of defeat serves as a subtext, a precondition, in writing about the west.[10]

Of interest in this regard, to some, at least, is the development of what its proponents call "new Western history." This subdiscipline purports to take a clear-eyed view of the West, not as frontier or potential Edenic space but instead as a convergence of diverse peoples—women, Indians, Latin Americans, African Americans, Asian Americans, as well as white Europeans—who have been engaged in invasion, exploitation, development, and conquest, with often tragic consequences. At its best, the adherents of the New Western history explore areas that have been

neglected and redress the balance in solid historical writing. At its worst
it becomes thesis-ridden and seems designed to create a space for
reputations to be made in the profession. It takes as its basis a quarrel
with a historian of a hundred years ago, Frederick Jackson Turner, and
his "frontier thesis." It also spends time arguing with a figure of fifty
years ago, Walter Prescott Webb (must historians use three names?), who
developed a view of the West based on its climate and topography. Much
of the polemic appears to be directed against the limitations of
historians themselves, who are the product of their times. A look at the
way we have changed our views of the American Revolution in the last
hundred years, for example, reveals how history is written from the
preconceptions of the era. This doesn't mean we reject the author we
find limited in perspective but only that we understand his or her
limitations while we read. The distaste for Jefferson and Madison that
shines through Henry Adams's monumental history of their
administrations cannot undercut his achievement in helping us to
understand what was occurring. I, for one, still find Adams and DeVoto
and Henry Nash Smith, and Wallace Stegner more useful and satisfying
than the more theoretical constructs in the work of Patricia Limerick or
Richard White. This may be one of the reasons I cannot call myself
a historian!

It does not require profound insight to recognize the distance
between the expectations for the West and the reality of what has
occurred there. Today's West is undeniably built upon the destruction
of previous cultures, the ravaging of the landscape, and the colonization
of its settlers. Having understood that, it is also possible to entertain the
idea that something new can be built upon the ruins of the old. In my
journeys along the path of Lewis and Clark I have been struck time and
time again by the "quality of life" displayed in some towns and cities
there. It is qualitatively different from what I have become accustomed
to accept as the norm during my years of living in the Northeast and the
Old Northwest. I had hoped to study this in detail, but the complexity

of fleshing out my hunches has defeated me. An entire literature has grown up around the urbanization of the West, since the cities are where eighty percent of its population lives. And I don't have the skills or the vocabulary to master it. Another approach would be to live among the people of the West in such towns and get to know them—in general, no people are more accessible and open to strangers—in order to tell their stories. But I don't have the journalistic abilities (in the best sense) of a Timothy Egan or a Blaine Harden for in-depth reportage, either.

And so I am left with my observations and my reading to construct an image of "the only true America." Like Wallace Stegner a generation or so ago, I find some grounds for optimism in the possibility of a fresh burst of life in the communities I visited. The dedication to fishing in Yankton isn't what interests me, but I respect the quest for the record catch. I will never dance along the riverfront in Sioux City, but I am glad there are people who do. I no longer make mountain trails and streams my pursuit, as I would if I lived in Dillon, but to know that I could is important. While I can imagine myself living as part of the arts community in Bismarck or Great Falls, I probably couldn't take the winters. If I chose to live in a city, it might be Portland, or if I looked to the bracing North Pacific, I could see myself in Astoria. What all these places have in common is their *energy*, their pride in doing things, and their cohesiveness. They may be appealing because they only tangentially share the major social problems of today's civic life—racial disharmony, extremes of wealth and poverty, collapsing infrastructures and services, and failing educational systems. And to incline toward them may be only another form of nostalgia. But I would hope not.

I end this investigation with an irony I would like to avoid but cannot. "The only true America" for Thoreau was a totally inward construct, a *personal* vision that each of us is capable of shaping, a projection of our own best place. Yet what emerges from my journey along the Trail is an impression of shared hopes and expectations, as expressed in what I can only call "civic energy." The Romantic impulse ends up looking for Enlightenment order! If it is true that Lewis and Clark "opened up" the West, it must be in some sense beyond economic growth or expanding settlement. Their Trail serves fundamentally as the pathway for the human spirit to flourish. The thinker Northrop Frye was fond of viewing all literature the world has ever produced as parts of one vast poem, whose theme is (I quote from memory) "the end of human effort in fulfilled desire." The Journals of the Expedition fit into that beguiling possibility, and, as such, become richer than the history they are a part of.

Thoreau's comments on "the only true America" remind me of the most important thing I think I have ever learned, the story of Astraea. In the world's Golden Age, so the story runs, Astraea, a divine young virgin dwelt among the people, who lived in perfect harmony. But the harmony did not last, and disputes arose which required mediation. All turned to Astraea, who dispensed such justice that all were satisfied. But in a later age, men began to ignore her judgements and they paid no attention to her in their quest for self-gratification. Ugliness among people and even warfare emerged. Astraea no longer had a place in this Brazen Age, and so she retreated from the earth. She dwelt in the heavens as the constellation Virgo, where she remains visible to this day, to remind anyone who looks upward of what life was once like, and she thereby offers ground for the hope that it may be like that again if she is to return. Her story is one of loss of harmony, but also its potential for coming again. We live amidst the rubble of what is possible, and yet judge our lives from a larger perspective than what we presently see. Landscapes of hope or despair? Lewis and Clark's west helps me to find the former.

1 *Letters*, I, 358.

2 "St. Louis Welcomes Lewis and Clark," in James. P. Ronda, ed., *Voyages of Discovery: Essays on the Lewis and Clark Expedition* (Helena, Montana Historical Society Press, 1998), pp. 203–205.

3 *Letters*, I, 352.

4 Henry Adams, *History of the United States of Americs During the Administrations of Thomas Jefferson* (New York, Library of America, 1986), p. 751.

5 Ambrose, p. 429, following Bakeless, p. 388, state this as a definite fact, but others do not.

6 *Letters*, II, 385–386, 390, 394–397.

7 Bakeless tells this story well, p. 69.

8 Bevis, p. 8.

9 Robert D. Kaplan, *An Empire Wilderness: Travels Into America's Future* (New York, Random House, 1998).

10 Bevis, p. 165.

Acknowledgements

It is impossible to properly give my thanks to the scores of people along the Trail who have contributed to this work. In all walks of life-from waitress to newspaper publisher, minister to campground staff, student to scholar-they have cheerfully given their time and their knowledge so that what I would present would be as accurate as possible. But a special word must be spoken for those stalwart members of the Lewis and Clark Trail Heritage Foundation, who at their annual conference go on non-stop about their interest and have been an unfailing source of information and energy. Among them it is only proper to single out for special attention the names of Bob Doerk, Bob and Florence Gatten, and Don Nell. Strode Hinds and Blair Chacoine who are no longer with us, belong in a special category as well.

The staffs of museums and libraries have unfailingly aided with my sometimes eccentric queries, always with good humor. Let me offer my thanks from east to west: to the Bartle Library of SUNY-Binghamton, Steele Memorial Library of Elmira, N.Y., Elmira College Library, the library of the University of Pittsburgh and the Carnegie Library there, especially the staff of the Pennsylvania Room, Museum of the Old Northwest at Marietta, Ohio, the Missouri Historical Society in St. Louis, the State Historical Society of Missouri at Columbia, the South Dakota Cultural Center at Pierre, the State Historical Society of North Dakota at Bismarck, the Montana Historical Society at Helena, and the Oregon Historical Society of Portland.

These thanks would not be complete without two more acknowledgements. Julia Miller and the staff of the Academic Advising Office at SUNY-Binghamton put up with my presence long after it was necessary. And my wife Pat has been the surest editor a writer could ask for. This would have been a better book if I had adopted more of her suggestions. None of the above, of course, can be responsible for the mistakes made here.